AFTER SPENDING 10 YEARS INTERVIEWING
500 SUCCESSFUL PEOPLE I DISCOVERED:

HERE'S WHAT REALLY LEADS TO SUCCESS

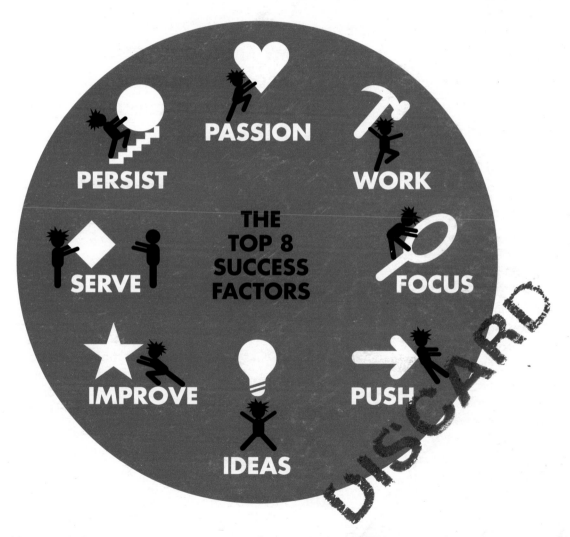

THE TOP 8 SUCCESS FACTORS

PERSIST · PASSION · WORK · SERVE · FOCUS · IMPROVE · IDEAS · PUSH

DISCARD

AND SMARTS, LOOKS, AND LUCK AREN'T ON THE LIST

Stupid, Ugly, Unlucky, and RICH
SPIKE'S GUIDE TO SUCCESS

INTRODUCTION

Boring!

Why I spent 10 years of my life on this book, when I could have been sitting on a beach.

6   **MY APOLOGIES FOR THE TITLE**

7   **ABOUT THE AUTHOR**

8   **THE START OF A JOURNEY**

14   **4 QUESTIONS ABOUT SUCCESS**

SECTION A
WHAT REALLY LEADS TO SUCCESS

This is the really important stuff - *The Top 8 Success Factors*

And the great thing is, they're all simple things anybody can do. Even me.

16   **THE TOP 8 SUCCESS FACTORS**

20   **PASSION**

42   **WORK**

66   **FOCUS**

86   **PUSH**

120   **IDEAS**

152   **IMPROVE**

172   **SERVE**

208   **PERSIST**

Don't chase success or money. Just do these 8 things and the rest will come.

But, just in case you wouldn't mind getting rich, see this chapter.

Know the things that don't lead to success so you don't waste time on them.

SECTION B
WHAT DOESN'T LEAD TO SUCCESS

270   **DEBUNKING 4 SUCCESS MYTHS**

273   **THE SMARTS MYTH**

293   **THE LOOKS MYTH**

306   **THE LUCK MYTH**

324   **THE MYTH OF REACH THE TOP & STOP**

If you think you'll succeed by just being smart, good-looking, or lucky, read this section.

What NOT to do after you succeed.

ACKNOWLEDGEMENTS

337   **THANKS**

338   **ACKNOWLEDGEMENTS**

To find quotes by a particular person, and the source of the quotes.

HERE'S THE MESSAGE OF THIS BOOK

You don't have to be special to succeed. Most successful people are ordinary, everyday people, who are not particularly smart, good-looking, or lucky. They succeed because of the 8 things they do — *The Top 8 Success Factors*.

AUTHOR'S NOTE: The author has made every effort to make this book as complete and accurate as possible. However, he is human and he makes mistakes. Just ask his wife. If you discover mistakes, please contact us and we will make every effort to make appropriate corrections.

Stupid, Ugly, Unlucky and Rich — Spike's Guide to Success
1st edition — includes index and sources.
ISBN 0-9739009-0-3

Printed in Canada.

This book is recyclable. Train of Thought Arts makes every effort to use recycled paper, as well as ideas.

Train of Thought Arts Inc., 230 Niagara Street, Toronto, ON, M6J 2L4, Canada

info@SpikesGuide.com

INTRODUCTION

People ask me, "Who is Spike?" Well, it all started one day by accident, when I drew this character on a sign and gave him spiky hair. Then, before I knew it, the little creep took over. Now Spike is everywhere in the book – and his agent is demanding that we put his name on the cover.

Spike represents all the ordinary people out there who reach extraordinary success. I'm a Spike, and so are lots of other guys and girls. That's the reason I made Spike very simple, so anybody can relate, no matter what their gender, nationality, or race.

(Editors note: The real reason he made Spike so simple is, even after 4 years at art college, the guy still can't draw.)

MY APOLOGIES FOR THE TITLE

First, I'd like to issue an apology to all the very nice people who were kind enough to give me interviews and whose quotes appear in this book. I can just picture your friends saying something like: "Hey, I hear you're in a book called *Stupid, Ugly, Unlucky and Rich*. I didn't know about the rich part, ha, ha, ha."

So, I apologize for the title, and I want you to know that *Stupid, Ugly, Unlucky* isn't referring to you. Honest! It's really referring to me. I mean, I'm as stupid, ugly, and unlucky as they come. Yes, I am. But not all successful people are like me. Some are very smart, good-looking, and lucky, and I'm sure you're one of them.

Oh, and, if you're offended because I put RICH in the title, I apologize for that, too. Yes, I'm aware success isn't just about money, and it was unbelievably crass of me to put that word on the cover.

In my own defense, I actually didn't want to use this title. I mean, the part about successful people not being the smartest, best-looking, and luckiest is a very small portion of the book. Really, this should be titled *The Top 8 Success Factors*, since that's the biggest, most important part of the book. The only reason I didn't call it that can be described in one word – boring!

Test readers overwhelmingly preferred *Stupid, Ugly, Unlucky, and Rich*, and said that's the book they'd pick up. I want people to pick up this book and read it, because it's like having a lot of successful people in the same room telling you what helped them

succeed, and then you can apply it to your own life.

In the end, I figured a mistitled book that people pick up and read is better than an accurately titled book that sits on the shelf. (I think that's called marketing.)

So, to all the successful people out there who appear in this book, please accept my sincerest apologies. I'll never use another title like this again. Mainly because you'll never give me another interview, and I'll never get to write another book.

ABOUT THE AUTHOR

To be honest, I really don't like talking about myself. ("Yeah, sure. You'd never know it from this book.") However, I figure I have to tell you something about my background, because in the back of your mind you're thinking, "What credentials does this guy have to write a book on success?" And the answer is, I have absolutely no academic credentials whatsoever. I mean, I barely passed high school and I struggled through college. To top it off, I don't even look like a successful person. Just your average, everyday guy.

Yet, I did achieve success in the real world, although not right away. After graduating from design college, I cycled through Asia for a year, then joined Nortel's R&D labs, where I spent my time bouncing around from research, to design, photography, advertising, and producing videos. I could never figure out what title to put on my business card, so I just left it off. Finally I figured out what I really do. I'm a de-mystic. I love taking complex subjects, like technology, and communicating them in a way that people are able to understand.

After 10 great years of doing that at Nortel, I started my own company, and for 25 years we've helped large high-tech companies communicate to their customers, whether it's by creating web animations, videos, brochures, or advertising. (Now comes the success stuff.)

In business for 25 years! Hey, that's a success. And we've taken home some big awards, including the top ones in the world for best corporate videos and scriptwriting. My photographs have appeared in international publications and I even shot a cover for *Playboy* magazine. But only once. My wife reminded me of the old Zen saying, "He who shoots bunnies may also get shot."

On the sports front, I've run a fairly fast marathon (26 miles/42km) in 2 hours, 43 minutes, and I still sometimes win my age group – "Old Farts Over 50." My wife Baiba and I have climbed 2 of the world's highest mountains, Kilimanjaro in Africa and Aconcagua in South America, before concluding that mountain climbing wasn't our sport. And we've been together for over 30 years, a success in itself these days (and probably a record in Hollywood).

When it comes to money, I was never really interested in it, or motivated by it, and I don't like to talk about it. But, like it or not, money is one indicator of success. So I guess I have to stand up and confess that I'm a... a ..a....a.......millionaire. Whew! Glad that's over.

The bottom line is, I don't just talk about success, I've achieved it in a number of ways. But just being successful doesn't make me an expert on the subject. What gives me the real credentials to write this book is the decade I spent asking hundreds of successful people what helped them succeed, and analyzing every word they said. So I still may not look like a successful guy, but I can sure tell you what leads to success. And that's what this book is all about.

THE START OF A JOURNEY

What REALLY leads to success?

This all started one day on a plane. In the seat next to me was a teenage girl and she was really excited because it was her first plane ride. It looked to me like it might also be her last, because she came from a poor family, her parents were separating, and she was going to stay with relatives. As I tapped away on my computer, she kept asking me about my work and what I did.

Then, out of the blue, she asked, "Are you successful?" I thought for a minute and said, "No, not really. Oprah, now there's a big success. Or my hero Terry Fox, a kid who ran thousands of miles on an artificial leg and raised millions for cancer research. Or Bill Gates, a guy who owns his own plane and doesn't have to sit next to some kid asking him questions." She laughed. But then I told her about some of my accomplishments in business and sports, and when I'd finished she said, "I think you've been successful. So, are you a millionaire?"

I didn't know what to say, because when I grew up it was bad manners to talk about money. But I

figured I'd better be honest, and I said, "Yeah, I'm a millionaire, but I don't know how it happened. I never chased money and it's not that important to me." She shot back, "Well, money is important to me. I don't want to be poor anymore. I want to get somewhere, but it's never gonna happen." I asked, "Why not?" "Well, you know, I'm not that smart. I'm not doin' great in school."

I said, "So what? I'm not smart. I barely made it through high school. I was never voted "Most Popular" or "Most Likely to Succeed." I started a whole new category, "Most Likely to Fail." I had no self-confidence, no big goals in life, and nobody thought I'd become successful, including me. I had absolutely nothing going for me, but I achieved success and also became a millionaire. So, if I can do it, you can do it."

Then she hit me with the big question, "What REALLY leads to success?" I thought for a while, but finally had to admit, "Sorry, I don't know. Somehow I just did it." As the plane landed and we said good-bye, I had a feeling she would do okay

in life, but I felt bad that I couldn't help her more. I couldn't stop thinking, "How did an ordinary guy like me make it?" Later, at a conference, I was standing in a room, surrounded by the top people in many fields – arts, sciences, sports, business – and suddenly it hit me: Why don't I ask them what helped them succeed and pass it on to others?

I ran out, bought a little tape recorder, and rushed back ready to do some interviews. Then the self-doubts set in. A voice in the back of my head said, "Why would anybody want to talk to me? I'm not a famous journalist. I'm a nobody." So I said, "Ah, forget it. It was a stupid idea anyway." And I started to put the recorder away.

Then, who did I see walking towards me but Ben Cohen, the famous co-founder of Ben & Jerry's ice

cream. I figured it's now or never, so I jumped out in front of him, butterflies in my stomach and ready for rejection, and said, "Ben, I'm trying to find out what leads to success, can I talk to you?" He said, "Sure, come on, let's get an ice cream." And over coffee and ice cream he told me what helped him succeed. Thank you, Ben!

I got up the courage to do some more interviews, and then more and more, and slowly my little success database grew. Now here I am, 10 years later, and I've done more than 500 interviews. I figured I'd spend a couple of months on this project, find out what leads to success, then get back to my regular life. Now I can't even remember what my regular life was like.

10
YEARS OF RESEARCH

500
PERSONAL INTERVIEWS

1000s
OF QUOTES FROM OTHER SOURCES

Below are some of the BIG NAMES I've interviewed. I'm often asked, "How do you get to these famous people?" I say, "It's easy. Go to a conference where they're speaking and stand outside the washroom. Then beg a lot." I also spent years combing through books, magazines, websites, radio shows, and TV programs to find more examples of what leads to success, and in these pages you'll see many quotes from other writers who actually know what they're doing. To find out the sources of the quotes, see the Acknowledgements section.

PLEASE, PLEASE, PLEASE TALK TO ME!

John Abele founder, Boston Scientific
Jeff Bezos founder, Amazon.com
Jay Chiat co-founder, Chiat/Day ad agency
Ben Cohen co-founder, Ben & Jerry's Ice Cream
Russell Crowe Oscar-winning actor
Daniel Dennett influential philosopher
Gideon Gartner founder, Gartner Group
Frank Gehry acclaimed contemporary architect
Terry Gilliam film director, Monty Python member
Jane Goodall renowned scientist/conservationist
Matt Groening creator of *The Simpsons*
Mae Jemison first black female astronaut
Norman Jewison Oscar-winning film director

Quincy Jones legendary music producer
Joe Kraus co-founder, Excite
Mitch Kapor founder Lotus
Norman Lear TV producer, *All in the Family*
Leon Lederman Nobel Prize in physics
Rupert Murdoch media mogul
Larry Page & Sergey Brin Google founders
Issy Sharp founder, Four Seasons Hotels & Resorts
Paul Stanley lead vocalist, KISS
Martha Stewart founder, Martha Stewart Living
Julie Taymore director, Lion King on Broadway
James Watson co-discoverer of DNA structure
The list goes on...

BUT SUCCESS ISN'T ABOUT JUST BIG NAMES OR MONEY

I was trying to discover what successful people all have in common, so I interviewed people in many different fields. This is just a partial list of the careers and titles of people I've interviewed. Look at all the options available. Wow! The days of only being a butcher, baker, or candlestick maker are over.

Actor	Director	Musician
Advertising Director	Doctor	Naturalist
Anesthesiologist	Economist	Neonatologist
Animal Behaviorist	Editor	News Anchor
Animation Director	Engineer	Nurse
Anthropologist	Entrepreneur	Parent of the Year
Architect	Environmentalist	Photographer
Art Director	Executive Consultant	Physicist
Artist	Executive Director	Planner
Astronaut	Explorer-In-Residence	President
Astrophysicist	Filmmaker	Primatologist
Athlete	Financial Analyst	Professor
Author	Financier	Psychiatrist
Ballerina	Game Developer	Psychologist
Biomedical Researcher	Geneticist	Publicist
Business Consultant	Glass Artist	Publisher
Cartoonist	Historian	Pulitzer Prize Winner
CEO	Humorist	Real Estate Agent
Chairman	Illustrator	Research Scientist
Chef	Interior Designer	Restauranteur
Choreographer	Interviewer	Rock Star
Classical Pianist	Jazz Musician	Salesperson
Columnist	Journalist	Scientist
Comedian	Juggler	Singer/Songwriter
Community Leader	Lawyer	Strategist
Composer	Librarian	Teacher
Correspondent	Manager	Technologist
Criminologist	Marketing Director	TV/Radio Producer
Deep-Sea Explorer	Medical Geneticist	Venture Capitalist
Designer	Mission Scientist	Veterinarian
Developer	Mountain Climber	Writer

Hey, look at all the cool careers!

Where I grew up, professions were very limited. I thought there were only 10 things in the world you could do and none of them looked interesting to me.

I didn't know there was a great job that was invented just for me. Then once you start exploring there are so many options out there.

Elinor Mackinnon
CIO, Blue Shield

THE BIG JOB WAS ANALYZING 10 MILLION WORDS

Over time, my little database on success grew from a few thousand to more than 10 million words! I couldn't believe it. The downside was I actually had to do something with all those words. So I started dissecting all the interviews, line by line and sorting them into all the categories people said helped them succeed. You think landing on the moon is tough? Try sorting 10 million words!

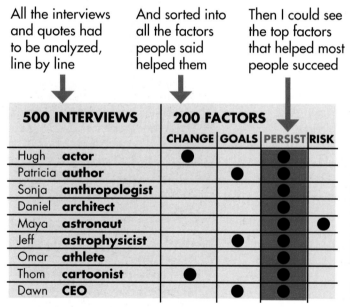

All the interviews and quotes had to be analyzed, line by line

And sorted into all the factors people said helped them

Then I could see the top factors that helped most people succeed

500 INTERVIEWS		200 FACTORS			
		CHANGE	GOALS	PERSIST	RISK
Hugh	actor	●		●	
Patricia	author		●	●	
Sonja	anthropologist			●	
Daniel	architect			●	
Maya	astronaut			●	●
Jeff	astrophysicist		●	●	
Omar	athlete			●	
Thom	cartoonist	●		●	
Dawn	CEO		●	●	

Do you know how much work it is to sort all this stuff?

AND NOW, AFTER 10 YEARS, I CAN ANSWER THE QUESTION

The little project I thought would take a couple of months has taken over my life. All I do is analyze and sort, analyze and sort. I'm obsessed with it. I no longer make any money. I gave up paying work years ago, while my business partner Thom Rockliff runs our company. Thank you, Thom!

I no longer have a personal life. (My wife says it wasn't that great anyway.) I can no longer just read the paper or enjoy watching an interview on TV, because I'm too busy analyzing what made the person succeed. I'm totally consumed with this

thing. I'll tell you, if I ever get my hands on that kid I met on the plane that started all this....

Actually, if I do see her again, I'll thank her, because I've never had so much fun in my life, and met so many interesting people. And now I have the answer to her question: "What really leads to success?"

So, wherever you are kid, thanks. This is for you. And for all the other people out there who want to get somewhere in life.

4 QUESTIONS

1. WHAT IS SUCCESS?

Some people say to me, "First you have to define success." Well, this book shows by example, so here are a few examples of success:

- Mother Theresa succeeded in helping the poor.
- Bill Gates succeeded in building a huge company.
- Ann Turner succeeded in building a small company.
- Vanthy Ly succeeded in inspiring and motivating her own children, plus countless other parentless children, and was named Parent of the Year.
- Terry Waite succeeded in staying alive, after being held hostage for 7 years.
- Matt Groening succeeded in creating a popular cartoon series called *The Simpsons*.
- Pam Reed succeeded in becoming the first woman to win the Badwater 135 mile ultramarathon run across Death Valley.
- Sam Sullivan, a quadriplegic, succeeded in becoming mayor of Vancouver.

These are just some of the hundreds of examples of success in this book. And what do all those people in common? They all achieved something, in big and little ways. So I like the simple definition of success: Achieving something.

2. DOES SUCCESS MEAN MONEY?

I'm sometimes asked, "When you say success, do you mean money?" As you can see by the previous examples, the answer is no. Success does not always mean money. Many people are working for rewards other than money, like ice cream, for example. Or the intangible rewards success brings, such as acknowledgement, recognition, the satisfaction from a job well done, or the just the great feeling we get by making a contribution in some way.

On the other hand, money only results from success. First we have to succeed at something, then we get the money. You'll find many millionaires and billionaires quoted in this book, not because I think it's great they're rich, but because it's a sure sign they've succeeded at something in a big way.

(Editor's note: The real reason he quotes rich people is because he's trying to get invited to their parties.)

ABOUT SUCCESS

3. DOES SUCCESS LEAD TO HAPPINESS?

Another question I often get is: "Does success lead to happiness?" And my answer is, "I don't care." At least for this book. The girl on the plane didn't ask me how to be happy, she asked me how to be successful. I can only handle one major topic at a time. The purpose of this book is to show what leads to success, not what leads to happiness. Sorry, I don't have much information on happiness, because I didn't ask 500 people what made them happy. I asked them what helped them succeed. But I can tell you this, from all outward appearances, successful people seem to be happy. I mean, many are just bursting with energy, and they smile and laugh a lot.

On a personal note, I can tell you that sometimes success made me happy and sometimes it didn't. At one point in my life I was successful by any measure – awards, money, recognition, helping people – but I was miserable and taking anti-depressants. So, at that point, success didn't lead to happiness for me. Although it did make somebody happy – the drug companies selling me the anti-depressants. (For more on that story see the final chapter.)

4. IS SUCCESS WORTH THE EFFORT?

Is it worth the effort to succeed at something in a really big way? Well, only you can answer that. And you can only answer it once you've done it. But I can tell you this – nobody has yet said to me that it wasn't worth it.

This is a book about success, but I'm not saying everybody has to become a huge success. We all achieve many little successes every day and sometimes we hit it really big. When I was a kid, I didn't care about being successful. It wasn't a priority at all. But I somehow stumbled into doing the things that got me there, and I achieved success in spite of myself. And, as you'll see in this book, I'm not alone. Many successful people don't chase success or money. They just do the right things and the rest comes.

I think there's "Terminal Success" in the same way there's "Terminal Velocity." When I did skydiving and jumped out of a plane, it didn't take long to reach terminal velocity, the maximum speed at which we fall. Terminal Success is sort of the opposite – the maximum height we rise, or the maximum height we want to rise. I think we all have an idea of how far we want to go, and what we're willing to go through to get there. Some people want to achieve huge success, for whatever reason, and others don't. Whatever works for you. The purpose of this book is to give you some tips if you do want to succeed.

So now let's get into the real content and look at *The Top 8 Success Factors*.

SECTION A

It's about time we got to the important part!

THE TOP 8 SUCCESS FACTORS

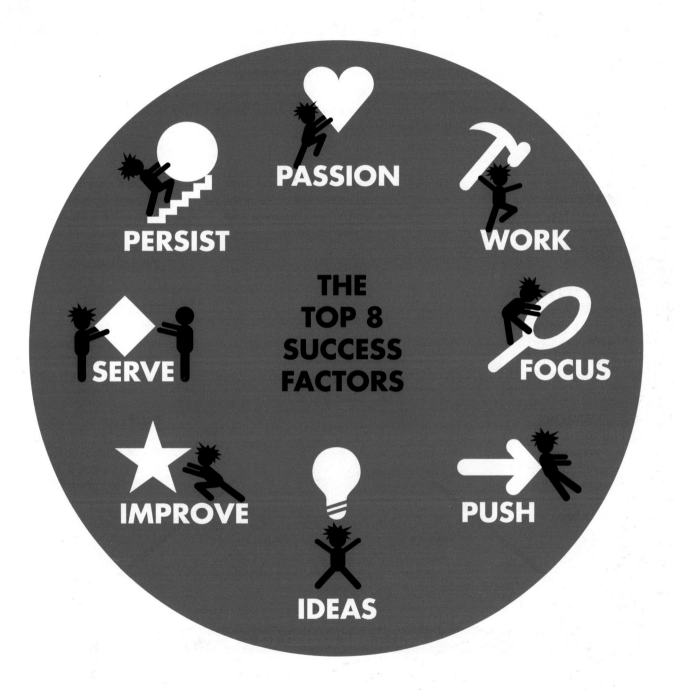

THE TOP 8 SUCCESS FACTORS

PASSION

WORK

FOCUS

PUSH

IDEAS

IMPROVE

SERVE

PERSIST

THE TOP 8 SUCCESS FACTORS

Here are the top 8 factors people say helped them succeed. These are the core for success in anything we do. We add other skills to this core, such as technical, analytical, and people skills. Just be sure to have *The Top 8 Success Factors* at your center. They'll be the foundation for your success.

There's no overnight success so we need to **PERSIST** through time, as well as failure, mistakes, criticism, rejection, and adversity. Just keep going and never give up.

Successful people **SERVE** others something of value. And not just in a charity sense. If getting rich is what you want, you'll need to serve other people something they want.

Keep trying to **IMPROVE**. Successful people are always improving themselves and what they do. Getting better at anything means practice, practice, practice, and always aiming to do your best.

Find your **PASSION**. Chase love, not money, and the money will come anyway. It can take a long time to discover your passion, so just keep looking.

WORK very hard. All successful people work their butts off. But they love it, so it's not work, it's fun. They're not workaholics, they're WorkaFrolics™.

FOCUS long-term on one thing, not everything. Short-term, develop the ability to ignore distractions, put your head down, and concentrate.

PUSH yourself through barriers like shyness and self-doubt. Push yourself beyond what's expected. Push yourself to do the impossible.

1.**PASSION**

8.**PERSIST** 2.**WORK**

7.**SERVE** 3.**FOCUS**

6.**IMPROVE** 4.**PUSH**

5. **IDEAS**

IDEAS are how we solve problems and take advantage of opportunities. Getting good at coming up with ideas isn't magic. Anybody can be creative.

TECHNICAL SKILLS

PEOPLE SKILLS

OTHER SKILLS ARE ADDED TO THE CORE

THE TOP 8 SUCCESS FACTORS ARE KEY TO SUCCESS AT ANYTHING
FROM BEING A ROCK STAR TO ROCKING YOUR BABY

So there I was, sitting at Starbucks trying to come up with a good example to illustrate *The Top 8 Success Factors*. My problem was too much choice. This book has hundreds of examples of successful people in many different fields, so who should I pick? How about Bill Gates in technology? Maybe Oprah in entertainment? Or architect Frank Gehry? Or Martha Stewart? I hate making these momentous decisions, so I was really struggling. Plus, it was impossible to concentrate because there were all these kids running around. "Hey, what is this, Mothers Day at Starbucks?" And then it hit me — MOTHERS! Now there's a great example of people who constantly apply *The Top 8 Success Factors* to their vocation of successfully raising a child.

PASSION The successful Mother loves what she does and has unconditional love for her child. Passion is an insufficient description of the way she feels. (Although it's not the same kind of passion that started it all.)

WORK Mothering is all about work. The successful Mom works her butt off, especially in the beginning, when it's 24-hour non-stop feeding and diaper changing. But there are also many giggles and grins, so it's work and fun all rolled into one.

FOCUS The successful Mother is more focused than a pilot landing a jumbo jet. All that matters in the world is that child, and nothing will distract Mom from making sure that he or she lands safely in life.

PUSH The successful Mother keeps pushing herself to do stuff she really doesn't feel like doing, whether it's those 3 a.m. feedings, or driving kids all over town. It's really double duty pushing, as she also helps her child push through barriers like shyness and doubt.

IMPROVE The successful Mother has both herself and her child on a continuous improvement program. For her it's about getting better and better at parenting, and for her child it's about getting better at everything from school, to sports, to getting a date.

IDEAS The successful Mom is always coming up with ideas that solve dozens of day-to-day problems, like how to get the puke stain out of the rug – or an idea for her kid's next science project, speech competition, or Halloween costume.

SERVE The successful Mother serves her child above all else, including herself. The little one comes first, she comes second. And a Mother never stops serving. Her kid can be 60 and Mom is still saying, "I just brought you a little something to eat."

PERSIST The successful Mother is a persistence machine, hanging in there through the whole life cycle of her child and persevering through the baby crap and the teenage crap, all the way to old age. And no matter what happens, she never, ever gives up on that kid.

Add it all up and *The Top 8 Success Factors* are as essential to achieving success in raising a child, as they are to success in any other vocation. And although this book focuses mainly on the career side of life, keep in mind these 8 factors also lead to success on the personal side, whether it's marriage, parenting, relationships, hobbies, exercise, or health. So, now let's get into *The Top 8 Success Factors*.

PASSION

1. **PASSION**   2. **WORK**   3. **FOCUS**   4. **PUSH**

PASSION LEADS TO SUCCESS

PASSION

22 **PASSION IS THE STARTING POINT FOR SUCCESS**
24 **SUCCESSFUL PEOPLE LOVE WHAT THEY DO**
26 **PASSION TURNS UNDERACHIEVERS INTO SUPERACHIEVERS** — 1.
28 **PASSION TURNS UNDERACHIEVERS INTO SUPERACHIEVERS** — 2.

5 TIPS FOR FINDING PASSION

30 **1. FINDING PASSION CAN TAKE TIME**
32 **2. EXPLORE MANY PATHS**
34 **3. FALLING INTO YOUR CALLING**
36 **4. FOLLOW YOUR HEART, NOT YOUR WALLET**
38 **5. DO IT FOR LOVE AND MONEY COMES ANYWAY**

MY STORY

40 **I LOVE WHAT I DO SO MUCH, I'D DO IT FOR FREE**

5. **IDEAS**   6. **IMPROVE**   7. **SERVE**   8. **PERSIST**

THE STARTING POINT IS
PASSION

The bottom line is **I love the actual job of acting**. I have a great passion for it.

Russell Crowe Academy Award for Best Actor

When people ask me "What's the most important thing for success?" I say there are 8 factors that lead to success in any field. They're all important, but I put PASSION at the top of the list, because if you love what you do, it will be so much easier to embrace the other 7 factors.

Actor Russell Crowe said to me, "I love telling stories, so it's very simple for me to do my job." He also said one of the great things about passion is it helps you decide what to do and what not to do. "I never make a movie unless I get a physical charge out of the script, and then I'll make that film. I'll make the film that I'm passionate about." Lisa Nugent, founding principal of ReVerb, says to "Follow the tug in your heart that's pulling you. Stay true to that and you'll find something fulfilling."

The tug in David Jensen's heart led him to a possible name for his executive recruitment company. "When we were discussing what we might call our company, one of my colleagues suggested calling it Passion. I asked why and he said, 'Because your personal passion is so strong.'" Yes, passion is powerful stuff. No wonder when I ask people what helped them succeed, the words *love* and *passion* are often the first words out of their mouths. Speaking of mouths, I know this is hard to believe, but even successful dentists like Izzy Novak love what they do. "I love dentistry. I can't imagine being anything else."

Sometimes passion is mistaken for ambition. Famous real estate developer Donald Trump seems to be one of those gung-ho guys, so we think he's driven by ambition, but he says it's all about passion, "I'm not ambitious. I just love what I'm doing, and if you love what you do, you do a lot of stuff. And then people say, 'Oh, you're ambitious.'" Passion makes all the difference in any field, whether it's the boardroom or the classroom. Brian Little, a psychologist voted by students as the most popular Harvard professor, says, "My personal project is teaching with a passion, and I'll do whatever I have to do to bring that project to fruition." Hey, I wanna be in that guy's class!

Let's conclude with singer Jon Bon Jovi, who sums it up well when he says, "Nothing is more important than passion...Whatever you decide to do in life, just be passionate about it."

> **You've got to have passion. You can't be successful unless you have passion for your work.**
> **Don Green** co-founder, Roots

> **I think there has to be a big passion in fashion.**
> **Alexander McQueen** acclaimed fashion designer

> **I care passionately about the things that I do. I really want to do them. I don't know where it came from, but I'd recommend it.**
> **Jennifer Mather** renowned psychologist, animal behaviorist

> **Passion is what makes you feel good. It's what makes you get up in the morning and want to do it.**
> **Freeman Thomas** car designer, new Beetle and Audi TT

> **Passion. Utter passion for what I'm doing is number one.**
> **Adam Bly** founder, *SEED* science magazine

SUCCESSFUL PEOPLE LOVE THEIR WORK

I absolutely loved it. **I loved hitting the golf ball**.

Tiger Woods golf superstar

I love astronomy.
I love research.

Jaymie Matthews astrophysicist

Passion is so important, here's another page of people saying they love what they do. I mean, I can't even begin to show the huge number of successful people who use the words love or passion when describing their work.

Dave Lavery, the NASA whiz who sends robots to Mars, said to me, "Passion is almost an insufficient description of the way I felt. I discovered something I really loved, the thing that turned me on and got me excited. It made me want to get up and go to work every morning, and not want to go to bed at night."

Many people who grew up poor tell me it was passion that pushed them to the success they have today. Graham Hawkes told me he "grew up on the wrong side of everything." But passion took him from "living in a derelict cottage with no money" to designing a revolutionary ocean deep-diving system, founding 5 technology companies, and holding the world record for the deepest solo ocean dive. Graham says, "People around me tell me I'm just totally passionate and driven about what I do. I think it's normal."

Craig Venter is another example. He says, "I came from a lower-middle class family. There was no excess money at all." So how did Craig become the millionaire geneticist who led private industry's decoding of the human genome? He says, "I think the most important things are passion and being willing to work hard. Those have taken me further than anything."

I'm not saying everybody loves what they do. I'm just saying most successful do, like acclaimed graphic designer Chip Kidd. "I can't imagine spending my days doing something that I didn't love. That is a wasted life."

And it's amazing what you can do, when you do love something. I mean, passion has enabled Aimee Mullins to set running records, even though she's missing 2 essential limbs for running – legs. They were amputated below the knee when she was a child. But with the help of artificial legs and real passion, she set a number of world records at the Paralympics. She's well-named, since "Aimee" comes from the word for "love" in French, and it's a big reason for her success on the track and in life. No wonder she says, "If it's your passion then inevitably you'll succeed."

Passion is huge. I think being irrationally passionate is extremely healthy. Gravitate towards the things you love.
Sandra Yingling president, VisibleWork.com

I love what I do. I've only missed 3 days in 4 years.
Carlos streetcar driver, Toronto Transit Commission

On my desk I have a picture of me at 2 years old and I'm on the phone. I am phone obsessed and I'm in the business I love.
Rick Moran VP, Cisco Systems

I've spent my life doing what I love doing. At a very early age I found that I loved history.
Margaret MacMillan professor, winner of England's most distinguished book award

Passion has really helped me. I tell my children to find their passion, the one thing you do really well, that you're here to do in this world, and do it.
Paula Silver, former president, Columbia Pictures Marketing, *My Big Fat Greek Wedding*

UNDERACHIEVERS

BECOME

SUPERACHIEVERS

ONCE THEY FIND THEIR

PASSION

UNDERACHIEVERS WHO BECAME SUPERACHIEVERS

Albert Einstein world's most renowned physicist

Bill Gates co-founder, Microsoft

Frank Gehry renowned architect

John Grisham best-selling author

Larry King famous talk show host

Issy Sharp founder, Four Seasons Hotels

Colin Powell U.S. Secretary of State

Michael Eisner CEO, Disney

In today's world, some kids are being pushed harder and harder to become overachievers, academically and in every other way. So I'm sitting here looking at my research and wondering why we want kids to overachieve, when so many successful people started out as underachievers. For example, who said this?

> "...sitting in my room being a philosophical depressed
> guy, trying to figure out what I was doing with my life."

It was none other than Bill Gates. Writer Janet Lowe says, "In the sixth grade, Gates was under performing in school, at war with his mother, and generally struggling with life. His parents decided to send him to a psychologist for counseling." Yeah, I can just hear people back then saying, "Boy, that Gates kid sure is an underachiever. He's never gonna go anywhere in life!" Of course, once he found his passion for software, Bill went on to achieve modest success (the understatement of the year).

Little Issy Sharp was another kid who must have seemed like a slow starter. He says, "School was not important to me. I was a terrible student." But when Issy found his passion for the building industry, he went on to create Four Seasons Hotels and Resorts, a leading luxury hotel chain.

And how about Michael Eisner? His sister was one of those grade "A" students and an excellent ice skater. Gee, compared to her, poor little Michael must have seemed like a kid going nowhere. He says he was interested in just existing and didn't have major goals. Boy, what a loser. Funny how once he found his passion in the entertainment industry, he became a famous CEO of Disney.

Linda Keeler, VP and general manager of Sony Pictures, says, "I got Cs all through high school and I was a very lazy student. It wasn't until I got out of college that I applied myself and became very successful, because I found my passion. When you have a passion, it makes a big difference."

Yes, finding your passion is like slapping a turbocharger on a car engine. It's the same engine, yet far more powerful. Passion, the greatest turbocharger of all, is what turns underachievers into SUPERachievers. As neurosurgeon Keith Black says, "The energy comes from within, if you love what you do."

In school I had average grades. It was only when I got out of school and found something I really liked and could get excited about – practicing optometry and building my own little business – that I got charged up.
Jerry Hayes optometrist, founder, Hayes Marketing

As a kid I was pretty undisciplined and easy going. I didn't really get a drive to do well until I was in my 20s.
Robin Budd accomplished animation film director

I wasn't driven when I was growing up. I was completely directionless. Movies were an unrealistic dream. I almost had to be forced into it.
Don McKellar award-winning actor, writer, director

I was a high school dropout. I was bored and I didn't have good grades. Then I figured out what I really wanted to do, went to college, and I became very focused.
Lee Smolin theoretical physicist, major contributions to loop quantum gravity

BEN SAUNDERS

AGE 13 REPORT CARD FRAMED OVER HIS DESK

Ben lacks sufficient impetus to achieve anything worthwhile.

Photo: Martin Hartley, www.martinhartley.com

Interesting how, once Ben found his passion for outdoor adventure, he could haul a 400 pound sled over 800 miles and became **the youngest person to ski solo to the North Pole.**

THAT'S THE **POWER OF PASSION**

Here's another page about successful people who got off to a slow start, because I can't stress enough the importance of letting kids develop at their own speed, instead of driving them to overachieve. Just help them find their passion, and they might surprise you with what they can do. Ben Saunders is a good example. He told me, "I don't have a degree. Academically, I did the bare minimum to scrape through. It's only when I was exposed to the great outdoors that it was like someone flicked a switch in my life, and I said, 'This is what I love.'" Once Ben found that passion he "switched" from underachiever, to superachiever, pushing himself a grueling 800 miles in arctic conditions, and becoming the youngest person to ever ski solo to the North Pole.

Ben is a young guy, but passion also works for old guys. Frank Gehry tried a university night course in architecture, then after a year he was told to quit because he didn't draw with feeling. He persisted and his passion for architecture eventually transformed him into one of the world's most sought after architects. Frank said to me, "I'm a late bloomer. My best works didn't come along until my 60th year. Take your time. Build it a brick at a time. And don't worry about it."

Richard Saul Wurman is another old guy slow starter. He said to me, "My life has not always been what the world would call successful. When I was 45, I didn't own one share of stock, one piece of real estate, I had just been fired from a job, I had no money in the bank, I had 2 kids in college, and an old stick-shift Honda Civic. At 45, you were supposed to have turned the corner in your life and I certainly hadn't." That all changed when Richard followed his passions into publishing and also created the famous TED conferences. Today he's a successful multi-millionaire. Slow starter, super finisher.

So parents, it's okay for your kids to get off to a slow start. If they're not Einsteins at 8, don't panic. Even Einstein wasn't Einstein at 8. Little Albert was the ultimate underachiever. He didn't speak until age 3, stumbled his way through school, and worked for years as a low-level clerk in a patent office. However, he followed his passion for physics, developed the Theory of Relativity and changed the world. I'm sure Albert would say that how fast you reach success is all relative. Today's underachieving kid can turn into tomorrow's Einstein, once they find their passion.

Do what sets you on fire. If you do what you love, you will succeed.

Joseph MacInnis physician, deep-sea explorer, author

Life really is too short to do something you don't like or enjoy. But realize there are steps to get there, so you may not do it right away.

David Carson leading graphic designer

You can't pretend with passion. It's gotta be there. You believe in something and that gives you the commitment and perseverance to stay with it.

Issy Sharp founder, Four Seasons Hotels and Resorts

Whenever I attempt to do things just to be successful I lose energy and get nowhere. But when I go after something I'm really passionate about, there's an energy that helps you succeed.

Nick Foster Academy Award for animation software

STRIVERS

KNOW THEIR PASSION AND HEAD STRAIGHT TOWARDS IT

SEEKERS

DON'T KNOW WHAT THEY LOVE AND NEED TO DISCOVER IT

A FEW **FAMOUS SEEKERS**

Paul McCartney The Beatles
Jack Welch CEO, General Electric
Bill Gates co-founder, Microsoft
Anita Roddick founder, The Body Shop
David Baldacci best-selling writer
Jim Kimsey founder, America Online

Martha Stewart homemaking guru
Andrew Weil doctor, integrative medicine
Billy Graham renowned evangelist
James Cameron filmmaker, *Titanic*
Story Musgrave dean of U.S. astronauts
Mitch Kapor founder, Lotus

We've seen that passion is important to success, and most successful people love what they do. But maybe you're sitting there thinking, "What's wrong with me? I don't know what I love." Well, join the club. You're not alone. Many successful people start off not knowing and it takes them awhile to find their true passion. People seem to fall into 2 categories:

STRIVERS know what they love and can strive straight towards it. An example is the girl who knows she wants to be a doctor from the time she's 10.

SEEKERS, both young and old, don't know what to do with their lives. They need to discover their passion, and once they find it they often achieve great success.

In my research, I found a lot of Seekers. Just look at the list of famous Seekers on the opposite page. We sort of assume that big names all knew what they wanted to do in life, but many didn't have a clue. Whether it's *Titanic* filmmaker James Cameron, or Beatle Paul McCartney, or homemaking guru Martha Stewart, they had to discover what they loved. So the next few pages are devoted to giving Seekers a few tips on the trip to finding passion.

The first tip is, don't feel bad if you don't know what to do with your life. Robert Ward didn't. He started without a destination and ended up working with the likes of Steven Spielberg and George Lucas, planning and designing theme parks for Universal Studios. He said to me, "Many of us who have done neat things, took a path that we never thought we would go down in the beginning. My background is painting and photography, and today I'm driving billion-dollar theme park projects. So I like to think I paint with bulldozers." Robert adds, "You don't always have to know what you want. Don't be afraid to say, 'I don't know what I want to do.' That will come in time."

But maybe we are afraid to say we don't know, because some people think it's better to be a Striver – "My son's only 12 and he's going to be a lawyer!" Sure, Strivers may have less anxiety, since they know where they're headed, but it's no better or worse. It's just one way. The other way is to be a Seeker who travels down uncertain roads, in search of unknown passions, and still arrives at the right destination. Maybe a new, undiscovered destination. The truth is, you don't have to know where you're going in order to get there.

I don't know where I'm going, but I'm on my way.
Carl Sandburg author, poet

I didn't really know what I wanted to do in life. I was a load tester, a penitentiary service clerk, a mechanic. I know I like this better.
Dan Aykroyd actor

People ask, "Did you always want to be an astronaut?" When I was a little kid, there were steam locomotives. There was no way I could have envisioned space travel. I didn't know where I was going.
Story Musgrave 6-time space shuttle astronaut

There's something in you that pushes you in a certain direction, and you just have to go with it. The hard part is figuring out what that is. I spent the first 30 years trying to figure out what that was.
Russell Campbell president, ABN AMRO Asset Management Canada

TO FIND PASSION
EXPLORE MANY PATHS

I needed to explore to find my passion. I started off as an engineer, then I went into management consulting, then product marketing, before I finally stumbled into venture capital.

Steve Jurvetson renowned venture capitalist, Draper Fisher Jurvetson

If we're Seekers and haven't found our passion, how exactly do we discover it? Well, unfortunately it's not going to drop into our laps as we sit at home with our feet up having a cold one. We've got to get out there and explore many paths. T.K. Mattingly, veteran astronaut and one of the real-life heroes of Apollo 13, said to me, "I've had a lot of experiences. I've been to places that provided opportunities to do things, and I just never said no. The more experiences, and the faster you get 'em, the better. They always pay off."

When Robert Munsch told me about his career search, it sounded like the plot for a funny video: "I studied to be a priest and that turned out to be a disaster. I tried working on a farm and they didn't like me. I worked on a boat; it sank. I tried a lot of different things that didn't work. But I didn't give up. I kept trying, and then I tried something that did work." I'd say it worked. Now a celebrated children's author, Robert has sold over 20 million books!

Wade Davis worked in a logging camp, then as a big game hunting guide, a park ranger, and a photographer. Then one day he knocked on the door of legendary plant explorer Richard Evans Schultes. "I said, 'I've saved up money and I want to go to South America with you to collect plants.' I didn't know anything about plants or South America, and 2 weeks later I was in the Amazon." That knock on the door led Wade down the path to becoming a noted anthropologist, ethnobotanist, best-selling author, and National Geographic Society "explorer-in-residence." Now, is that a cool title, or what?

Exploring to find your passion doesn't mean you need to go all the way to the Amazon like Wade Davis. Another Davis, Elli Davis, told me she just went down the street. "I was a teacher, but I liked to read the real estate ads, and I used to look at open houses on weekends. I was afraid to try real estate, but if I'd never tried it, I would never have known how good I could be at it. You must try it. Just do it." By just trying it, Elli found her real path to passion and rose to the top of the real estate profession.

So, if you haven't found your passion, keep exploring and looking. And it doesn't even require sight. As Erik Weihenmayer, the first blind climber to summit Mt. Everest, says, "Follow your bliss, down dead-end alleys and to unseen places; it will lead you to a lifetime of happiness."

To find the things you really like, you need to explore and look around.
Michael Hawley professor, director, MIT Media Lab

Throughout life, if I had an opportunity to do something, I just went and did it. You never know what you're going to end up liking unless you try it.
Ted Stout founder & CEO, ROI Institute

Earthlink didn't happen instantly. Before that I had a window washing business, a candy store, a couple of coffee houses, a computer graphics company…Try a lot of things. You are always learning.
Sky Dayton founder, Earthlink

Try lots of things. Don't stick with it if you don't like it. You can change jobs many times in your life. I've done many, many jobs.
Gail Percy anthropologist, National Geographic Society

FALLING
INTO YOUR
CALLING

I fell into what I do and **I didn't know I loved it until I fell into it.**

Dawn Lepore CIO, Charles Schwab

They say you have to find your calling. But if it's a "calling" shouldn't it call you? I mean, your phone should ring and a deep, Darth Vader-type voice says, "You will become a brain surgeon!" And you go, "Gee, okay, thanks!" And you become a brain surgeon. But that's not how it works. Instead of a calling it should really be named a falling, because many successful people fall into their passion by accident. Architect Susan Ruptash says, "I fell into architecture. I was sitting in the guidance counsellor's office in high school, at the deadline to apply for university, without a clue what I should do. I started flipping through university calendars and stumbled on architecture. I thought, 'That looks interesting. I'll try it out for a year.' Here I am 20 years later. I discovered I loved it."

Optometrist Jerry Hayes says, "I stumbled into being an optometrist. I always wanted to be a dentist, so I went and talked to my local dentist, and he said, 'Why would you want to be a dentist? Become an optometrist instead.' I didn't even know what it was, but it turned out to be a better path, because I didn't have enough hand dexterity, and the best dentists are good with their hands." Freeman Thomas used his hands to draw things and he became a famous car designer, responsible for the Audi TT and updated Beetle. You'd think he was born to do it, but he says, "I fell into design. I was always drawing, but I never knew it could be a career. I had to fall into it. And it was only after I found it, that I knew it was what I wanted to do."

Michael Furdyk, who turned his passion for computers into a number of successful online companies and became a millionaire at the age of 17, told me, "It was kind of an accident, which is the way I think these things usually happen. But you also have to be proactive about it." He makes a good point. We can't just sit, waiting for our calling to call. It happens by getting off our butts, trying different jobs, going down different paths, then one day turning a corner and falling into what we're meant to do. As fabric design innovator Jack Lenor Larson says, "I fell in love with weaving, like falling into a trap, and I never wanted to get out."

If you haven't found something that makes you feel that way, keep looking. Be open to falling into your calling. And don't worry about hurting yourself. Just the opposite. It will make you feel absolutely wonderful.

I fell into the health care industry by default when I got an admission into a pharmaceutical college. And it became an addiction for me.
Aman Gupta CEO, Imprimis Life

I stumbled into personal computers and actually hit upon something that I was passionate about.
Mitch Kapor founder, Lotus, designer of Lotus 1-2-3

You don't always choose your careers. I think careers choose you. I became a lawyer by accident.
Ken Hertz lawyer, digital copyright expert

I wanted to be a pro baseball player but didn't make it. Then on vacation at the beach I saw some weird animals and thought, "Wouldn't it be great if I could somehow study the motion of these creatures?" And that's exactly what I'm doing.
Robert Full renowned professor of integrative biology, University of California, Berkeley

FOLLOW YOUR **HEART** NOT YOUR **WALLET**

Hey, what about me?

GO FOR THE **ZING** NOT THE **KA-CHING**

I am absolutely passionate about what I do. **I would pay someone to let me do what I do.**

Carol Coletta radio producer, Smart City

How do you find your passion? It's obvious, follow your heart. But the problem is, there's this other thing called a wallet we're often tempted to follow. Money is not easy to ignore, yet most of the successful people I talked to said they've always been motivated by hot passion, not cold cash. And that even goes for people who deal with money, like Wall Street investment banker Lise Buyer: "Don't necessarily pick the job that has the highest salary attached, because that's not where you'll find your success. Pick the one that fires you up. What gets me out of bed in the morning is absolute love of the job."

I'm not saying money isn't in the minds of some successful people, especially those who come from poor backgrounds. But even they tell me that passion, not money, was the real motivator. In fact, many walked away from money to do what they loved. Renowned graphic designer David Carson told me he gave up a good teaching salary to follow his passion for design: "I was never motivated by money. I worked for many years for little money. There were days when I couldn't get to the office because I didn't have money for gas. The goal was not money or fame. The goal was to do something I really enjoyed." Now David is both famous and very well off. So is science historian, author, and TV producer James Burke, but he says, "The least important things are fame or money. I mean, I'm perfectly happy to write books and articles and never come out of my room. It's not recognition. It isn't money, because I'm no good with money. I just like making the product."

Donovan and Green co-founder Nancye Green may have that color as her last name, but she says to forget about the green stuff and do what you love. "Forget how much money you're earning. Find a way to put food on the table, but feed your heart. I didn't care about having a lot of money. What I cared about was how excited I could get about what I was doing, and the rest would follow – and it did."

Let's conclude with 2-time world curling champion Colleen Jones, who says, "The feelings I've gotten through the sport have been million-dollar whoops of joy.... I just play for the joy of it. I think I'd be a different curler if I was playing for the money." So don't go for the million dollars. Go for the "million-dollar whoops of joy." Follow hot passion and you'll probably end up with the cold cash anyway.

I do it because I love it. Money is icing on the cake.
Simone Denny pop singer

Money is not a guiding light for me. On my deathbed I want to look back and say I had a rich life, and that doesn't mean making millions and millions of dollars.
Darlene Lim post-doctoral fellow at NASA, "Top 20 under 20" winner

If you're in photo journalism, you don't do it for the money, you do it because you get to fly on Air Force One, shoot the Superbowl, and meet famous people. You're not stuck in a rut and that's way more important than the money.
Kevin Gilbert award-winning photojournalist

The people who make it to the top – whether they're musicians or great chefs or corporate honchos...are the ones who'd be doing whatever it is that they love even if they weren't being paid.
Quincy Jones famous music producer

DO IT
FOR
LOVE

THE
MONEY
COMES
ANYWAY

Yes, I've made a great deal of dough from my fiction, but I never set a single word down on paper with the thought of being paid for it.... I did it for the buzz. **I did it for the pure joy of the thing.**

Stephen King best-selling novelist

Successful people chase passion, not money, and the interesting thing is, many end up very rich anyway. Basketball superstar Michael Jordan, said, "I play the game because I love it. I just happen to get paid." A lot, I might add, since Michael became one of the highest-paid sports figures.

Bill Gates says money wasn't the motivation when he and Paul Allen started Microsoft. "Paul and I, we never thought that we would make much money out of the thing. We just loved writing software." And by loving it they became 2 of the world's richest men. Sometimes, we think rich people go for the money, when they really go for the passion, and sort of stumble into the money as a result. Geneticist Craig Venter told me he's been described as an accidental millionaire. "I went into biology thinking I was going to be poor my whole life. There's nothing I've done because I was trying to get money. I've been pursuing my passion, and money has come along with it a few times. Don't pursue money."

Acclaimed adventurer Ben Saunders told me he used to be skeptical about the love/money connection. "Years ago somebody said to me, 'Do what you're passionate about and the money will follow.' And I thought, 'What a load of bullshit.' I was barely surviving, borrowing money to buy bus tickets to go to another rejection. And now, finally, it's happened. I'm making a good living, purely because I absolutely focused on what I'm passionate about, did it to the best of my ability, and didn't even think about money."

So, why does following your heart also fill up your wallet? *Simpsons* creator Matt Groening, who became very rich doing what he loved, summed it up for me: "I think that when you do what you love, you bring passion and enthusiasm to your job, so you are much more motivated to do a good job, which means you're more likely to be successful and to make more money." Makes sense. And the opposite is also true. People who chase money seldom get rich, because they're so focused on the dough they don't do what will really make them wealthy, like follow their passion. Comedian Rick Mercer says, "I've seen people do things for money, and it generally backfires. You have to work for the love of what you do. That's the most important thing."

The bottom line is, do what successful people do and follow your heart, not your wallet. In the end, your wallet will be happy you did.

I was never motivated by money. I was motivated by passion and ideas, and the money came. *My Big Fat Greek Wedding* had no money and we made $251 million domestically, all done with love and passion.

Paula Silver
former president, Columbia Pictures Marketing

I really believe if you do what you love, you will make money at it. If you do something just because you want to make money at it, you will not succeed. You will be fighting an uphill battle.

Elinor MacKinnon
CIO, Blue Shield

I'm a millionaire several times over, but I've never gone after the money. I've always wanted to do nice things. I built the nicest restaurant in town, the nicest office building, and the nicest subdivision. I did it because I loved it.

Millionaire who asked to remain anonymous

MY
LOVE
STORY

I never had any wild goals to be incredibly successful or make millions. I just had this gut feeling that if I followed my passion and did what I loved, somehow it would all work out.

Sounds easy, except for one little problem. At first I didn't have a clue what I loved. I wasn't a Striver who knew what to do with my life. I was a Seeker who needed to somehow find my passion. It's like dating. You don't quite know what you want, but you'll know it when you find it. So I tried lots of stuff and suffered through a lot of really bad career "dates," like drilling holes in metal on an assembly line and moving furniture. Some people might love that work, but not me.

School wasn't much help in finding my passion. There was no love lurking in math, history, English or, least of all, economics. I wasn't interested, so I got terrible marks. Without passion, I was the underachiever who people thought would never amount to much. Only one thing really interested me – drawing. My school was in the dark ages and had no art classes, so I just sketched on my own when I should have been learning math. It never occurred to me that drawing could be a career because it was just so much fun.

At the end of high school, my friends were all running off to become accountants or lawyers and I still had no clue what to do with my life. Then one day, I was walking past the guidance counselor's office and the door was open, so I went in and asked him what I should do. The guidance counselor asked just one question – "What do you love to do?" (It's only now that I realize what a great question that was. The guy should get a medal.) I said, "I love to draw cars." He suggested becom-

ing an industrial designer. I didn't even know what it was, but off I went to college to study design, and it was like being hit by Cupid's arrow. Suddenly I was energized. Passion took me from being the high school underachiever, to graduating at the top of my college class. Gee, there's power in that passion!

I loved design, then my passion morphed to photography, marketing, video, and writing. I finally realized my true love is taking complex information and making it simple. And that passion to communicate has always been my driving force – not money.

A number of times I've walked away from great-paying jobs to do poor-paying jobs that I was more passionate about. Once was when I had a terrific job with a large corporation, working with good people, traveling the world, and taking home a fat paycheck. But I wasn't doing what I really loved, photography. So I thought I'd leave, start my own company, and just do photography. My heart said, "Yeah! Go for it." My wallet, and all my friends, said, "Are you crazy? You can't walk away from all the money. You'll starve!" My heart won the argument, so I left and started my own company. True, at first there wasn't much money, but I didn't care. I was doing what turned me on. Which meant I worked hard at it, and eventually much more money poured in than I ever would have made in my old job.

So here's the acid test for knowing if you've found your passion – Would you do it for free? If you answer, "Yes!" then you've found your passion. If you answer, "No!" then just keep looking. As famous fabric designer Jack Lenor Larson says, "You have one life, it better be the one you love."

WORK

1. **PASSION**   2. **WORK**   3. **FOCUS**   4. **PUSH**

WORK LEADS TO **SUCCESS**

WORK

44   **ALL SUCCESSFUL PEOPLE WORK VERY HARD**

9 WORK TIPS

46   **1. BE A WORKAFROLIC – WORK AND FUN ALL ROLLED INTO ONE**
48   **2. SUCCESSFUL PEOPLE HAVE FUN WORKING**
50   **3. REMEMBER, IT'S NOT EASY FOR ANYBODY**
52   **4. FORGET TGIF - THINK TGIW - THANK GOD I'M WORKING**
54   **5. BE PREPARED TO WORK LONG HOURS**
56   **6. LOSE THE SNOOZE WHEN NECESSARY**
58   **7. REMEMBER THAT WORK TOPS TALENT**
60   **8. A WORK ETHIC WILL CARRY YOU THROUGH LIFE**
62   **9. TRUST THAT YOUR HARD WORK WILL PAY OFF**

MY STORY

64   **I'M A WORKAFROLIC - WORK, PLAY, FUN ALL ROLLED INTO ONE**

5. **IDEAS**   6. **IMPROVE**   7. **SERVE**   8. **PERSIST**

SUCCESSFUL PEOPLE
WORK REALLY HARD

I'm a real hard worker. I work and work and work all the time. Never believe that others will do your work for you.

Martha Stewart founder, Martha Stewart Living

The 2nd of *The Top 8 Success Factors* is WORK. As Nez Hallett III, CEO of Smart Wireless, said to me, "You have to work like there's no tomorrow. If you're going to be successful at anything, the key thing is to work hard." Yes, work is the basic entry fee for success, and all successful people work very hard. For me, that means it's often really tough to get an interview with them. Like the time I talked to Esther Dyson, a world expert on emerging information technology who was ranked number 12 in *Upside Magazine's* Elite 100. She said, "Hard work is part of success, but I enjoy the work and I work a lot. Which is why I'm not going to stay and talk to you much longer." Esther laughed as she left me in a trail of dust and went back to work. But I wasn't hurt – much – because I know working hard is a major reason why people like Esther and Martha and Oprah have risen to the top of their fields.

Author Peter C. Newman said to me, "I'm a very hard worker. I've always worked 2 jobs. I've always written books from 4 in the morning, until about 9 or 10 o'clock, and then had a regular job." And architect Susan Ruptash said, "In my first jobs, I always tried to work harder than anybody else. I've always wanted to be the first person in the office in the morning and the last one to leave at night. The hard work led to opportunities, and that's probably a key to early success for anybody."

Like it or not, it's a competitive world and working hard can give you an edge. Ted Turner said that edge is what helped him win him the America's Cup world sailing championship: "You can't win races without working harder than the other guys." Ted also said, "Nothing ever came easy. My first eight years of sailing I didn't even win my club championship. But I just kept working and working and working. That's the secret of my success." Work was also the secret to Google's success. Co-founder Larry Page said to me, "We started working on Google 8 or 9 years ago when we were at Stanford. Since then we've worked on it really hard, 24 hours a day. You can't just have inspiration. It's maybe 10% inspiration and 90% perspiration."

Perspiration, sweat? Yech! Working hard can get pretty messy. But, as journalist Heywood Hale Broun said, "Sweat is the cologne of accomplishment."

Thinking about physics, I do 24 hours a day. I do it in the bathtub, I do it on the john, I do it while I'm taking a walk.
Leonard Susskind one of the top theoretical physicists

Be committed to working very hard...I work like a demon, I really do.
Sherry Cooper economist and global strategist

All good things come from hard work and doing your best.
Greg Zeschuk "Game Developer of the Year"

Work is a big part of my life. I think about investment pretty much 24 hours a day, 7 days a week.
François Parenteau top independent analyst

Working hard is one of the keys to success. I had no big breakthroughs. I just kept going and worked hard. Even now, I'm the first to arrive in the morning.
Michael Frankfurt lawyer, Frankfurt Garbus Klein & Selz

SUCCESSFUL PEOPLE
AREN'T WORKAHOLICS
THEY'RE REALLY

WORKAFROLICS™

Absolutely have fun working. If you're not having fun, you're doing it for the wrong reasons.

Jay Chiat co-founder, Chiat Day advertising

Now let's look at 9 tips about WORK. The first tip is to find work that's fun for you, because if you enjoy what you're doing, even hard work becomes easy.

The problem is, many folks put a strong dividing line between work and fun. They see fun as something that takes place after work, and some even see work as a bad thing. I was out for a run and I heard a radio program about the evils of work. They painted a picture of hard-working people as workaholics, slaving away with a frown on their face, so addicted to work that it ruins their health and life. I stopped in my tracks and thought, "That's not right." I've talked to hundreds of successful people. Sure, they work very hard, because they want to achieve something, but they also have fun working. Bell Mobility chairman Bob Ferchat said to me, "I was never a workaholic, but I always worked 7 days a week because I was interested in what I was doing. It wasn't work. It was fun." I thought, instead of workaholic we need a new word to describe successful people who enjoy their work. Then it popped into my head – successful people are WorkaFrolics™.

WorkaFrolics have no dividing line between work and fun. It's both rolled into one. You can tell Jimmy Pattison, billionaire chairman of The Jim Pattison Group, is a WorkaFrolic when he says, "Business is my recreation. I'd rather go to a bunch of factories, meeting with our people, than go to Hawaii and stay on the beach, I can tell you that." Dave Lavery, who's in charge of building the robots NASA sends to Mars, is a WorkaFrolic. He told me, "There are way too many sleepless nights. We work our fingers to the bone, but it doesn't seem like work. It's fun, it's what we want to do. We don't want to put things down in the evening and go home."

Everybody can find some type of work they really enjoy. Mathematics professor Arthur Benjamin told me he even has fun doing math: "My goal in life is to make more people love mathematics, and see that there's really a fun side to it that doesn't always get shown in school." Arthur is a true WorkaFrolic, and he summed it all up when he said, "I feel happy doing work that I love. Before my father passed away, I asked him, 'Dad, what's the secret to a happy life?' and he said, without any hesitation, 'Find work that you really enjoy.'"

Become a WorkaFrolic. Have your work and fun all rolled into one.

I love to work. Work for me is pleasure, happiness. So, I work 90% of the time, and I sleep the rest. I don't go on a vacation. That's not what gives me pleasure. Work gives me pleasure.
Eve Ensler award-winning author, *The Vagina Monologues*

Business is ideas and fun and excitement and celebrations, all those things.
Jack Welch CEO, General Electric

I've always liked working. I think the biggest mistake I ever made was to retire. I didn't realize how much I really did love work. Now I'm back.
Diane Bean VP business development, Manulife

I work hard, but I've always had fun doing what I'm doing, and still do. I go to work every day and behave like a child and get paid for it.
Sheldon Wiseman CEO, Amberwood Productions

If I can't laugh and I don't see that there's fun in it, I always ask: **"Why am I doing this?"**

John Tyson VP, Nortel

Successful people are WorkaFrolics – they have fun working. And by fun, I don't mean it's always the "ha ha" kind of fun. Perhaps fulfilling is a more appropriate word to describe the work of a nurse taking care of patients; yet, even in those circumstances, there are moments of great joy. Other words people use to describe their work are enjoyable, gratifying, and engaging. But often they just use the simple word – fun. As famous inventor Thomas Edison said, "I never did a day's work in my life – it was all fun."

Renowned architect Jack Diamond put it this way: "It's not hard work if you get a bang out it. I do what I do because it's fun. I think that's the secret to success." Darlene Lim, post-doctoral fellow at NASA and winner of a "Top 20 under 20 years old" award, says, "I love to have fun and work makes me feel good. I think hard work is probably 95% of the equation, but it doesn't seem difficult because it's enjoyable."

Having fun at work drives people at the top. Bill Gates says he does his job because it's a fun job. And having fun also drives people like Bill up to the top in the first place. I mean, if you have fun working, you naturally work hard at it, so you do well, get promotions, and rise higher. That's why the top ranks of companies are full of WorkaFrolics, such as Ian Craig, president of Nortel Wireless Networks. "We always have a lot of fun. I say, if you ain't havin' fun, you ain't doin' it right." I saw Ian work, and the way he kept thousands of people motivated wasn't with a whip, it was with his wit.

There's a strong link between fun, energy and success. Comedian Martin Short says, "My agenda has always been just to have fun because if you are having fun you can always find the energy you need that drives you." Yes, when people have fun, things get done. CNN founder Ted Turner says, "Struggling hard to achieve something is the most fun I get...People have the most fun when they're busting their ass." And for many successful people the fun doesn't wear off over time. Famous talk show host Larry King says he's having as much fun now as when he started out making 55 bucks a week.

Warren Buffett could easily retire, since he's one of the world's richest people. But the fun still drives him. "When I go to my office every morning, I feel like I'm going to the Sistine Chapel to paint." Do you feel that way when you go to work?

Stick to what you're interested in. Don't be alarmed if it looks like fun.
Lorne Michaels
creator, *Saturday Night Live*

The biggest kick is sitting down and making something.
Milton Glazer
preeminent graphic designer, "I Love New York" logo

My passionate belief is that business can be fun, it can be conducted with love and a powerful force for good.
Anita Roddick
founder, The Body Shop

The only way a kid is going to practice is if it's total fun for him...and it was for me.
Wayne Gretzky
superstar hockey player

I played for fun for 9 straight years. We happened to win championships.
Michael Jordan
basketball superstar

IT'S NOT EASY

FOR ANYBODY

It never came easy. It took a lot of very hard work.
Some people don't understand. They seem to think that great things will happen just because they're wonderful.

Sherwin Nuland clinical professor of surgery, Yale

Success doesn't come easy to anybody, but the problem is we think it does. I remember driving home at 4 in the morning after working non-stop for days, thinking, "Nobody else has to work this hard." But now, after interviewing more than 500 successful people, I know success always requires hard work. Not one person told me it came easy.

Of course, some occupations look easy. The actors we see on TV don't really seem to be working that hard. However, I've directed films and I can tell you the best actors are also the hardest-working ones. Oscar-winning actor Russell Crowe said to me, "Films are a lot harder than people think. I've been training for this one for over 6 months and there's still another 2 months shooting to go. And I've been on this script for 7 years." Okay, what about singing? Now there's a cushy job. But pop singer Simone Denny says, "The perception of people outside show business is that it's glamorous. What I'm doing it's 95% work, 5% glamour. It's constant hard work."

Some people think retail is easy. Just open the door of your store and sit there waiting for customers to walk in. Well, when retail pioneer J.C. Penney was asked the secret of his success he said: "The answer is summed up in two words: hard work." Today nothing has changed, according to Michael Budman, co-founder of Roots clothing: "I have to work very hard. I love the business, but it takes a lot of time and energy and effort and creativity." Hey, what about opening a restaurant? People think that's a fun, easy job. Drew Nieporent, owner of Nobu and other top New York restaurants, says to think again: "It's never been easy. I've had to work very hard."

There has to be some easy job out there. Hey, I know! Now with the internet and all the cool technology out there, maybe we can do "virtual" work instead of actual work. Let me ask Jeff Bezos, founder of amazon.com. I mean, he built his business on technology and the internet. What's that? Jeff says: "I don't care what you want to do, you're gonna have to work hard." So much for virtual work. Guess we have to stick to the old-fashioned kind.

I have yet to find a person who achieved success without working hard. If you find one, let me know. I'll put them in the "Oddities of Nature" display in the museum, right next to the man they discovered who would actually ask people for directions when he was lost.

> **Easy street is a blind alley.**
> **Wilson Mizner** screenwriter

> **I wasn't the funniest guy growing up, but I was the guy who worked on being funny the hardest.**
> **Chris Rock** comedian

> **The superstars I've directed, like Jim Carrey, are incredibly hard workers.**
> **Ron Howard** Academy Award-winning director

> **What happened to me is just an example of the American dream, of somebody busting their ass and working hard.**
> **Bruce Willis** popular actor

> **I work hard. I mean, writing is never easy, and anyone who says writing is easy is either a bad writer or a liar.**
> **Wade Davis** explorer-in-residence, National Geographic Society

FORGET TGIF Thank God It's Friday

THINK
TGIW

Thank God I'm Working

It's not a 9 to 5 thing where at 5 o'clock you just turn off your work and go home and kick back. **It's something you love and it's with you all the time.**

Jaymie Matthews
astrophysicist, mission scientist for MOST space telescope

If you ask a successful person what TGIF means, you just might get a blank stare. People who succeed in life really don't understand the "Thank God It's Friday" attitude. They're not the ones on a Friday afternoon lined up at the door, like the start of the Indy 500, ready to rush out when the clock strikes 5. Instead of TGIF, successful people think TGIW, "Thank God I'm Working." They're not afraid of hard work, they're afraid of no work. As famous graphic designer David Carson, says, "It's not about the hours. I put in a lot of hours, but I'm enjoying it. I'm not watching the clock. I'm not waiting till 5 o'clock to go home."

Success takes a lot of work and effort. That's why, instead of a 9 to 5 attitude, successful people really have a 5 to 9 attitude. When others are leaving at 5, they stay and work until 9. As inventor Thomas Edison said, "I am glad the eight-hour day had not been invented when I was a young man. If my life had been made up of eight-hour days, I do not believe I could have accomplished a great deal." Best-selling author Stephen King writes his novels every day of the year, including Christmas and his birthday. But, why wouldn't he work those hours when he's having so much fun doing it? "For me, not working is the real work. When I'm writing, it's all the playground, and the worst three hours I ever spent there were still pretty damned good."

When you think about it, working a set number of hours a day is actually a new invention. Switzer Communications president Jessica Switzer says, "I grew up on a farm. You never stopped working, so I don't have a 9-to-5 mentality. It definitely instilled an around-the-clock work ethic in me." Hmmm… I wonder if that could be why scores of successful people grew up on a farm. Working hard in the fields prepared them to work hard in any other field of endeavor.

Yes, successful people work long hours and often get little sleep. (Can we get some sad violins playing?) Wait, on second thought, we don't need to shed a tear for them. They're WorkaFrolics who love what they do and they're having fun. It's the people who yell "TGIF" and rush off at 5 o'clock we should feel sorry for, because they're probably in the wrong job. As WorkCard chief strategist Kathleen Lane says, "Stress isn't working 15 hours at a job you like. Stress is working 15 minutes at a job you dislike."

You can't be highly successful punching a time clock and saying, "My 8 hours are up. I'm done for the day."
Randall Larsen founder, Institute for Homeland Security

A lot of these things are hard and take a lot of work. Saying you are only going to work so many hours on something sounds good, but life doesn't work that way.
Janet Baker CEO, Dragon Systems

People say to me, "How many hours a day do you work?" and I just say, "Till I'm finished."
Elli Davis top real estate agent

With my fledgling start-up business, I was working more than 12 hours a day for long periods of time. But I was so absorbed in it, I never felt like it was hard work. It was exhilarating.
Jerry Hayes optometrist, founder Hayes Marketing

IF YOU LOVE YOUR WORK IT REALLY ISN'T HARD BUT THE HOURS ARE

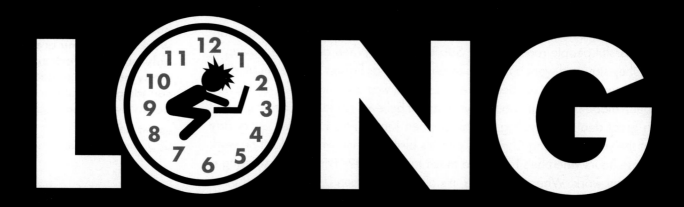

LONG

I just worked my tail off – 12 and 14 hour days for many years. No one said it was easy, but it was worth it.

Kimberly King president, King & Associates Strategic Alliances

The other day I saw an article that stated: "There is no correlation between success and hours worked." When I read that, my blood boiled, because it's simply not true. Based on my research, every successful person works long hours. I mean, even after he was very rich, Bill Gates worked most nights until 10 o'clock and, get this, he only took 15 days off in 7 years. (And he probably spent them on his computer.) Oprah says, "I would never see daylight. I'd come into work at 5:30 in the morning when it was dark and leave at 7:00 or 8:00 when it was dark. I went from garage to garage."

When we're starting out on the road to success, there's a big learning curve and that usually means extra hours. During his first year on the job as mayor of New York City, Rudolph Giuliani worked every single weekend, and in 8 years he only missed one day due to sickness. Renowned architect William McDonough says, "When I was starting out, I always worked long hours. I did 90 hour weeks when I was apprenticing." And musician Ed Robertson told me the early success of The Barenaked Ladies was due to tireless hard work: "We toured for 26 months straight and we earned the fan base one person at a time. We never took a break. "

Successful people will sometimes cruise along for a while, working 8 hour days, but then along comes a project or goal that takes over their life, and the hours shoot up. When filming *Star Wars,* George Lucas worked 16 hour days for 6 months with no days off. David Cohen, writer for *The Simpsons,* says that when he was developing the *Futurama* TV series, "I worked 100 days in a row, at one point, without a day off." Ben Saunders told me that his Arctic adventure meant skiing non-stop for months, hauling a 400 pound sled. Now that's work: "I skied for 72 days and only had 3 days off. You never really fully recover from one day to the next. So you wake up more and more tired." Yes, tired but happy, when the work paid off and Ben became the youngest person to ever ski solo to the North Pole.

Chiat/Day advertising co-founder Jay Chiat summed it up well for me when he said, "Be willing to work whatever it takes. It doesn't have to take long hours, but if it does take long hours, you have to be willing to do it." I believe him, and I guess that's why I'm sitting here writing this at 3 a.m.

I'll work 2 years straight, 7 days a week, 14 hour days, if I'm in love with a project.
Steve Schklair CEO, Cobalt Entertainment

I had to work as hard as I could, 24 hours a day, to make it work. Which is what I did. If you think you're gonna make it without work, fat chance.
Ron Rice founder, Hawaiian Tropic

I worked 12 hour, 15 hour days, 7 days a week for many, many years.
Lisa Nugent founding principal, ReVerb

We were working 16 to 20 hours a day, 6 days a week. Salma [Hayek] was on the set 20 hours a day. The woman is tireless.
Julie Taymore acclaimed director, *Lion King* on Broadway

In the schools of architecture, there's still very much a culture of blood, sweat, and tears. There's lack of sleep, all-nighters, and pouring absolutely every ounce of your being into the work that you do.
Susan Ruptash architect, Quadrangle Architects

LOSE THE SNOOZE
WHEN NECESSARY

I learned how to work very hard when I was working for IBM. I worked in one key department where **we used to often stay up almost all night for 2 or 3 days**.

Gideon Gartner founder, the Gartner Group

On a daily basis, there doesn't seem to be any link between success and how much you sleep. Thomas Edison only slept 4 to 5 hours but Einstein slept 8 to 10 hours. (He said it was all relative.) Successful people have different sleep patterns, but the one thing they all have in common is the willingness to go without sleep when it's necessary.

Best-selling author David Baldacci started writing books while he was a lawyer. That, and family life, took up the daylight hours, so the only time he could write was from 10 at night until 3 in the morning. But he discovered that writing at night actually had some advantages: "It was in the middle of the night creating my little fictional worlds that I was most lucid, my most energetic." City TV president Moses Znaimer told me the advantage of working at night is fewer disturbances and more focus: "For years I've schooled myself not to need much sleep. I like to work through the night. You become enormously productive because the distractions aren't there."

Dave Lavery often works through the night in order to manage a $1-billion NASA solar systems exploration program. One of his courses in college was apparently *Sleep Less 101*: "What helped me get through college as an undergraduate was to learn to do without sleep. Massive overdoses of caffeine helped. I was able to put in 20 hour days, and not suffer a mental breakdown." Today Dave still only sleeps 3 hours a night – and he drinks lots of Diet Coke. Famous filmmaker Terry Gilliam learned to go without sleep when he was creating those wonderful animations for *Monty Python's Flying Circus,* with panic deadlines to meet every week: "I'd literally work day and night when we were doing a series. I'd be going 7 days a week, usually with 2 all-nighters, churning out artwork."

It's not just outside forces that cause lack of sleep. Paul Allen says that when he and Bill Gates founded Microsoft, it was their own passion that kept them awake: "We stayed up until all hours of the night because we just loved working on software so much. It was a fun time." The bottom line is, get the sleep you need on a daily basis. But, on occasion, be prepared to lose the snooze, in order to do a good job, handle a crisis, meet a deadline, or do what you love. You may not get much sleep during those times, but you'll sleep like a baby the rest of the time.

You can sleep when you're dead, is my motto.
Jaymie Matthews astrophysicist

Just get stuff done, man. Don't sleep. This is a business where, you know, nobody waits for anybody. You gotta just continue to keep your foot on the throttle, and always just get things done, and be proper with the way it's done.
Choclair hip-hop star

All single-handed racers sleep in 20-minute catnaps. Sleep for 20 minutes, wake yourself up, check the horizon, check the performance of the boat, go right back to sleep....Once you're into that routine you can do it indefinitely.
Derek Hatfield sailed around the world alone

Personally, I enjoy working about 18 hours a day. Besides the short catnaps I take each day, I average about 4 to 5 hours of sleep per night.
Thomas Edison famous inventor of the light bulb

Everyone has some talent. **Hard work is the real weapon in life.**

Martin Brodeur hockey goaltender

Sometimes, when you're busting your buns, you can't help thinking, "If I'd just been born with more talent I wouldn't have to work hard." Well, it might re-assure you to know that what really makes people exceptional is work, not talent. Professor Michael Howe and colleagues at Exeter University examined outstanding performances in many areas and couldn't find anyone who reached the highest levels of achievement without thousands of hours of work and practice, whether in music, mathematics, chess, or sports.

I'm not saying the Shakespeares, Picassos, Einsteins and Edisons of the world don't have some natural affinity for what they do, but the key seems to be that they work harder and longer than other people. Look at child prodigy Mozart. Everybody said the kid had talent, but he still had to work 12 hours a day for over a decade in order to produce his first acknowledged masterpiece. Then there's Michelangelo, who produced some of the world's great art, yet he gave work, not talent, the credit for his genius: "If people knew how hard I worked to get my mastery, it wouldn't seem so wonderful after all."

Talent may provide an early advantage, but many people lose their edge by not putting in enough effort. Michael Jordan slacked off, until the coach cut him from the varsity basketball team. That little wake-up call made Michael realize he couldn't rely on talent alone and he began to practice harder. Soon he became one of the hardest-working players, and he even bullied the other players if they weren't putting in the effort. (There's nothing worse than a reformed slacker.) So after a lot of work and practice on the basketball court, he became the Michael Jordan that coaches wanted to hire, not fire.

We overvalue talent and undervalue work because we don't see what goes on behind the scenes. We see the "talented" dancer's 15 minutes of fame, not the 15 years of work that went into it. We see the "talented" gymnast's perfect score of 10, not the 10 years of struggle to get there. We see the 200-page book, not the 20,000 hours the "talented" writer spent sweating over it.

The truth is, whether you have a natural gift of talent or not, there's an even greater gift you can give yourself, and that's the ability to work hard.

When people say to me, "Oh, it must be so wonderful to have a God-given talent," I say, "That's a lot of crap." Artists are disciplined. It's not a case of waiting for inspiration. You've gotta work.

Ken Danby renowned artist

I think numbers and I have always gotten along. But my talent, I'm sure, is just the matter of the time and hours I've put into it. To get good at anything really requires practice.

Arthur Benjamin "America's Best Math Whiz"

Nobody's a natural. You work hard to get good and then work hard to get better.

Paul Coffey hockey player, record goals by a defenceman

People would say to me, "You're so lucky to be talented," and I was always puzzled by that because every single drawing was a struggle for me. I spent a lot of time learning to draw.

Robin Budd animation film director

I WANTED A PONY AND ALL I GOT WAS A

WORK ETHIC

The first qualification for success in my view **is a strong work ethic**.

Henry Ford II president of Ford

When I was a kid I desperately wanted a pony. I was gonna be a cowboy, so a horse, or at least a pony, was a basic requirement of the job. I mean, galloping around on a broomstick just didn't cut it. I begged Dad for a pony, but he never gave in. Instead, he gave me something that turned out to be much better – a work ethic. Dad was a WorkaFrolic™ who always worked a lot and enjoyed it, and by watching him, I picked up that same ethic.

I've discovered that a strong work ethic is a common pattern among successful people in all fields. I know this is hard to believe, but even successful rock stars have a strong work ethic. I've seen many Rolling Stones concerts and I can tell you that Gene Simmons of Kiss is right when he says about the Stones, "They've maintained the work ethic of a brand-new band. They go out there every night and they deliver." A work ethic helps nurses, like Janell Jacobs, deliver better health care: "A work ethic not only affects you, it affects the people you work with. In my line of work it affects the care of patients. If somebody doesn't do their job it affects a patient's well-being."

How do you pick up a work ethic? By hanging around people who have one, and often that means parents. Anita Roddick, founder of the Body Shop says, "I was brought up in a large Italian immigrant family with a work ethic...we worked every weekend, every evening, and every holiday in the café." Architect William McDonough's family also had a strong work ethic, which meant William had to work more than many other kids: "We had to pay our own way through school. I had 2 paper routes, and shined shoes, and worked every vacation." *Time* magazine called William "a hero for the planet" so I'd say his work ethic paid off for him, as well as the world.

But what if you were born into a family without a work ethic? Well, just find a WorkaFrolic who likes to work – a mentor, boss, coach, or role model – and hang out with them. In no time, their work ethic will rub off on you. The trick is to be with people who have fun at work, not those who make fun of work.

In hindsight, a work ethic is the best gift Dad ever gave me, although at the time I really would have preferred the pony. But material things and money soon disappear. Instead give kids a strong work ethic and it will carry them off into the sunset, and on to success.

I think what my dad gave me at a young age was an appreciation for hard work leading to results.
Silken Laumann
world-champion rower

I have always worked hard. It's my cultural background and you can see it in my family. Many of my relatives have 2 jobs. It's the work ethic.
Elinor MacKinnon
CIO, Blue Shield

I grew up in a household that gave us a work ethic. I never thought of work as being hard.
Issy Sharp founder, Four Seasons Hotels and Resorts

I come from a family that has an incredible work ethic...When I was 12, I said to my dad, "When do I get my first allowance?" He said, "When you get a job." So I got a job the following day at a bicycle store, and became their number one salesperson.
Kenneth Tuchman
founder, TeleTech

TRUST THAT YOUR HARD **WORK WILL PAY OFF**

I've always believed that if you **put in the work, the results will come.**

Michael Jordan
basketball superstar

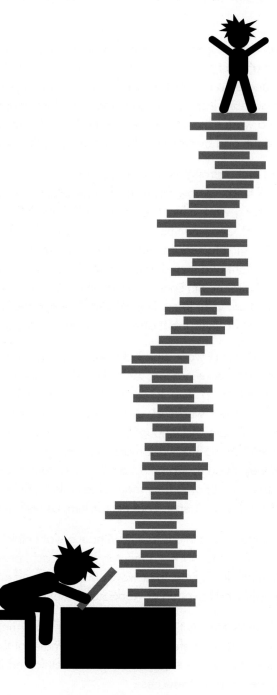

Sometimes, when you're putting a lot of effort and hours into something, you wonder if it will ever pay off. I remember times when I was working all night, and in the back of my mind I'd be thinking, "Is it worth it? Maybe this is all for nothing, so why bother?" Usually I'd just shove those doubts aside and keep going. Now, in hindsight, I'm glad I did because eventually the work did pay off and I learned to trust that it always would.

Wayne Schuurman, president of Audio Advisor, told me that it was a trust in work that helped him get out of hot water when his company was in financial trouble: "I had to come up with a genius way of saving the business. And my genius way of saving everything was to get up in the morning and go to work. I had friends that this happened to, and they stopped working and goofed off. But I went to work every day and worked as hard as I could. I didn't stop. I just kept pushing. And eventually it worked out." As golf superstar Tiger Woods says, if you have a strong work ethic it's amazing how good things will just unfold.

Trusting work is like trusting the wind. When I first started windsurfing, and there was a really strong wind, I'd stand upright on the board and try to pull the sail around, but the wind would catch it and I'd become a human projectile, catapulted across the board into the water. After watching me wipe out about 200 times, a guy who actually knew what he was doing came over and said, "When it's really blowing, the way to get going is to fall backwards and then, just before you hit the water, pull the sail around into the wind. It takes a leap of faith because you think you'll land in the water, but you have to trust that the wind will hold you up."

I tried it and, like magic, it worked. From that moment on I remembered: Trust the wind. So when it was blowing hard, I'd just fall backwards, the wind would catch the sail and hold me up. It's the same when life is blowing hard, and you're putting in lots of hours, and not sure if it's really getting you anywhere. At times like that, just fall into work, keep going, and trust that the effort will hold you up and pay off, because in the end it will. Renowned college football coach Lou Holtz once said: "No one has ever drowned in sweat. " I'd go a step further and say: A lot of sweat is like a river that carries you along and keeps you afloat.

> **You must have faith that your work ethic and your discipline have prepared you to be successful.**
> **Rick Pitino**
> renowned basketball coach

> **Keep it in your mind: "I can make this work because I'm gonna work hard!" The self-confidence that you can out-work the other guy will carry you through a lot.**
> **Jerry Hayes** optometrist, founder, Hayes Marketing

> **Sometimes when I'm working on a book I get stuck. And for that whole stuck period, the only thing that can save you is to get to the desk and keep working, because you've done this before and you'll work it out.**
> **Joseph Mark Glazner** author

> **Know that hard work is going to pay off. It may not pay off today, but the longer you stick with something the more it pays off. You just have to put time in on the treadmill and trust that it is going to make a difference.**
> **Kate Laidley** VP, JN4D

MY **DAD** THE WORKA**FROLIC**

TAUGHT ME **WORK** AND **FUN** CAN **BOTH BE ONE**

How did a guy like me, who couldn't make it on smarts, looks, or luck, actually do okay? It's simple. I worked hard. Yes, I'm a WorkaFrolic™. I picked it up from my father, who always brought work home with him and was happiest sitting at our dining room table, tapping away at his old adding machine. Dad never let on that he really liked work. He'd always say "Well, back to the old grind!" But you knew he couldn't wait to get back to the old grind. He never preached to me about working hard – he just did it.

I could see that he was happy working, and I became a WorkaFrolic, too. Oh, not right away, since I was a typical, lazy teenager. I'm a slow learner so it took time for Dad's work ethic to surface. It was when I went to college to study design that the work ethic finally kicked into gear. Possessing no real talent, I started off at the bottom of the class and had to work my butt off just to avoid flunking. So, while my classmates were out partying, I was in my room working on design projects. Then a funny thing happened. The really talented people in the class started to rest on their laurels and worked less, while I worked more. I started to pull ahead, and at graduation I was the one awarded a traveling scholarship.

That experience showed me the value of work and it became my secret edge in the business world. I joined a big company and worked very hard for 10 years. Then I started my own company and my eyes were opened to what work really was. Actually, they were held open by toothpicks, so I could make it through the long hours. Over the years, most days have been 12 to 16 hours, including many weekends. And when a panic deadline is staring me in the face, sleep goes out the window. But those times, when I'm up against the wall, busting my buns to meet a challenge, have been some of the best experiences of my life.

Wait a minute! I'm talking a lot about work. What about play? The truth is, I probably play more than most people. It's just that it's disguised as work a lot of the time. The thing is, I don't see any dividing line between work and play. They're intertwined. When I have fun working hard at the office, it's play. And when I pedal my butt off biking, it's work. There's no difference. Both involve fun, work, and play.

Oh, sure, it's nice to sit on a beach, but the best vacations my wife Baiba and I take are the ones where some effort is involved. Like the time we ran through the Himalayan mountains for a week, or when we ran up the Inca trail to Machu Picchu, or along the Great Wall of China. They were all fun experiences. We were running around and playing like kids, having loads of fun. But, I can tell you, running up a mountain is also a lot of work. Well, maybe more for Baiba, since she has to carry me. Guess that's why she says, "If it hurts, it must be a vacation."

So, work hard and play hard, and often they're the same thing. And the irony is, by working hard, life actually becomes easy. How's that? Well, I love my work and have fun doing it so it really isn't hard. And it gives me enough money to pay other people to do the things I really do find hard. To me, fixing my car is hard – or for that matter, fixing or building anything – but I can afford to pay other people to do it.

That's why I say, if you want life to be easy, work hard. Become a WorkaFrolic.

FOCUS

1. **PASSION**   2. **WORK**   3. **FOCUS**   4. **PUSH**

FOCUS LEADS TO SUCCESS

FOCUS

68 **FOCUS ON ONE THING**
70 **START BY THINKING WIDE, THEN NARROW DOWN AND FOCUS**
72 **BE SINGLE-MINDED NOT NARROW-MINDED**
74 **SUCCESSFUL COMPANIES FOCUS ON ONE THING**

CONCENTRATION

76 **BE ABLE TO PUT YOUR HEAD DOWN AND CONCENTRATE**

3 CONCENTRATION TIPS

78 **1. TO CONCENTRATE, ELIMINATE DISTRACTIONS**
80 **2. USE MENTAL BLINDERS TO BLOCK OUT DISTRACTIONS**
82 **3. IT'S EASY TO CONCENTRATE IF YOU'RE INTERESTED**

MY STORY

84 **FINALLY I STOPPED DABBLING AND FOCUSED**

5. **IDEAS**   6. **IMPROVE**   7. **SERVE**   8. **PERSIST**

You have to be focused. The single universal quality among every successful person I know is **they all have an incredibly high level of energy focused on one thing.**

Jay Chiat co-founder, Chiat/Day advertising

The 3rd success factor is FOCUS. Successful people say it's important to focus on one thing, and one thing only. Renowned filmmaker Norman Jewison said to me, "I think it all has to do with committing yourself and focusing yourself to one thing. I believe to do one thing well brings not only satisfaction, it also brings a kind of confidence. We become very confident when we know we can do one thing well."

Professor of mathematics Arthur Benjamin says, "I think every successful person spends an intense amount of time focused on one activity they really love." Arthur's focus on math turned him into "America's Best Math Whiz." When I talked to Dean Kamen, instead of asking what leads to success, I asked, "What leads to failure?" And the first thing he said was, "To be a failure, don't focus." Dean's focus on technology solutions for health problems led him to over 150 patents, and the invention of some very cool devices like the first portable insulin pump, the heart stent, and the Segway human transporter.

Focus is all about specializing in something and becoming an expert at it. Joseph MacInnis says, "You need to have a specialty, which is the platform upon which you stand very firmly. In my case, I was a physician, but I specialized in physiology and divers working at extreme depths." That focus helped Joe become the first person to dive under the North Pole and also be among the first divers to explore the wreck of the Titanic. Psychiatrist and Stanford professor Ken Woodrow says, "You do have to be an expert in some area in order to bring something to the party and give back in a meaningful way."

Developing expertise means we can't just do something for a week, then fly off and do something else. Achieving success at anything – a career, goal, a project – means staying focused on that one thing for months, years, or even decades. It took downhill skier Picabo Street 22 years of focus to become a gold medalist in the Olympics. It's interesting that many successful people's area of focus and expertise can be described in 5 words or less.

Martin Luther King - civil rights expert   **Martha Stewart** - homemaking expert
Frank Gehry - sculptural form expert   **Albert Einstein** - Relativity expert
Michael Jordan - dunking expert   **Bill Gates** - software expert

Can you describe your area of focus and expertise in 5 words or less?

Focus is absolutely critical. Many people work really hard, but they're not focused. They're flying around trying to do too many things, and the work they're doing becomes diluted.
Susan Ruptash architect, principal, Quadrangle Architects

I followed my dream and I just stayed focused. And I didn't give up. Focus.
Peter Max renowned pop artist

I laser in on something, and I end up very, very focused. I can just really disappear into obsession with one thing.
Chris Anderson chairman, TED conference

It's infinite focus. I spent almost 5 years developing the search engine.
Louis Monier developer of the Alta Vista search engine

After a number of years of focus you reach a point of proficiency. For me, it was about 20 years, working at it pretty intently.
Gary Burton Grammy award-winning vibraphonist

At first you go wide and let yourself wander a little bit to figure out the best way of getting there. But, at the end of the day, **it requires long-term focus to get there.**

Adam Bly founder, *SEED* science magazine

Success means narrowing down and focusing on one thing, not being scattered. But wait! (Here comes the disclaimer.) *Don't focus too soon.* At the beginning of anything – a career, a goal, a project – we need to do the opposite of focus. We need to start by thinking wide.

That's why they invented schools, so we get exposed to many different subjects and discover what turns us on. And, believe it or not, all those seemingly useless subjects come back later to help us in the one thing we focus on. Bob Rogers, founder of BRC Imagination Arts, says, "In school, some people ask, 'What does this course have to do with anything?' But, eventually it all relates. It's only in retrospect that you find out every single course was useful."

Studying to be a doctor requires intense focus, but Sherwin Nuland, a famous clinical professor of surgery at Yale, told me he started out by thinking wide: "I didn't focus early in my career. I thought broadly. You want to learn everything you can get your hands on. By the time I went to medical school, I'd learned about literature and history, and you're much better when you focus, because you bring all of these wide things to the table."

Google co-founder Larry Page said to me, "You should focus on one important goal. It takes a long time to do these things and you need to be pretty single-minded. But you also need to really understand all the different parts. At Stanford, we built the whole search engine, so we had to understand all the parts, we had to interact with the world, and we had to innovate in different areas like business, not just computer science, to make our system work."

Yes, thinking wide is important at times, but if we continue to do it for too long our energy is dispersed in many different directions. We become dabblers in many things and masters of none. So, at some point, we need to shift gears, narrow down, and focus in on one area. As Don Norman, author of *The Way Things Work,* says, "You have to think broadly in the beginning, but you're never going to finish anything unless you focus."

When you focus the sun's rays through a magnifying glass, it can generate enough energy to create a fire. So use the same principle in your own life. Focus all your energy intensely on one thing, and it will help fire up your own success.

> **When I'm trying to plan out the landscape, then I try to think very broad. But when I'm trying to accomplish something, I'm very focused.**
>
> **Deborah McGuinness** senior research scientist, Stanford

> **When you're young and have the time and energy, get as broad an education as you can, because that comes back to help you later on.**
>
> **Douglas Dorner** surgeon, senior VP, Iowa Health

> **You need to think broadly, because you have to take pieces from here and there and fit them together into a specialty – and then it clicks.**
>
> **Josef Penninger** renowned medical geneticist

> **You explore the landscape and then you focus deeply in one area. You survey and then you drill down.**
>
> **Kim Rossmo** criminologist

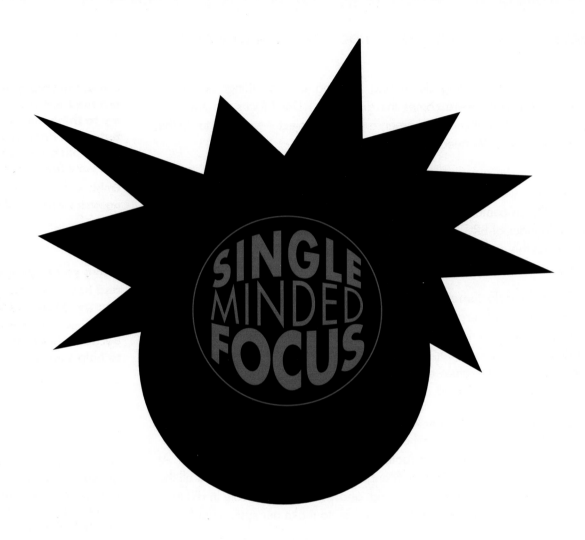

You must be single-minded. Drive for the one thing on which you have decided.

George Patton famous army general

We have a million things on our minds every day. But we can't succeed at a million things. It's hard enough to succeed at just one thing. That's why it helps to develop a single-minded focus. Philanthropist John D. Rockefeller Jnr. said, "Singleness of purpose is one of the chief essentials for success in life..."

A single-minded focus enabled Cathy Rigby to take home Olympic gold in gymnastics. She says, "I couldn't think of anything else but winning a gold medal." Scientist Eva Vertes was only 15 when her single-minded pursuit to wipe out Alzheimer's disease led her to a major discovery and possible cure. She told me, "Focus and dedication are important. You have to devote your whole life to one thing for a while. I devoted my life to getting started in Alzheimer's. Getting started is the hardest part, and if you don't have focus and determination you'll just go off on tangents."

A single-minded focus enabled astrophysicists working on the MOST space telescope project to do something nobody else could do – build a suitcase-sized satellite costing $10 million, compared to the $2 billion cost of the huge Hubble space telescope. Jaymie Matthews, astrophysicist and mission scientist for the MOST space telescope, told me, "Focus is the key word for our success. We pulled this off on such a tight budget and short time line because we did one thing exceptionally well. We didn't try to make the Swiss Army knives of telescopes that did a lot of things." Lawyer Susan Grode works with successful people in many fields and she said to me, "One of the things I've observed among many of my clients is how single-minded they are in pursuit of a goal. It can be constructing a new city, a new sculpture, their next joke, but they're absolutely single-minded in that pursuit. And they refuse to let the world deter that focus."

A word of caution. Don't confuse single-minded with narrow-minded. Narrow-minded means refusing to accept new information. But successful people are like sponges, always absorbing new stuff from many different areas, because it gives them new perspectives they can apply to their single-minded pursuit. So even though you're focused on one thing, keep poking your head up, looking around at the world, and absorbing something new. Take it all in, then switch gears and get back to the single-minded focus that will really help you succeed.

I think you have to be very single-minded to stay focused enough to really break through whatever you're doing. I was single-minded to the point of being obsessive.
Thomas Dolby musician

I began to enjoy the single-mindedness of training, riding hard during the day and holing up in the cabin in the evenings.
Lance Armstrong champion cyclist

I have a singular focus. I've kind of become obsessed with work, and obsessed with the product.
Rick Mercer comedian

I have this vision that is constantly evolving in my head. I go to sleep thinking about it, and wake up thinking about it, and have the shower beating me on the back while I am thinking about it.
Kenneth Tuchman founder, TeleTech

SUCCESSFUL COMPANIES

FOCUS

What it takes to make a company successful is
laser-like focus on just one thing.

Bill Gross chairman, idealab

Successful people focus and so do successful companies. When Bill Gates started Microsoft he didn't try to do everything under the sun. He focused on one thing and one thing only, saying, "Microsoft is designed to write great software. We are not designed to be good at other things. We only know how to hire, how to manage, and how to globalize software products."

Domino's Pizza thrived because they focused on pizza, and within that they focused on speed of delivery. When founder Tom Monaghan was asked the secret of his success, he said, "A fanatical focus on doing one thing well." Warren Buffett became the world's most successful investor by focusing. He said, "I can't be involved in 50 or 75 things. That's a Noah's Ark way of investing – you end up with a zoo that way. I like to put meaningful amounts of money in a few things."

In the mobile email market, some companies tried to make a device that did everything, but Research in Motion focused on doing only one thing really well – always-on email that automatically comes to your BlackBerry. That focus gained them an early lead in the market, which is why Jim Balsillie, co-CEO of RIM, says, "Focus. The more experienced I get, the more I realize that great focus is an excellent competitive strategy." Some companies succeed at one thing, like widgets, so they think, "Why not try banking or ice cream?" Those diversions often fail because they lack the intense amount of focus needed to succeed. Research in Motion founder Mike Lazaridis cautions that, when you're successful, instead of losing focus, you actually need to focus deeper. And that approach kept BlackBerry at the head of the wireless email pack.

Bill Tatham maintained his focus. He started Janna Systems, a customer-relationship software business, in his basement and focused on serving the small niche of financial services firms. As the company became more successful, Bill refused to diversify. He says, "The key was our maniacal focus. You have to learn to say no to opportunities that don't fit your strategy." Bill's focus paid off big-time when he sold the little business he started in his basement for over a billion dollars. The moral of the story is, if you want to your business to go from basement to billions – focus.

In business, being able to focus on a micro-niche is ultimately very important.
Gerald Durnell CEO, ProTech Publishing

My focus is only on the health industry; I do nothing else.
Anula Jayasuriyk venture capitalist, Draper, Fisher, Jurvetson

If you look at my company Earthlink, I just focused on the things that had not been invented yet and spent all my time on those.
Sky Dayton founder, Earthlink

My thinking has always been fairly broad, but I've learned that in business you do need to focus. I think the biggest mistake that people make is that they tend to lose their focus on a commodity or what the real business is, and they let their attention drift.
Gord Lownds founder, Sleep Country

DEVELOP THE ABILITY TO CONCENTRATE

I have a ferocious ability to concentrate. I can say, "I am going to do this," and close the rest of the world off. And I think that matters an awful lot in any job.

Jennifer Mather animal behaviorist

Focus actually has 2 parts: Focus and Concentration. We tend to use these words interchangeably and I always wondered, "What's the difference?" So I looked in the dictionary and it said the definition of focus is "to concentrate" and the definition of concentrate is "to focus." Whew, glad they cleared that up! But having focused, or concentrated, on the subject for years, here's how I see it: Focus is more long-term, like focusing on a career or a big goal; concentration is more short-term, like concentrating on getting something done right now. Both focus and concentration mean zeroing in on one thing and blocking out everything else.

The ability to concentrate is something that helps many people succeed. Golfing great Tiger Woods has an incredible ability to concentrate. He says that when you're about to hit that ball, it has to be the only thing you're thinking about, the only thing that matters at that point in time. Everything else has to be pushed aside or shut out, including all the screaming fans. Which brings up a good point. Concentration doesn't necessarily mean being alone in a quiet place. Tiger's ability to concentrate really pays off when he's inundated by noisy fans yelling so loud his ears are ringing. He just blocks it all out and performs. And being able to concentrate on where he wants that little white ball to go, has taken Tiger to where he wants to go.

Olympic gold medal hurdler Edwin Moses says, "Concentration is why some athletes are better than others. You develop that concentration in training. You can't be lackluster in training and concentrate in a meet." Lindsay Sharp, who heads up the National Museum of Science and Industry in London, told me, "It's very hard to concentrate, so you have to practice a lot and it gets built up like any muscle. I wasn't taught. I learned how to study in the middle of an airport. So now, if I'm focused on reading or writing and there's a fire siren going, I don't even hear it."

Being able to snap into concentration mode will help you no matter what you're doing, whether it's finishing a project, writing a letter, painting a wall, doing a term paper, working on a court case, or winning a game. But if you can't concentrate, how do you concentrate long enough to learn how to concentrate? Turn the page for a few tips.

The secret of my success? Concentration.

Chris Evert tennis legend

When every physical and mental resource is focused, one's power to solve a problem multiplies tremendously.

Norman Vincent Peale author, *The Power of Positive Thinking*

My formula for success is simple: Practice and concentration – then more practice and more concentration.

Babe Didrikson Zaharias golfer, track and field great

Concentrate all your thoughts upon the work at hand. The sun's rays do not burn until brought to a focus.

Alexander Graham Bell inventor of the telephone

I'm very focused before and during a performance. Once I'm finished my performance, then I'll look around.

Naida Cole acclaimed pianist

ELIMINATE

DISTRACTIONS

SO YOU CAN **CONCENTRATE**

Keep focused on what you want, even though there may be a lot of **distractions**.

Clement Mok founder, Studio Archetype

Concentration is important, so here's 3 tips to help you concentrate. The first tip is to eliminate distractions. A distraction is anything that's either fun or noisy. This includes TV, music, cell phones, video games, parties, the opposite sex, or just plain sex. Things that are not fun or noisy are rarely distracting. I mean, when was the last time you were distracted by broccoli or a librarian?

Every day, scientists are busy inventing new distractions, although it's not easy since they're constantly getting distracted. TV has grown into a huge, widescreen, panorama, stereo-sound, gazillion-channel distraction. And with cell phones, email, surfing the web, and chat lines, it's a wonder we can concentrate for more than a second before something rings, beeps, or warbles. Successful people need concentration time, so they find ways to eliminate those distractions. Great horror novelist Stephen King gives some advice to aspiring writers, like me: "If possible, there should be no telephone in your writing room, certainly no TV or video games for you to fool around with. If there's a window, draw the curtains or pull down the shades unless it looks out at a blank wall. For any writer, but for the beginning writer in particular, it's wise to eliminate every possible distraction."

Then there's Warren Buffett. He became one of the world's richest men by constantly living in a state of no distraction – Nebraska. He says, "I used to feel, when I worked back in New York, that there were more stimuli just hitting me all the time....It's much easier to think here." Hmmm... I wonder if fewer distractions could be the reason why small towns produce so many successful people? I haven't done a statistical survey, but I can tell you I'm no longer surprised when a successful person tells me they grew up in a place like East Cupcake, or a cabin in the middle of nowhere. And they often go back to a place like that when they need to concentrate. When Wade Davis was writing a book, he went to a cabin in the wilderness, where he worked 14 hours a day for 7 months, with no distractions, and came back with the best-seller *The Serpent and the Rainbow*.

A cabin in the woods! Gee, maybe that's what I need. I mean, there are so many distractions here in the city, I'm having real trouble focusing long enough to finish this chapter on focus. I'm sure I'd get a lot more writing done in a cabin in the woods. I wonder if they get satellite TV?

You can surf the internet or watch TV and get distracted very easily. Writing means that you have to tune everything out and just focus on that.

Meredith Bagby CNN reporter, author

I find the most successful people are willing to forego many of the diversions that occur along the way, in order to stay true to their goal.

Susan Grode lawyer

I stay focused. You can't do it all so I actually cut out a lot of extraneous things. I haven't watched television for 18 years. I don't miss it.

Steve Jurvetson renowned venture capitalist

I grew up in a rural environment, and I think it helped form my thinking processes, because there's not a lot of distractions. You can spend a lot of time inside your own mind thinking about things.

Elinor MacKinnon CIO, Blue Shield

USE **MENTAL BLINDERS** TO BLOCK OUT DISTRACTIONS

I did my doctoral thesis in a bar because I loved the noise. **I could concentrate even with all the noise around me**.

John Seely Brown chief scientist, Xerox

When we need to concentrate, we can't always find a nice quiet place without distractions, so it helps to be able to mentally block them out. You know, the same way leather blinders on horse's eyes keep them focused straight ahead and block out distractions on the side. Well, successful people develop mental blinders, and when they need to concentrate they just go "click" and shut out all the noise and distractions.

Quincy Jones developed mental blinders through years of composing music wherever he happened to be, whether it was sitting on the floor in a hallway or surrounded by noise and commotion backstage. He said to me, "I do have the ability to focus. I really love chaos, but you can remain calm in the midst of it, because you become totally focused while the chaos spins around you." Quincy told me his buddy Steven Spielberg has developed the same ability.

Some people use good noise to block out distracting noise. Stephen King says, "I work to loud music – hard rock stuff like AC/DC, Guns 'n Roses, and Metallica have always been particular favorites – but for me the music is just another way of shutting the door." Xerox chief scientist John Seely Brown said to me, "I did my doctoral thesis in a bar, because I loved the noise. I could concentrate, even with all the noise around me. We call that 'state of flow.' Once you get into it you can totally focus on what you are doing and it doesn't matter what's happening around you." Gee, I thought all those people in bars were partyers and it turns out they could be academics.

J.K. Rowling wrote the first *Harry Potter* book in a café, writing with one hand and taking care of her baby with the other. I'm like J.K. Rowling, except without the baby and the millions of books sold. After years of being surrounded by activity while I wrote scripts and speeches, I can now put on mental blinders and write better in a noisy coffee shop than in my quiet office. The only downside is, after all the caffeine they have to peel me off the ceiling. The moral of the story is, develop the ability to put on your own mental blinders and block out distractions. As master architect Mies van der Rohe once said, "Less is more." And in this case, less distraction is more success.

> When I focus on something, usually it's as though I've got blinders on. I lock on that.
> **Laurie Skreslet** first Canadian to summit Everest

> It's like I put the lenses over my eyes, and I see the whole world only in those terms for a little while.
> **John Girard** CEO, Clickability

> I can write with noise in the background. I worked in newspapers for many years and you're in a big room with lots of noise and people around.
> **Robert Fulford** journalist

> [Michael Jordan's] ability to stay relaxed and intensely focused in the midst of chaos is unsurpassed.
> **Phil Jackson** basketball coach, Chicago Bulls

> In my early career, I tended to keep my head down and never look up. There are a lot of surgeons who have blinders on and are very intense about their work.
> **Douglas Dorner** vascular surgeon

HAVING TROUBLE CONCENTRATING?

ATTENTION **D**EFICIT **D**ISORDER

IS SOMETIMES

INTEREST **D**EFICIT **D**ISORDER

It's crucial to be interested and passionate about what you're doing, **otherwise it's hard to concentrate** on it.

Lindsay Sharp museum director

What's the easiest way to concentrate on something? It's simple. Be interested in it. Of course, there will always be things we need to do that aren't the least bit interesting and we need to learn to concentrate on those too. But if you can find things that interest you, it'll be a lot easier. As David Jensen, chief executive of Brooklands Executives recruitment, says, "I can concentrate on things that interest me. But give me a task, whether it's academic or sporting or something that I'm not interested in, and I fail at it. So I tend to hone in on the things I find interesting."

These days you hear a lot about kids with ADD – Attention Deficit Disorder. It can be a serious illness, but I think ADD is sometimes IDD – Interest Deficit Disorder. The kid just isn't interested in the stuff they're told to concentrate on. But it's funny how they can concentrate like crazy on something they do find interesting, like an exciting video game or the latest trendy shoes. Maybe Bill Gates had IDD. He got poor grades in school subjects that didn't interest him and his parents even sent him to counselling. But once Bill found something that did spark his interest – computers and software – his ability to concentrate kicked in big-time.

I, too, suffered from IDD, since most school subjects didn't interest me. Especially English, and writing essays on boring things I couldn't care less about. My attention wandered so much they had to send out search parties to find it. No wonder I ended up with a 66 in 12th grade English. Now, fast forward to when I was out in the real world producing videos. I hired writers to develop scripts, but they were often unacceptable, so one day I started writing them myself, without any training and purely out of interest. Suddenly I had no trouble concentrating. You couldn't tear me away from writing. I focused on it, got better, and even won an award for the best corporate video script in the world. So let's see... I went from getting a mark of 66 writing essays in high school to a top award writing video scripts, and the only difference was *interest*, the magic ingredient that made it easy to concentrate.

The truth is we all find it hard to concentrate on some things and easy to concentrate on others, and a lot of it has to do with following your interests and doing what you love. Now, if I could only find a way to get interested in cleaning up the house...

Find things that you like a lot, so you're willing to focus on them. I don't focus on things I don't like.
Nathan Myhrvold chief technology officer, Microsoft

A lot of people's success in business is more determined by their level of interest rather than their ability to do it. If you're not interested, it's hard to do it, no matter how important it is.
John Caldwell president, CAE

It's knowing your interests and working at those. I'm definitely not lazy, but I'm lazy about doing things that don't interest me.
Cliff Read award-winning product designer

In order to work at something, I need to be interested in it. I'm very bad at working hard at something I don't care about. If I care about something, I'll do whatever it takes.
Chris Anderson chairman, TED conference

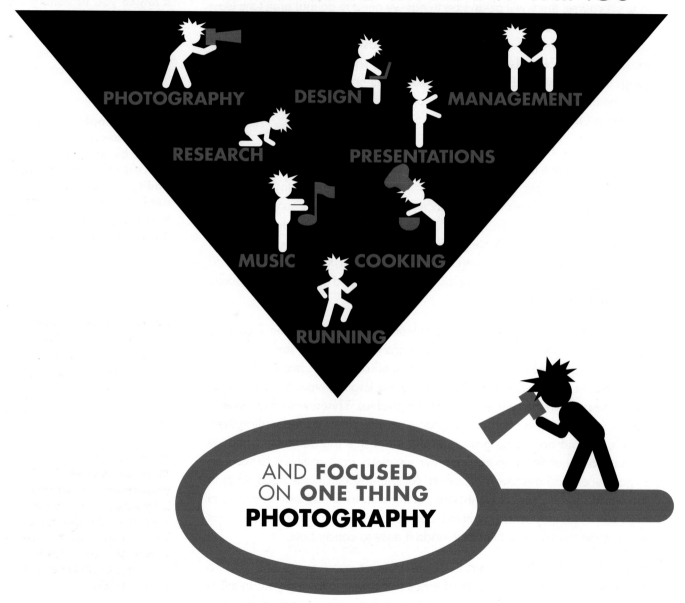

I STOPPED DABBLING IN MANY THINGS

PHOTOGRAPHY DESIGN MANAGEMENT

RESEARCH PRESENTATIONS

MUSIC COOKING

RUNNING

AND **FOCUSED** ON **ONE THING** **PHOTOGRAPHY**

If you had to come up with one word that sums up why, at one point in my life, I wasn't living up to my full potential, it would be "dabble." I mean, after spending 10 years in the work force I was still dabbling in many different areas: research, design, project management, presentations, writing, and advertising photography. On the personal front, I was dabbling in sailing, rowing, and running – plus taking music, cooking, and French classes. Running all over the map meant I never stopped in any one place long enough to become really good at it. And, let's face it, there isn't much demand for professional dabblers. When you look in the classifieds for a job you don't see ads like this:

> "Senior Dabbler required for growing midtown firm. Three years minimum experience, preferably accumulated only 20 minutes at a time. Candidate must have only superficial knowledge. Those with any real expertise need not apply. Preference will be given to those with a short attention span and an MDA – Must Dabble Always."

I realized that if I was going to get anywhere I had to focus and become an expert at something. I loved photography, but it was always a sideline. Now it was time to focus on it and see how far I could take it. So I left my well-paying job at the big corporation, started my own company, and focused all my energy on photography. The personal dabbling in music, French, and cooking classes had to go. (No big loss – my real strength was eating, not cooking.) The focus paid off, and I finally started to achieve success. I became a pretty good advertising photographer, my work appeared in international magazines, and I even shot a cover for *Playboy*. But, as I mentioned in "About the Author," I only did one *Playboy* shoot. My wife reminded me of an old Zen saying: "He who shoots bunnies may also get shot."

Over time, my passions morphed from photography to marketing to video production to writing. But, at any one time, I focused on only one thing. No dabbling. And each time the intense focus paid off in terms of quality, satisfaction, awards – oh, and I almost forgot – money. The bottom line is, if you really want to reach your potential, FOCUS.

Don't just dabble. Really get into it. Read, understand, practice, learn.
Robert Young Pelton writer, *Fielding's World's Most Dangerous Places*

To do a good job at something you've got to concentrate in one area, not be a jock-of-all-trades.
Ted Turner broadcasting and entertainment tycoon

My father always said, if you want to be a star, don't be versatile.
Jason Robards movie star

Focus has helped me. There are so many things going on out there, and if you don't have that ability to sort the most important from the less important, you really can't use your time effectively.
Larry Burns head of R&D, General Motors

PUSH

1. **PASSION**   2. **WORK**   3. **FOCUS**   4. **PUSH**

PUSH LEADS TO SUCCESS

88 **JUST KEEP PUSHING YOURSELF**

PUSH THROUGH SHYNESS
90 **MANY SUCCESSFUL PEOPLE ARE SHY, BUT PUSH THROUGH IT**
92 **SHYNESS ISN'T ALL BAD – IT CAN HELP YOU SUCCEED**
94 **TO GET OVER SHYNESS PUSH YOURSELF IN FRONT OF PEOPLE**

PUSH THROUGH SELF-DOUBT
96 **SUCCESSFUL PEOPLE HAVE SELF- DOUBT**
98 **SOME TIPS TO HELP YOU PUSH THROUGH THE DOUBT**
100 **USE DOUBT TO PUSH YOU HIGHER**

9 WAYS TO PUSH YOURSELF
102 **1. GET A CHALLENGE TO PUSH YOU**
104 **2. GET A GOAL TO PUSH YOU**
106 **3. GET A DEADLINE TO PUSH YOU**
108 **4. GET SELF-DISCIPLINE TO PUSH YOU**
110 **5. GET A MOTHER TO PUSH YOU**
112 **6. GET OTHERS TO PUSH YOU**
114 **7. GET COMPETITION TO PUSH YOU**
116 **8. GET A TOR-MENTOR TO PUSH YOU**
118 **9. PUSH OUT OF YOUR COMFORT ZONE**

5. **IDEAS**   6. **IMPROVE**   7. **SERVE**   8. **PERSIST**

PUSH
YOURSELF

Push yourself. Man, that's huge. Always. **Physically, mentally, you've gotta push, push, push.**

David Gallo marine scientist, director, Woods Hole Oceanographic Institute

I used to think all successful people were driven and ambitious. I mean, that's how they're usually portrayed on TV. But in my research, I discovered a huge group of people who say they aren't particularly ambitious or driven. They just keep pushing themselves.

Adventurer Ben Saunders said to me, "I'm not the driven, controlling type. I'm a pretty laid-back character and I kind of go with the flow. But I do push myself extremely hard, and I expect high things from myself." Ben pushed himself all the way to the North Pole on a pair of skis. Graham Hawkes pushed himself to become the world record holder for the deepest solo ocean dive, plus he's founder of 5 technology companies. Graham said, "I always think of myself as a kind of humble person who doesn't push. But I really think I do push. It's in there somewhere, and somehow it came out." World-champion rower Silken Laumann says, "As a rower, I'm average size and average weight. In order to beat some of the really big, strong, single scullers that I compete against, I need a little extra edge. And I think that extra edge, to a great extent, is the mental ability to push myself."

Oh, I should clarify that pushing yourself doesn't mean being pushy, like those people who are always pushing in front of you in line. (Don't you hate that?) I've interviewed a lot of successful people and none came across a pushy. As Steve Schklair, CEO of Cobalt Entertainment, said to me, "I'm not a pushy kind of guy, but I push myself." So does renowned architect William McDonough: "When I'm working on a project, I may not know what the result will be, but I know that we're going to keep pushing until we all succeed."

The ability to push ourselves helps get us through the down times and all the stuff we don't want to do. Top real estate agent Elli Davis says, "Some days, I'm just in a bad mood. I don't want to call this person again and again and again. I just push myself." Legendary management consultant Peter Drucker sums it up by simply saying, "Push, push, push and you see results."

Successful people push themselves through shyness, doubt, and fear. They push boundaries. They push limits. They push beyond what's expected. It all comes down to pushing themselves in one way or another. And that's how they discover what they're really capable of. So just keep pushing yourself.

> **I pushed myself. I think it's important. I've always pushed myself.**
> Michael Stadtlander world-renowned chef

> **Push yourself. Try hard. You don't just sit and wait for life to happen to you.**
> Leslie Westbrook marketing consultant

> **I worked hard. Just loaded up and pushed through. I absolutely push myself.**
> Steve Jurvetson prominent venture capitalist

> **I've had to push myself, and had to stretch in ways that I didn't know I could possibly stretch.**
> John Girard CEO, Clickability

> **I push myself, and I push my employees and partners and everybody else. I think it's important to push. If you push you get to a new level of ability.**
> Wallace Eley president, Crossey Engineering

MANY SUCCESSFUL PEOPLE ARE

SHY

BUT THEY KEEP PUSHING THROUGH IT

One big internal barrier many people need to push through is shyness. I'm constantly amazed at how many successful people are, or were, extremely shy, but over time they push themselves through it. Elli Davis started out shy: "As a teenager, I was quite insecure, quite shy really. I kept everything inside." But Elli pushed through the shyness and became a top real estate agent.

The people we see on stage and screen don't seem the least bit shy. But, as actor Rip Torn says, many big-time actors and performers also have big-time shyness: "I think most actors are shy. I really do. The greatest actors can disappear." Top fashion model Erin O'Connor is shy: "I was a very, very tall, awkward girl in school. I am painfully shy." But Erin keeps pushing through the shyness as she struts down those fashion runways with hundreds of eyes glued to her. People may be shy in some situations, yet not in others. Brooklands Executives CEO David Jensen says, "I was not shy. I was always very outgoing. But I'm not very good at walking into a crowd and networking with strangers. In that context, I'm shy. There's self-doubt and apprehension, and I don't want to force myself on people."

The good news is, based on the reams of shy successful people, shyness won't stop you from succeeding. As conclusive proof, here are 2 shy guys who won the ultimate success indicator, the Nobel Prize. James Watson won it for finding the structure of DNA, but he was so shy he couldn't find a date. James said to me, "I had one arranged date in college and it was a failure. I was shy with girls." So was Nobel Prize-winning physicist Richard Feynman, who writes, "I was not very good socially. I was so timid that when I had to take the mail out and walk past some seniors sitting on the steps with some girls, I was petrified: I didn't know how to walk past them!" Hey, I can relate!

Now comes the "but." Yes, these 2 Nobel Prize winners started out shy, but they both pushed past it, over time. Richard Feynman became known for his fascinating lectures that he gave to large audiences. James Watson said to me, "You can be shy, but with some people you shouldn't be shy. It's a weakness if you don't know other people."

The bottom line is you can be shy and still succeed. Many successful people do. But like them, you also need to keep pushing yourself through the shyness. It's worth it. Like James and Richard, you might even win a really big prize.

I really admire people who can get in there and mingle and just work a crowd but not me! I like people, but I'm shy.

Ralph Famiglietta Emmy Award-winning art director

I was always shy at school. I don't like being the center of attention. I hated dances in school. I'd be the one at the back. I wasn't the life of the party.

Ben Saunders adventurer

I'm not as outgoing as maybe I might express in my music.

Choclair hip-hop star

I've always been a little bit shy, so it's a problem for me to knock on a door to make a cold sales call.

Jerry Hayes optometrist, founder, Hayes Marketing

I make my living talking to people. I've been in front of audiences of 1000 people. I just love it. But put me in a room full of strangers at a cocktail party and I'm terrified. I can't make small talk.

Steven Schwartz author

Shy Helps You

SHYNESS IS NOT ALL BAD
IT CAN HELP YOU SUCCEED

SHY PEOPLE SPEND MORE TIME

READING	**LEARNING**	**FOCUSING**
LISTENING	**OBSERVING**	**IMAGINING**

When I was young I was tongue-tied and very shy. It was terribly painful not being part of the group and not having any dates, but **it gave me the ability to be more observant, and a listener, and a watcher.**

Albert Maysles renowned documentary filmmaker

So I got to thinking, if there are countless numbers of successful people who are shy, then shyness can't be all bad, can it? Could it be that, in some crazy way, shyness actually helps people succeed? I discovered the answer is yes. Shy people may spend more time alone, putting more hours into reading, learning, focusing, using their imaginations, and actually getting good at doing something. Wayne Schuurman, president of Audio Advisor, told me that being shy helped him become an expert in his field: "I am shy. The whole audiophile community is reclusive. In order to be really good at it, you have to spend a lot of time alone listening to equipment and music."

By hanging out at a party, you may pick up a hot date, but you won't pick up any of the cool skills that require a lot of concentration and practice on your own. Author, speaker, and sales expert Steven Schwartz says, "Because I was shy, I spent millions of hours practicing magic and creating my own effects. It sharpened my creative abilities and also helped me develop a performer side that's enabled me to do well in sales." Arthur Benjamin, "America's Best Math Whiz," told me that spending a lot of time alone helped him hone the skills that made him famous: "I spent a lot of time alone, because I was kind of socially awkward. I wanted kids to play with me, but I wasn't the first pick for the football team. So I spent a lot of time doing math and practicing magic tricks. I really enjoyed it. And when I learned magic, I got a lot of attention. I went from just being a nerd to, 'Hey, show us a trick.'"

In a strange way, shyness can also pay off in a crowd, because shy people spend more time listening and observing than talking. So if you're shy, you may not be the life of the party, but you might see what's going on at the party better than others. One of my heroes, Albert Maysles, said to me, "When I was young I was tongue-tied and very shy. It was terribly painful not being part of the group and not having any dates, but it gave me the ability to be more observant, and a listener, and a watcher. I trained myself to see things that other people don't see and I developed a very sharp eye for what should be filmed." And with that shy, sharp eye, Albert became one of the world's great documentary filmmakers.

So shyness isn't all bad, even though it might feel that way at times. The trick is to use it, then lose it. Keep the good things you learn from being shy, but keep pushing yourself through it. Now, let's look at how to do that.

I was very shy as a kid. I spent my childhood pretty much as a nature nerd, and I spent a lot of time outside by myself. But I developed a sense of focus, an ability to see the patterns in the natural world.

Janine Benyus biologist, educator, author of *Biomimicry*

I was shy as a kid, and I still am. When you're shy and an introvert, you spend more time internally with the ideas in your head and you really focus.

Chris Anderson chairman, TED conference

I was a shy child, so I think I've grown into an understanding of other people, and a caring for other people.

Jennifer Mather renowned psychologist, animal behaviorist

I was shy as a child. And when you're shy, you learn to be quiet and absorb what's going on around you, which is important.

Irene Pepperberg scientist, renowned for researching the cognitive abilities of parrots

TO GET OVER SHYNESS
PUSH YOURSELF IN FRONT OF PEOPLE

I am less shy now than I used to be, because I have been thrust in front of more people than I had ever imagined. I get to play with wonderful people like Steven Spielberg and George Lucas. You learn very quickly, if you want that opportunity you can't afford to be shy.

Robert Ward senior VP, design and planning, Universal Studios

Shyness isn't all bad, but if we stay inside our cocoon, it's hard to become a butterfly and really go places. Many opportunities come through interaction with other people, and if we're too shy to open our mouths, we miss out on those opportunities. So how do we get over shyness? The advice I get from successful people who are shy, is to just keep pushing yourself to speak, whether it's to one person or a group. Overcoming shyness is all about practice, practice, practice. And sorry, it's one thing you can't practice alone in your room. Organizations like Toastmasters and Dale Carnegie provide good opportunities to practice. Or you could do what author and CNN reporter Meredith Bagby did: "I was the shyest kid around. So, to get over it I put myself in situations such as debating, where I was forced to get up in front of an audience and speak."

Bell Mobility chairman Bob Ferchat used a different strategy: "I was diagnosed as shy, inarticulate, and I also had significant speech impediments. I couldn't say 'R's or 'L's. I stammered when I got in front of a group and I'd be so nervous I could barely speak." Gee, you'd think Bob would just lock himself away in a room and never come out. But instead, he did just the opposite: "To get over it I became a teacher and began to give lectures. And, over time, your fear and shyness go away, and speaking even becomes a strength."

People in some professions tend to spend more time in front computer screens than talking to other people. Boston Scientific founder John Abele was like that, but he kept pushing himself to get out and interact: "When I got out of college, I was more of a technical guy and I was very shy. So I put myself in situations where I had to deal with people. By pushing myself to do that, I gradually became more comfortable. And, by the way, it's fun." Did he say fun? You might be thinking, "Hey, it's not exactly fun when I'm so afraid to speak to a group of people that my stomach is in knots!" Well, if you cringe at the thought of talking to a massive crowd, like 3 or 4 people, just start with one person. GIAC consulting founder Eilish McCaffrey says, "I tend to be pretty shy, so when I first walk up to somebody I feel a little uncomfortable. But, you know, once I'm talking, everything's fine. My advice is just do it."

So just do it. Push yourself to get out there and talk to somebody. Oh, and don't worry about putting your foot in your mouth. By pushing past shyness, your foot will be taking a giant step towards success.

I made presentations to groups of 5 or 10 people for years. Then I pushed myself into circumstances where I have to talk to 300 people. I just said, "What's the worst that can happen?"

Russell Campbell president, ABN AMRO Canada

I teach one day a week. I am still actually a little shy, so teaching is something of a performance and I become someone else.

David Macaulay renowned author and illustrator

I used to be shy, until I had to appear in front of audiences of thousands of people.

David Ossman writer, comedian, *The Firesign Theatre*

I spend a lot of time thinking and reading, and not as much time bouncing off other people. But in MIT I am constantly bombarded by brilliant students, so the environment forces me to interact more than I naturally would, and that's helped me get over my shyness.

Michael Hawley professor, director of the MIT Media Lab

SUCCESSFUL
PEOPLE
HAVE
SELF
DOUBT

I always had self-doubts. I wasn't good enough.
I wasn't smart enough. I didn't think I'd make it.

Goldie Hawn actor

Another internal barrier people need to constantly push themselves through on their way to success is self-doubt. What? You mean they aren't the super-confident types we think they are? No, they aren't. In fact, many successful people tell me they have more self-doubt than self-confidence. Drew Nieporent has created some of the world's best restaurants, including New York's Nobu, yet he said to me, "I'm always questioning. I have tremendous self-doubt." So does Jerry Hayes, optometrist and founder of Hayes Marketing: "I think you always have self-doubt. One of the traits of successful people is you have the ability to sometimes just put your head down and push through it, even when you're questioning, 'Oh, boy, is this the right thing to do?'"

Sometimes you don't know if what you're doing is the right thing, simply because it hasn't been done before, so it's only natural to have self-doubts and insecurity. Actor Faye Dunaway says, "Great artists never know if they're making the right choice." I would add, they also never know what kind of reception their work is going to get. Writer and editor John Robert Colombo says, "Every day is riddled with self-doubts. Are people going to like this?"

Even famous people who we think should be full of confidence have to push through doubt. Stefan Sagmeister, a famous graphic designer who has created album covers for some of the top bands including the Rolling Stones, said to me, "I have self doubt, and I have enough meetings with rock stars to see that all of them also have serious self-doubts. I thought it was something that would go away with success, but I think it's always there."

When Stefan told me that, I had an instant flashback to a few years ago when the Rolling Stones played at a small club before taking their big show on the road. I was a few feet from the stage, and when Mick and the boys walked on, you could tell they were full of self-doubt. I couldn't believe it! Here's the world's greatest band and they had no idea if the fans would still like them. It wasn't until they started playing and the crowd went wild, that you could see the self-doubt literally melt from their faces and they actually smiled.

There's no doubt about it, you're going to have doubt. There are 2 tricks to handling it. First, keep pushing through it so it doesn't stop you. Second, turn it around and use it as a driving force that can actually help you succeed.

Most people are just as insecure as you are, they just mask it better. Really, all of us are lost, all of us are struggling, all of us are vulnerable.

Eve Ensler award-winning author, performer

You either think you're good or you think you're terrible. It depends on what morning it is.

Gerald Durnell CEO, ProTech Publishing

I have self-doubt every minute of the day. I'm just a bundle of all that. But I know that's me.

Richard Saul Wurman creator of TED Conferences

I don't think any writer, any time in their career, feels secure about their work. We're a very insecure bunch.

Jane Urquhart writer

I had tremendous self-doubts about me, but I had the sense that I could help somebody else. Have self-doubt but keep on going in spite of it.

Ken Woodrow M.D., professor of psychiatry, Stanford

FIND WAYS TO PUSH
THROUGH THE SELF-DOUBT

I have self-doubts. But those are the times when you just have to believe that you're going to get through it, so you **keep going in spite of the doubts.**

Lisa Davis director of communications, AARP

Self-doubt may feel like crap, but it only becomes destructive if it shuts you down and brings you to a complete standstill, so you quit a project, stop making movies, back out of a race, or cancel a performance. Self-doubt is often there, lurking in the background, so here are 4 strategies you can use to push yourself through all the insecurity and keep going:

1. The "Done It Before" strategy. When you encounter self-doubt, briefly look back at your successes and accomplishments. Don't linger too long in the past, just look at similar things where you've succeeded, so you can say, "I've done it before, so I can do it again." It's a strategy that works for Tiger Woods: "I've got a putt, like say the one I had to make at the PGA last year to force the playoff, all I'm thinking about is: You've done this a thousand times on the putting green. Just step up and relax and hit the putt." The "Done it Before" strategy works as well in the boardroom as it does on the golf course, according to Diane Bean, senior VP of business development for Manulife: "It's experience. At first you think, 'Oh, I don't know anything and I'm going to screw it up.' And then you learn to figure it out and you go on to the next one. After a while you realize that while you don't know anything about it now, you will know something about it and be able to manage it."

You may be thinking, "Hey, what if I'm just starting out and I have tons of self-doubt, but I don't have any experience or success to look back on?" Well, the next 3 strategies are for you.

2. The "Outrun It" strategy. Here you forget about looking back, and you also forget about the self-doubt lurking in your mind. Just block it out and keep moving forward so fast that you leave doubt in a trail of dust. Famous horror writer Stephen King uses this strategy: "There's plenty of opportunity for self-doubt. If I write rapidly, putting down my story exactly as it comes into my mind...I find that I can keep up with my original enthusiasm and at the same time outrun the self-doubt that's always waiting to settle in."

3. The "Confident/Doubt" strategy. Here you counter-balance the times you really doubt yourself, with the times you're full of confidence. Grammy Award-winning musician Gary Burton describes it well: "I think every artist bounces between I'm great and I'm shit. There are moments when you feel like, 'Oh man, I'm lucky I got this far.' Then you switch gears and do something you're really happy with, and you think, 'This is really great!'" Acclaimed graphic novelist Seth uses the same approach: "I fluctuate between believing I'm creating a good book and the black dread that each page I'm drawing is slowly revealing what a dim-witted, sentimental idiot I am." If you adopt the "Confident/Doubt" strategy, remember to keep bouncing back and forth between confidence and doubt, and don't stay on one side too long.

4. The "Sleep It Off" strategy. Sheldon Wiseman, CEO of Amberwood Productions, says, "I have self-doubts. Many of them are horrendous and you wonder if you can persevere, but I don't let them overwhelm me and I get over them quite quickly. A good night's sleep helps. When I'm fresh I can do almost anything."

Hey, maybe I'll try the "Sleep It Off" strategy. I need something, because at this moment I really have serious doubts that I'll ever be able to come up with a good ending for this page. So good night.

USE DOUBT TO PUSH YOU HIGHER

I think you try and **use self-doubt as ammunition** rather than fearing it and shutting down.

James Truman editorial director, Condé Nast magazines

The previous page has 4 strategies to handle self-doubt. Now here's a 5th strategy, a big one: Use the self-doubt to push you higher. Often there's a reason we doubt ourselves. If the voice in my head is saying, "I'm not good enough," maybe it's right. Maybe I'm not good enough and I have to get better. Animation film director Robin Budd says, "I find most really talented people are incredibly insecure. They're always thinking that they're not really that great. There's always something gnawing at them inside, but that's also a motivating factor that pushes them forward."

You'd think that after selling millions of records, being awarded the Nobel Prize or winning an Academy Award, all self-doubt would vanish and be replaced by glowing self-confidence. However, the great ones don't let that happen, because deep down they know the self-doubt keeps them producing their best work. Nicole Kidman has won an Oscar for best actress, yet she says, "Every time I star in a film, I think I cannot act. I can always come up with a list of actresses who would do better and try to convince the director to cast someone else." Instead of security blankets, successful people have insecurity blankets that keep them from sitting back and resting on their laurels.

Many consider Frank Gehry to be the world's greatest architect, yet he says, "I approach each project with a new insecurity, almost like the first project I ever did. I get these sweats. I go in and start working. I'm not sure where I'm going." Frank actually calls it "healthy insecurity," and if he has too much confidence, then he knows something's wrong. "When I can predict or plan it, I don't do it. I discard it." Jeong Kim, president of Lucent Optical Networking, says he always felt that other people were better than him, and that pushed him to work extra hard to keep up with them. I can relate, because I've always felt everybody in the room is better than me, and that pushes me to try and measure up, so I work my butt off to excel at whatever I'm doing.

The bottom line is, never lose all your self-doubt, no matter how bad it feels, and it can feel pretty bad. Donald Sutherland has acted in over 100 films, yet he says, "I throw up on the first day of every movie." Yech! The great paradox is, this thing that feels so bad can also be the catalyst that keeps you on your toes and pushes you to do your best and succeed. So use it, don't lose it. Just try to avoid the throwing up part.

> **You have to have the self-doubt to allow you to look at the work critically and try to make it better.**
> **Seth** acclaimed graphic novelist

> **If you feel you're not good enough, you can harness that feeling and use it to motivate you to move forward rather than holding you back.**
> **Jessica Switzer** president, Switzer Communications

> **There has to be self-doubt, or you would never grow as a person. Self-doubt is questioning and you should always be questioning yourself and the world around you.**
> **Darlene Lim** post-doctoral fellow at NASA

> **I find self-doubt to be a very powerful motivator, in the sense that "I really should have done a better job on this." But I don't tend to get depressed.**
> **Michael Schrage** MIT Media Lab fellow

> **Without insecurity we'd all get so unbelievably big-headed that we would just become total assholes.**
> **Stefan Sagmeister** renowned graphic designer

GET A **CHALLENGE** TO **PUSH** YOU

Sometimes **I set impossible tasks and challenge myself** to do them.

Gord Lownds founder, Sleep Country

Let's look at 9 ways successful people keep pushing themselves. This will give you lots of options when you need a little push. The first way is to get a challenge to push you. Richard Branson, famous CEO of Virgin Records and Virgin Airlines, says, "My interest in life comes from setting myself huge, apparently unachievable challenges and trying to rise above them." Richard rose to the challenge, literally, when he became the first to fly a hot air balloon across the Atlantic Ocean. (They say a lot of CEOs are full of hot air and Richard took full advantage of it.)

It's appropriate that filmmaker James Cameron won Oscars for his movie *Titanic* because he says the more titanic the challenge, the more he enjoys it. With movies like *Terminator* and *Titanic*, James set almost impossible challenges for himself, and met them with amazing visual effects never seen on the big screen before. Barenaked Ladies musician Ed Robertson told me he pushes himself with challenges a little more than his wife would like: "I love wave boarding and snow boarding. I like adventure. Doing that sort of stuff keeps you human and humble." Ed's latest challenge was getting his pilot's license: "It was challenging to do something that was really hard and I wasn't necessarily cut out for. But I felt as much satisfaction from getting my pilot's license as I did from selling 6 million records. I worked at something and achieved it. It made me proud and happy."

When I asked Ben Saunders how he pushed himself to ski 800 miles to the North Pole, he said, "I do it for the challenge. That's when you see the best qualities in people. I certainly learn the most about myself when I'm up against a challenge." Of course, all challenges don't have to be huge ones like Ben's. For Stephan Van Dam it was just the challenge of leaving his home in Switzerland and going to America: "As a kid of 21, I came to New York and went through the school of hard knocks. It was a real challenge for me, but I think you need to take on these challenges in order to propel yourself forward." Stephan not only went to New York, he became an expert on the city and produces brilliant, award-winning maps of New York.

So propel yourself forward with a challenge. It's both scary and fun, but it can take you to new places, in more ways than one.

> **I'm not happy when I'm not challenged.**
> **Tom Cruise** actor

> **I like new challenges, and I think that pushes me. I like the adrenaline.**
> **Diane Bean** senior VP business development, Manulife

> **I think surgeons like to be challenged. I've always liked a challenge.**
> **Douglas Dorner** vascular surgeon

> **It's not about the money. It's still the challenge of going to work and going out on a limb with new technology.**
> **Norbert Frischkorn** president, Frischkorn Audiovisual

> **Not all surfers are big-wave surfers. Those who are have a certain passion and a deep desire to challenge themselves by surfing waves of that magnitude.**
> **Ken Bradshaw** record for biggest wave ever surfed

GET A **GOAL** TO **PUSH** YOU

I need a goal to push for. Then I reach that plateau, and I go look for another goal.

Norbert Frischkorn president, Frischkorn Audiovisual

Goals are another way successful people push themselves to get moving. Randall Larsen, founding director of the Institute for Homeland Security, told me it was a goal that pushed him: "When I was in high school, I was not a very good student. But after Vietnam I realized I really wanted to fly air force jets. But I couldn't do it without a college degree. So, even though I wasn't a very good high school student, just average IQ, I got my college degree in less than 3 years, while I was also working 40 hours a week. It wasn't so much the degree I was after. I had a goal. I had to have that sheepskin to be an air force pilot."

Comedian Rick Mercer says the good thing about goals is they push you to do things you may not really like, but are necessary to get what you want: "I failed memorization in school. But when I had the goal of getting up on stage, I pushed myself to do memory work. And I could memorize an hour-and-a-half monologue." Another example is violinist Adrian Anantawan, who told me, "I have to practice the violin for hours each day. Sometimes it can be difficult to get through an entire session. I just have to keep on remembering what I'm doing it for – the goal."

Some people find their goals early in life. Many physicians say they set themselves the goal of becoming a doctor by the time they were 10. Oprah was 12 when she spoke in a church and set herself the goal of speaking for a living. I'd say she's more than reached that goal. Eva Vertes wasn't much older than Oprah when she gave herself the goal of discovering a cure for Alzheimer's disease. She just kept pushing towards that goal, and it paid off when she discovered a compound that prevents the death of brain cells, a step toward curing Alzheimer's. For her breakthrough, Eva was awarded $30,000 at the Intel International Science and Engineering Fair. Wow! Not bad for a 10th grade science project. Eva says, "I push myself and set impossible expectations. And that pushes me more. It's important to have that level of pushiness. If it's your own goal, then you'd better be the one pushing, because no one else will push you to get to that goal."

So, if you're having trouble pushing yourself, get a goal to push you. Like Eva, it might lead you to discover something new – what you're really capable of achieving in life.

It's important to have a goal, no matter what that goal is. Something out there that you're pushing for, stretching for.
John Girard CEO, Clickability

Although we don't want to set unrealistic goals that frustrate us, we also have to keep pushing ourselves.
Rick Pitino basketball coach

I usually need a goal to help me stay focused and disciplined.
Laurie Skreslet first Canadian to summit Mt. Everest

When a goal matters enough to a person, that person will find a way to accomplish what at first seemed impossible.
Nido Qubein speaker, entrepreneur

Goal setting is not a mind game. It is a process of developing the internal willpower to accomplish what you have set out to do.
Joan Samuelson Olympic marathon gold medalist

GET A **DEADLINE** TO PUSH YOU

I find that **being pushed by a deadline actually helps my creativity.** I don't like the pressure, but the work that comes out of it seems to benefit.

Robin Budd animation film director

There's nothing like a deadline to get people moving. Physicist Maurizio Vecchione says, "I'm deadline-driven. Things don't get done until the deadline is there." Award-winning photojournalist Kevin Gilbert says, "Gotta have deadlines. If I don't have a deadline, I just procrastinate."

Barry Friedman is one half of the juggling Raspyni Brothers, who aren't really brothers, but they are very funny. When I asked Barry how they keep coming up with great new material for their act, he said, "Man, there's nothing like a deadline for a good push. We just sit there, and push our brains, and go, 'We've got to do something new.' And something always comes." If ideas didn't come they'd be standing in front of a huge audience that's not laughing, wishing they were dead. That's why it's called a deadline.

When you think about it, deadlines should really be called alive-lines because they immediately bring you alive and push you into action. Great music composer and producer Quincy Jones says that composers usually only write 2 or 3 minutes of music a day, but with the fear of a deadline hanging over their heads they can compose up to 10 or 12 minutes. He says, "There's nothing more terrifying than facing a forty-four, or hundred-piece orchestra, with the producers, directors, and editors looking over your shoulder and having no music to play."

When J.K. Rowling started writing *Harry Potter*, it wasn't her publisher who imposed deadlines, it was her baby daughter: "I used to put her into the pushchair and walk her around Edinburgh, wait until she nodded off and then hurry to a cafe and write as fast as I could. It's amazing how much you can get done when you know you have very limited time. I've probably never been as productive since, if you judge by words per hour."

The pressure of an imminent deadline can push us to do our best work. Journalist Walt Mossberg is constantly under a deadline to churn out his personal technology column for the *Wall Street Journal*, and he told me, "Deadlines are your friend. Some of the best work people do is done right up against a deadline. It's when your wits are really tested."

So take Walt's advice and treat deadlines as your friend. I know what you're thinking: With friends like that, who needs enemies?

Deadlines are absolutely necessary in a creative environment. The deadline forces you to stop tossing ideas around and start implementing.

Susan Ruptash architect

A spacecraft launch is pretty serious deadline pressure. You've got one chance and you can't miss it. So you'll find a way to make it work, no matter what.

Dave Lavery NASA whiz who sends robots to Mars

I've written hundreds of TV shows, but I also have a file in my computer of things that aren't finished because they don't have built-in deadlines. If I had deadlines, I would do them.

Rick Mercer comedian

I would rather have deadlines. I find that imminent execution sharpens the mind. I write about 2,000 words a day, but with a desperate deadline I've written 5,000.

James Burke award-winning science historian, author

PUSH YOURSELF WITH **DISCIPLINE**

OPTION A

SELF DISCIPLINE

OPTION B

DISCIPLINE BY **OTHERS**

GO FOR SELF-DISCIPLINE.
OPTION B COULD INVOLVE BIG, SCARY GUYS WITH WHIPS.

Another way successful people push themselves is by using discipline. Now I know what you're thinking – "Discipline! Oh no!" When you hear that word you know fun is not involved. But discipline really isn't that bad. It's just saying NO at times. Like saying NO to going out with friends when you need to finish the project. Or saying NO to the potato chips when you're trying to lose weight. Or saying NO to watching TV when you need to prepare for the meeting. Issy Sharp, founder of Four Seasons Hotels, says, "I think discipline is very important. It gets you to do things that aren't always as comfortable or pleasant as maybe those other things that you might want to do, but you've gotta get them done."

When it comes to discipline, there are 2 options: 1. DISCIPLINE BY OTHERS. This is the least preferred method since it may involve big, scary guys with whips and chains pushing you to be disciplined. Instead, go for 2. SELF-DISCIPLINE. This is the self-service option, where you push yourself. Dawn Lepore, CIO of Charles Schwab, says, "I'm very self-disciplined, maybe too much to tell you the truth, but I think that's important in achieving your goals." Greg Zeschuk used to be a doctor, and now he's "Video Game Developer of the Year." How's that for a switch in careers? Medicine and video games may seem worlds apart, but Greg says being disciplined has helped him succeed in both worlds: "Self-discipline is very important. There are barriers, and the challenge in your life is to climb those barriers and get past them, and you can only do that if you are disciplined."

Self-discipline is how award-winning author and performer Eve Ensler pushes herself on stage, night after night, to perform her wonderful plays: "I wasn't disciplined in my youth, but now I'm very disciplined and I think it's a key part of success. You have to just keep showing up and doing the work." Superstar Celine Dion has the self-discipline to keep showing up, and also to do whatever it takes to keep her singing voice in top shape. This includes no dairy products and, get this, Celine even has the discipline to say NO to ice cream. (Gasp! There go my dreams of being a singer.)

The moral of the story is, use self-discipline to push yourself forward towards success. And if your "self" can't muster up the discipline, then go find some big, scary guy with a whip to help out.

Pop didn't teach me golf. He taught me discipline.
Arnold Palmer golf legend

Discipline is important for me. Rigid discipline.
T.K. Mattingly Apollo 13 astronaut

Artists are very disciplined. It's not a case of waiting for inspiration. You've got to work.
Ken Danby artist, renowned for his realistic paintings

I'm a very disciplined kind of person. Making up your mind about what you want and then living consistently with it requires discipline.
Dave House president, Nortel Networks

My dad said that everyone ends up taking out the garbage. So it's important to do the hard stuff that's no fun, as well as the easy stuff. It ain't a bed of roses! It requires a lot of self-discipline.
Bill Joy chief scientist, Sun Microsystems

IT'S NOT EASY TO PUSH YOURSELF
THAT'S WHY THEY INVENTED
MOTHERS

I push myself...Well, **my mother pushed me.** So find somebody to push you.

Frank Gehry acclaimed architect

Sometimes it's really hard to push yourself, and that's why they invented mothers. Award-winning jazz pianist Linda Martinez said to me, "My mother pushed me. I practiced piano 7 hours a day only because my mother told me to." Great inventor Thomas Edison also had a mother behind him: "My mother was the making of me. She was so true, so sure of me, and I felt I had some one to live for, some one I must not disappoint." Olympic gold medal boxer Lennox Lewis says he felt like his mother was in the boxing ring with him, constantly motivating him and keeping him focused.

Legendary pop music star Ray Charles became blind at the age of 6, but his mother pushed him to be self-reliant. Ray said, "Everything I am today is because of her…At home she made me cook meals, dress myself, haul water, even chop wood with an ax…She used to tell me, 'I may not live to see what you do in this life, but there is one thing I know you will never do: You will never hold a tin cup and beg.'" Champion cyclist Lance Armstrong's mother pushed him to keep going when things got tough. In one of his early races when Lance was struggling and wanted to quit, his mother pushed him on, saying: "Come on, son, you can do it." When Lance told her he'd bonked and couldn't go any further, she told him he couldn't quit, even if he had to walk to the finish line. So Lance walked to the finish line.

Some Dads also make great pushers. Derek Hatfield was on a trans-Atlantic sailboat race when his mast broke and he was ready to quit. He made it to land and phoned his father saying, "Bring the trailer. I'm dropping out of the race." His father replied, "I'm not bringing you the trailer. You get back on the boat and go to the finish line." Derek finished the race and went on to become one of the few people who have ever sailed around the world alone.

Grandparents can also push you. That is, if they're not too busy spoiling you rotten. Alexander Rose, executive director of the Long Now Foundation, says, "What helped me succeed the most was working with my grandfather to bring in the hay every year. 100 degree heat, lifting 75 pound hay bales, I learned what hard work was. I didn't want to do the hay lifting – I was forced to do it. My grandfather wouldn't let me quit." The moral of the story is, find someone to push you. It will help you develop the skills you need to make hay in any field.

All I am, I owe to my mother.

George Washington first president of the United States

My mother said to me, "If you become a soldier, you'll be a general; if you become a monk, you'll end up as the Pope." Instead, I became a painter and wound up as Picasso.

Pablo Picasso 20th century's most famous artist

My mother and aunt were 2 professional women who were very supportive of me to study sciences. My Dad also played a supportive role. All 3 family members helped give me the confidence to believe I could do whatever I wanted to do.

Cynthia Trudell first woman to head an auto manufacturer

It was my grandmother who bought me my first video game and I owe her a great debt because I went from playing to programming and I was encouraged to keep going further.

Omar Wasow executive director, BlackPlanet.com

LET **OTHERS PUSH** YOU

TEACHERS COACHES
CLIENTS COLLEAGUES
MENTORS BOSSES

Coach Sutton...pushed me to go harder and harder and get better and better... **he just pushed me real hard and that helped me get to the NBA.**

Tony Allen basketball player, Boston Celtics rookie

It's great if you have a mother, father, or other family member to give you a push when you need it. But what if you don't? Then just find somebody else to push you. It can be a teacher, boss, colleague, client, coach, or mentor, just to name a few. Eve Shalley, senior VP at Intrasphere, says, "Ask for support from other people. If you know that you want to be a good pianist, but you're lazy about practicing, then ask somebody else to remind you it's time to practice. It's a support system. Get support wherever you can get it."

In the movie world, directors are like mothers with megaphones. Nicole Kidman was preparing to act in the film *Moulin Rouge* when she had second thoughts, called the director and said, "'I think you're going to have to recast it because there's no way my voice is going to be good enough and I can't do the role and you've made a big mistake.' Luckily, he didn't believe me and he pushed me forward." Yes, all the way to a "Best Actress" Golden Globe Award. In the sports world, you can always get a coach to push you. When Jamal Mashburn was starting out he asked renowned basketball coach Rick Pitino for a push, saying, "I want to be a professional ball player...I know that in order to get there I have to work hard. You'll make me do that." Rick kept pushing Jamal and he became a star on the basketball court.

If you can't find a big coach to push you, try a little librarian. Huh? Well, Robert Munsch, a popular children's author with over 20 million books sold, says his success might not have happened without a push from a librarian: "It was my hobby to tell stories to kids. I didn't think it was a job. It took a librarian to kick me and say, 'You should publish. Those are wonderful!'" Teachers can also be good at pushing you forward, according to my colleague Thom Rockliff, who says, "I wanted to buy a meter to test electrical signals, and my computer teacher said, 'You're not going to buy it, you're going to build it.' So I got the parts and built it. And my theatre arts teacher pushed me to act out scenes, which helped me gain confidence and overcome my shyness. Those teachers just kept pushing me, and it's interesting that the world I work in now is a fusion of those 2 areas: computers and entertainment."

So if you're having trouble pushing yourself, remember there's somebody out there who can help push you along. The only problem is, who's gonna push you out the door to find them? Sigh!... This success stuff is so complicated.

I was not allowed to quit when things got tough. I was not allowed to give up acting and try something else. I was just not allowed. There was always somebody there who gave me encouragement or help.

Morgan Freeman Academy Award-winning actor

I really need a network to push me. I'm a natural procrastinator. I'm not a natural doer. My husband is boom, boom, boom – he does things. I need people who keep calling me and saying, "Did you do this? Did you do that?" I really need that support system.

Lakshmi Pratury director, American India Foundation

I have an image in my head of this person named Norton that I met at TRW. He always showed me when I wasn't doing super well. So if I'm sloppy or lazy, I always imagine that he's going to walk up, look at the program, and tell me, "Look, here's a better way to do that."

Bill Gates founder, Microsoft

COMPETITION

GET COMPETITION TO PUSH YOU

I love the competition. I love pushing myself to the limit.

Amber Trotter fastest female cross-country runner in U.S. high school history

Another great pushing force is competition. If you're a competitive runner you're staring your competitors in the face – or worse, their butts, which can really stink or really push you. Roger Bannister, the first man to break the 4-minute mile, said he wouldn't have pushed himself as hard without competitors John Landy and Wes Santee hot on his heels.

Not that I'm in the same league as those champion runners, but I can relate. My fastest running times haven't come when I'm alone on the track. Only when a keen competitor is hot on my heels do I dig down and push myself harder than I thought possible. Hey, even Oprah is pushed by competition. When she was training to run a marathon, Oprah says personal trainer Bob Greene figured out how to get her going: "Now, if Bob wants to push me, he'll say, 'See that woman in the pink suit? You can take her.' And I'll kill myself to run past her. I never realized how competitive I am. But I am."

Sure, sports people are competitive, but how about those scientists? Well, James Watson says it was competition from another scientist that pushed him and Francis Crick to discover the structure of DNA: "We kept telling the people in London that Linus Pauling was going to move on to DNA. If DNA is that important, Linus will know it, he'll build a model and then we'll be scooped....and boy, I was scared." And with that competitive fear pushing them, James and Francis finished first in the race to DNA. (Wild cheering from all the spectator scientists in the stands.)

If you're a filmmaker, every time you go to a movie you see your competition projected on the big screen in front of you. When James Cameron went to see *Star Wars*, it turned out to be a defining moment because he saw the cool special effects George Lucas was doing, and James felt he was being left behind. That competition pushed him to get off his butt and actually become a filmmaker. Then he went on to produce great films like *Terminator* and win "Best Picture" for *Titanic*.

Competition is all about keeping you on your toes and doing your best. Instead of hating your competitors and being intimidated by them, see them as a pushing force that helps you get the most out of yourself. So, go find some competitors and thank them for helping you. Then push yourself so far ahead of them you'll leave them in a trail of dust.

Your competitor is a gift. He or she gives you the opportunity to do your best.

Jerry Lynch
sports psychologist

What did I think about on the bike for six and seven hours?...I told myself over and over that this was the kind of race in which I had to always push if I wanted to stay ahead.

Lance Armstrong
cyclist, 7-time Tour de France winner

There's a competitiveness that comes out every now and then. Sometimes all I can think is, "I'll show them. And I'll solo up 2 pitches just to get ahead of the other climbers.

Laurie Skreslet
first Canadian to summit Mount Everest

I was trying to keep up with the boys or beat them at their own games. I still try to beat the boys in business. I'm very competitive.

Ruth Fertel founder, Ruth's Chris Steak House

MENTORS
SUPPORT YOU

TOR MENTORS
PUSH YOU

My parents said I would never amount to anything, but that spurred me on. I was going to show them.

Norbert Frischkorn president, Frischkorn Audiovisual

Many people say that mentors were important to their success. Mentors provide an important support role, however this chapter is about PUSH, so let's look at another group of people who don't really support you. They push you, and not necessarily in a nice way. I call them TOR-MENTORS, since they give you a kick in the butt, rather than a pat on the back. Tor-mentors are people who bully you, ridicule you, or put you down. You can let them destroy you, or you can use them as a powerful force that actually pushes you to one up them, prove them wrong, or prove yourself. And sometimes that pushes you further than you ever thought you could go.

Top classical violinist James Ehnes says he owes his success to a teacher tor-mentor: "My teacher in New York was just a master at pushing the right buttons to get my dander up and force the challenge. And I worked very, very hard because it would have just killed me to think that someone didn't think I was capable of doing something. I'd say, 'Well, I'll show you I'm capable.' And I'd find a way to do it even if it almost killed me."

Basketball superstar Michael Jordan was a first-class tor-mentor, once called the most psychologically intimidating bully that basketball has ever known. He said he did it to push his teammates to perform better on the basketball court. "If you don't bring your level up to compete with me then I'm going to completely dominate you, and I'm going to talk trash to you and about you while I'm dominating. That's my way of getting my teammates to elevate their game." And Michael's tormenting helped push his team to the top.

My 12th grade math teacher Mrs. Murray, was a master tor-mentor. She'd get me up to the blackboard and if I couldn't answer her math question – Whack! – her cane struck me on the back. I really struggled with geometry so I got whacked a lot, but it pushed me to say, "I'll show her!" And it made me work a lot harder to understand geometry. Interesting how the highest marks on my final 12th grade report card were in Mrs. Murray's math class.

Now, I'm not advocating tormenting anybody. It's no fun. But tor-mentors like Mrs. Murray, and some of my tough clients, have pushed me to do some of my best work. So, if you find yourself at the mercy of a tor-mentor, use them as a force to push you forward. Then, when they see how successful you've become, it will really torment them for the rest of their lives.

Probably one of my biggest motivators was my dad saying I wouldn't amount to anything. I was really pissed off and I think it's been unwinding ever since, just to prove him wrong.

Edward Burtynsky renowned photographer

When I said I was going to go off and do writing, a boss said, "You'll be lucky if you ever make a dime." That kind of pushed me to really try and work hard.

Amy Tan best-selling author, *The Joy Luck Club*

My sister-in-law was a motivating factor...She didn't want me to date her little sister because I wasn't good enough...and I wanted to prove to this lady that she was wrong...I put her name on a 5-by-7 index card and taped it on the wall directly at eye level. Every night I would raise my head and see her name and that would make me want to put my head back to work.

Bill Bartmann founder, Commercial Financial Services

PUSH OUT OF YOUR COMFORT ZONE

You only ever grow as a human being if you're **outside your comfort zone.**

Percy Cerutty famous running coach

One of the nice things about success is that it brings comfort. Maybe it brings you a new house, a fancy car, an exotic vacation, or comfortable furniture. But here's the paradox: Success brings you comfort, but you can't be comfortable and successful at the same time. That's why you see billionaires, who could easily sit back and get comfortable, go to a lot of trouble to keep pushing themselves out of their comfort zones and keep challenging themselves. Richard Branson, billionaire founder of Virgin records and airlines, who could easily sit back in comfort, says, "Once we get comfortable as a company, I like to push the boat out again. My wife keeps saying, 'Why? Why? You're fifty. Take it easy. Let's enjoy it.'...If I put all my money in the bank and drink myself to death in the Caribbean, I just think that would be a waste of the fantastic position I've found myself in."

Award-winning photojournalist Kevin Gilbert says, "I love the comforts of life, but I don't want to get too comfortable, because then you get lazy and I would rather be on edge a little bit. When I get too comfortable I need to move on, try new things, be in different places." Brad Edwards, director of research at the Institute for Scientific Research, finds, "You have to keep pushing. Once you back off, you stop progressing. I've seen lots of good scientists get to a certain point, then just take it easy. And that's basically where they stay for the rest of their careers."

Norbert Frischkorn, who has run a successful audiovisual firm for over 25 years, told me, "You can't say, "Well, I've had a little bit of success, now I'll take 7 weeks off, and play golf. Then you'll fall behind. You'll lose your edge." Bell Mobility chairman Bob Ferchat says it's all about growth: "If you go through life feeling comfortable, you won't grow. You create discomfort for yourself because you want to grow in some way." Bob's right. I mean, just ask any baby who has new teeth coming in.

So, if you've been sitting there with your feet up, feeling cozy for too long, it's time to push yourself out of your comfort zone. If you're uncomfortable speaking to groups of people, then go speak to a group. If you're uncomfortable biking, then hop on a bike. Whatever you're uncomfortable doing, go do it and be prepared to grow. So, excuse me while I go take out the garbage. Hey, it's a start!

You can become very comfortable in a situation, and you need to take risks and go to where you're not comfortable.

Freeman Thomas
head of advanced product design, DaimlerChrysler

The waves here are 25ft. or higher and that allows me to get out of my comfort zone.

Layne Beachley
world champion surfer

If you are always seeking to be comfortable you'll have a very limited life. If you're willing to face discomfort, then you'll always grow and you'll always expand your boundaries.

Leslie Westbrook
marketing consultant

The ultimate measure of a man is not where he stands in moments of comfort, but where he stands at times of challenge and controversy.

Martin Luther King, Jr
civil rights leader

IDEAS

1. **PASSION**   2. **WORK**   3. **FOCUS**   4. **PUSH**

IDEAS LEAD TO SUCCESS

IDEAS

122 **IDEAS LIGHT THE WAY TO SUCCESS**

124 **EVERYBODY IS CREATIVE, INCLUDING YOU**

126 **IDEAS MAKE A BIG DIFFERENCE IN EVERY FIELD**

11 WAYS TO GET IDEAS

128 **1. HAVE A PROBLEM – IDEAS ARE SOLUTIONS TO PROBLEMS**

130 **2. IDEAS COME FROM LOOKING AROUND**

132 **3. KEEP LISTENING – EARS ARE ANTENNAS FOR IDEAS**

134 **4. BEING CURIOUS LEADS TO IDEAS**

136 **5. ASKING QUESTIONS LEADS TO IDEAS**

138 **6. BORROW AN IDEA, THEN BUILD IT INTO A NEW IDEA**

140 **7. MAKE CONNECTIONS BETWEEN DIFFERENT THINGS**

142 **8. MAKE MANY MISTAKES – OUT OF GARBAGE COMES GOLD**

144 **9. KNOW WHEN MISTAKES ARE GOOD, OR BAD**

146 **10. WRITE DOWN IDEAS, BEFORE THEY FLY AWAY**

148 **11. ALWAYS CARRY A P.E.N. PERSONAL ECONOMIC NOTETAKER**

MY STORY

150 **HOW I GOT A BIG IDEA**

5. **IDEAS**   6. **IMPROVE**   7. **SERVE**   8. **PERSIST**

IDEAS
LIGHT THE WAY TO SUCCESS

I intend to conquer the world, but instead of conquering with bombs
I intend to conquer with good ideas.

Ted Turner founder, CNN

There was a popular song called "You Light Up My Life." It was referring to a person but it could have been talking about ideas, because good ideas really can light up your life. One lit up the lives of Bill Gates and Paul Allen when they had the idea to start the first microcomputer software company. Bill said, "We had ideas that the giants of the time missed." Yes, ideas were the big advantage 2 little guys like Bill and Paul had over the giant companies.

Ideas also lit up the life of Jack Welch and helped make him CEO of General Electric. He said, "My job is to find great ideas, exaggerate them, and spread them like hell around the business with the speed of light." With all this lighting up, no wonder the symbol for ideas is usually a light bulb over somebody's head. (Historical note: Before the invention of the light bulb, candles would appear over people's heads when they had an idea, but everybody's hair kept catching on fire, so Edison invented the light bulb.)

The light bulb is a perfect metaphor for an idea, because it lights up our thinking in the same way that electricity lights up our environment. Physicist Leonard Susskind told me big ideas are rare in his profession. "Almost all the time you're confused and you're going nowhere. And then, maybe 5 times in your career, you get that sense of open daylight – that "Aha" moment – and you see where to go. It's a short-lived thing, and it's also an addictive high, looking for it, pushing for it." The feeling may be short-lived, but those 5 ideas have made Leonard one of the world's top physicists.

Ideas light the way for us to solve problems, take advantage of opportunities, and move forward. Disney CEO Michael Eisner said, "The fragile spark of an idea can spread to become a great work of art, or a movie, or a political movement, or an automobile, or a Space Shuttle, or a new communications technology. But these blazing achievements can only happen if the initial idea is cared for, protected, and nurtured until it is ready to spread."

Ideas are a powerful source of mental energy, and if you can generate better ideas, you have the energy to go further in life. A single idea has taken many people from nothing to something, from the bottom to the top. The trick is to come up with those ideas and, as you'll see in this chapter, there's no magic. Just do some simple things, and a big idea could light your way to success.

> **I have big ideas. It's been my business and I work hard at the ideas.**
> **Paula Silver** former president, Columbia Pictures Marketing

> **The most important thing is that you're taking your imagination as far out as it can go.**
> **Norma Kamali** fashion designer

> **You create something and you can see it and taste it and feel it. It's addictive. I'm so hooked on creativity I just can't stop.**
> **Jerry Della Femina** influential advertising guru

> **When people ask me, "How do I start my own business?" I say to them, "You have to have an idea that everyone else thinks is crazy, and you go ahead and do it anyway."**
> **Bill Low** CEO, AudioQuest

> **Man's mind stretched by a new idea never goes back to its original dimensions.**
> **Oliver Wendell Holmes Jr.** renowned jurist

EVERYONE CAN COME UP WITH
GOOD IDEAS

BUSINESS IS AS CREATIVE AS THE ARTS

Deals are my art form. Other people paint beautifully on canvas or write wonderful poetry. I like making deals, preferably big deals. That's how I get my kicks.

Donald Trump famous real estate developer

Warning! I'm now going to use one of the scariest words in the English language. No, it's not taxes. Are you ready? Brace yourself. It's CREATIVITY! Sorry, I had to say it, because generating ideas involves creativity. The problem is, many people think they're not creative because they can't do something that's considered creative, like draw or paint. For example, Elli Davis, a very successful real estate agent, said to me, "I don't think I'm creative. I'm not really artsy." Yet Elli is very creative in the way she interacts with clients and comes up with ideas to handle sales situations. And that's what creativity is all about – coming up with ideas. It has nothing to do with having a pencil or paintbrush in your hand.

Sleep Country founder Gord Lownds says, "There's a lot of creative or intuitive inspiration that business people use to solve problems." Based on my experience, he's right. I work in both the business world and the art world and I've found business people to be just as creative as the artsy crowd, except in business your canvas is a spreadsheet, business plan, or client list. My accountant is creative when he has a great idea to lower my taxes. I just wish he could be more creative. Business people are so uncomfortable with the word creativity they even came up with their own word for it – innovation. Gideon Gartner said to me, "At the Gartner Group, everything we did was an innovation." One of Gideon's innovative ideas was to produce technology reports that were only one page long, instead of huge reports nobody had time to read. That one idea to do one-page reports helped put the Gartner Group on the map.

Cathy Enz is a professor of innovation at Cornell University, a real expert on creativity, and Cathy says that Ali Kasikci is one of the most creative thinkers she knows. So, who the heck is this Ali Kasikci? Maybe an artsy filmmaker, or writer, or artist? No, he's the general manger of the Peninsula Beverly Hills hotel, and his ideas, like anytime check-in, have made it one of the top hotels in the world.

I've seen so many examples of great ideas from business people, I think they're the real artists of our times. As artist Andy Warhol said, "Making money is art and working is art and good business is the best art." The bottom line is, you don't have to be artsy to be creative. We're all creative.

> **Any activity becomes creative when the doer cares about doing it right, or doing it better.**
> **John Updike**
> novelist, essayist and critic

> **I think creativity exists in everyone. Some of us have antennae that are better than others, but we all have them and they can be honed and anybody can be creative.**
> **Mary Furlong,**
> CEO, Third Age Media

> **Working in technology does have a creative aspect. Solving problems is creative. If you want to challenge your brain go learn about the inner workings of a database management system.**
> **Elinor MacKinnon**
> CIO, Blue Shield

> **I am definitely on the creative front, but I am also business-oriented. I always approach business problems and opportunities from the creative and aesthetic viewpoint.**
> **Sky Dayton**
> founder, Earthlink

BE A **FOUNTAIN** OF **IDEAS**

Everybody is a kind of fountain of ideas. You've got 100 billion neurons in your brain, and when you think of the number of potential ways a thought can go through the brain, you've got one hell of a machine in there.

James Burke award-winning science historian

Ideas make a big difference in every field. But we tend to associate ideas with fields such as arts or sciences, not ones like sports or medicine. I mean, when I think of surgeons, I think scalpels, not ideas. Yet, when a surgeon is operating, the ability to quickly come up with ideas to solve problems can mean life or death. Surgeon Douglas Dorner says, "I think the best surgeons are creative. Every surgical procedure has some slightly different twist and the best surgeons are the ones who come up with ideas to deal with the twists that we're given."

Athletics seems to be about strength or speed, not ideas. Yet, the best athletes are very creative, because they're continually coming up with ideas on how to enhance performance. For example, high-jumpers used to dive forward over the bar until Dick Fosbury had the breakthrough idea to turn in the air and go backwards, making it easier for his legs to clear the bar. The Fosbury Flop was anything but a flop. Dick's idea won him a gold medal, set a new Olympic record, and became the high-jumping technique still used today.

For many years I was part of the design group in a big corporation and, unlike the stodgy engineers we worked with, we saw ourselves as hotshot creative types, able to magically come up with brilliant ideas. Then one day I was struggling, trying to figure out where to put a logo on a building, and I just couldn't come up with a good idea. Bill Moss, one of those uncreative engineers, walked over to my desk, pointed down at the drawing, and said, "Why don't you put the logo over there?" It was the perfect solution, and one of those times when you realize everybody can be creative – yes, even engineers. Crossey Engineering president Wallace Eley said to me, "We're always looking for bright ideas to solve problems and do things. It's just that artists are normally seen as creative, and engineers frequently are not. It's a matter of pushing a lot of engineers to be creative."

My mission is to help people see there's nothing stopping them from generating great ideas, no matter who they are, or what field they're in. That's what our minds are designed to do – come up with ideas. As award-winning science historian James Burke says, "Everybody is a fountain of ideas." So, let's look at 11 ways to get ideas. Do them and, you too, will be able to gush forth with the great ideas you need to succeed.

The best way to have a good idea is to have a lot of ideas.

Linus Pauling Nobel Prize-winning chemist

I think a lot of lawyers are quite creative, despite what people might think. Law is basically a lot of writing, and many executives in the film and television business are former lawyers.

Jamie Brown former lawyer and CEO of Frantic Films

Some people create with words or with music or with a brush and paints. I like to make something beautiful when I run. I like to make people stop and say, 'I've never seen anyone run like that before.'...It's being creative.

Steve Prefontaine legendary runner

The genius creates good ideas because we all create good ideas. That is what our combinational, adaptive minds are for.

Steven Pinker professor of psychology, MIT

IDEAS ARE SOLUTIONS TO

PR⊙BLEMS

I demystified the creative process.
I just saw it as an exercise in problem
solving. **I went at every single job
as a problem to be solved**.

Matt Groening creator of *The Simpsons*

The first way to get ideas is to have a problem. I mean, ideas are really just solutions to problems, so if you have no problem, there's no reason to come up with ideas. The human mind is really a problem-solving engine. Problems go in one side, and ideas to solve them come out the other. And it's a good thing we have that idea engine sitting on our shoulders, because no matter what field we're in, much of our time is spent problem solving. Jay Chiat, co-founder of Chiat Day advertising, says, "The agency business is problem solving. But I think that's what life is. What am I gonna eat tonight? That's a problem."

Yes, day-to-day life itself is full of big and little problems just begging for ideas to solve them. Usually when a sentence starts with "How," we have a problem in search of an idea: "How can I get a date?" "How can I be a better person?" "How can I earn more?" These are all problems in search of ideas. Some people think the word "problem" is too negative so, instead of problems, they talk about "challenges." But let's face it, challenges are just problems with a makeover so they don't seem so bad.

Emmy Award-winning news anchor Forrest Sawyer is typical of many successful people who see problems as a good thing: "I used to go out with the military in the field and I'd say, 'Boy, that's a big problem.' And they'd say, 'That's not a problem sir, that's a challenge.' 'Okay, sorry, wrong word.' I think problems are good. My mind just goes from problem to problem, in the best sense of the word." Catherine Mohr, product engineering manager at Aerovironment, feels the same way: "I came into engineering because I was interested in the problem solving side of it. Engineers solve problems, and that was very attractive to me."

Bill Gates says, "I guess you could say that I approach business as a kind of problem-solving challenge...life's a lot more fun if you treat its challenges in creative ways." So, when you've got a horrendous problem, do what Bill does – try flipping it around and looking at it as a problem-solving challenge. It may be the last thing you feel like doing, but if you can get those ideas flowing, you'll find problem solving is actually fun. And, like Bill's idea of starting a little software company, you just might come up with a great idea that will solve your problem – and lead to great success.

> **I get the most fun out of being given a difficult problem, and coming up with ideas to solve that problem. It's very satisfying to do that.**
>
> **David Jensen** CEO, Brooklands Executives recruitment

> **I like problem solving. At sea you have a small crew and you are thousand miles from land, so you always have to think on your feet.**
>
> **David Gallo** marine scientist, director, Woods Hole

> **Problem solving is what keeps your mind going. I make every project I do intentionally more difficult, just because the problem solving is fun and interesting.**
>
> **Rick Smolan** creator of the *Day in the Life* book series

> **What makes a really good photojournalist is being a problem solver. Whether you're in the Gaza Strip with Molotov cocktails coming at you, or you've got 2 minutes to photograph a company CEO, you've got to problem solve and make it happen.**
>
> **Kevin Gilbert** award-winning photojournalist

TO GET IDEAS LOOK AROUND

My mother always told me, **"You have to be observant."**

Mae Jemison astronaut

Another way to get ideas is to simply keep your eyes open and be observant. Observation is so important in getting ideas, I think we should change IQ to EYE-Q. Even Marilyn vos Savant, a woman with one of the highest IQs ever recorded, says EYE-Q is more important than IQ: "To acquire knowledge, one must study; but to acquire wisdom, one must observe."

Ron Rice told me how a simple observation took him from the lifeguard stand to the millionaire's club: "I was a lifeguard sitting on a lifeguard stand on the beach. I saw the suntan lotion being sold and it was all old and mundane. And I thought, even with my limited chemistry knowledge, I could make something a hundred times better than what was out there. And I created Hawaiian Tropic and I gave it the Hawaiian atmosphere. It was an instant success."

Moving from the beach to Wall Street, Lise Buyer told me how EYE-Q helped her become a successful investor: "It isn't about what happens in your office, and it isn't about what numbers you can invent on your computer. It's about what's going on outside your door. Are the kids' sneakers Nikes or are they Reeboks? No amount of computer modeling is going to tell you what people are buying. So my advice is, be observant."

EYE-Q even helped physicist Richard Feynman win the Nobel Prize. One day he was in the Cornell University cafeteria and he saw a student throw a plate in the air (must have been before they invented Frisbees). In the book *Surely You're Joking Mr. Feynman!*, Richard wrote, "As the plate went up in the air I saw it wobble, and I noticed the red medallion of Cornell on the plate going around. It was pretty obvious to me that the medallion went around faster than the wobbling." So Richard went away and worked out the motion of the mass particles, which led him to a breakthrough in physics. He writes, "The diagrams and the whole business that I got the Nobel Prize for came from that piddling around with the wobbling plate." Gee, I look at a plate and all I see is food. Richard looks at a plate and wins the Nobel Prize. Now, that's what I call observant!

So, to get good at coming up with ideas, I'd say forget about IQ and work on your EYE-Q. As famed New York Yankees manager Yogi Berra said, "You can observe a lot by watching."

A good animator looks and studies everything they see, from sitting on a bus, to watching a friend walk up the stairs. Observation is really important.

Robin Budd accomplished animation film director

The real voyage of discovery consists not in seeking new landscapes but in having new eyes.

Marcel Proust great writer

[Charles Oakley] didn't say much, but he was always observing. Charles has a way of taking everything in.

Warren Williams godfather to basketball star Charles Oakley

When you have creative block, look at the world. When I used to run out of ideas I'd go down to the National Gallery in London and just start walking through and – boom, boom – ideas started coming out of the paintings.

Terry Gilliam renowned filmmaker, *Monty Python, Brazil*

EARS ARE ANTENNAS FOR IDEAS

The key to success is to get out into the store and listen to what the associates have to say...Our best ideas come from clerks and stockboys.

Sam Walton founder, Wal-Mart

If you want to be great at coming up with ideas, remember this: Ears are antennas for ideas. I mean, it's amazing how many great ideas come simply through listening. Medical geneticist Josef Penninger told me his medical breakthroughs often come by keeping his ears open: "That's the most important thing. Listen to people. It starts you thinking, 'This guy gave me a little idea.' Then you talk to somebody else, and you put it all together."

If you want to be a great songwriter, it pays to listen. Carl Perkins wrote "Blue Suede Shoes" after listening to somebody at a high school prom tell his date not to step on his blue suede shoes. "I Started a Joke" was a song without a melody, until one night, as they flew over Germany, the Bee Gees listened to the hum of the jet engines and turned it into a tune. Paul McCartney and John Lennon got the idea for "A Hard Day's Night" by listening. Ringo would often get words mixed up, and one night after a grueling concert, he said, "It's been a hard day's night!" The idea-light turned on in Paul and John's heads, and they went away and wrote one of the Beatles' most popular songs.

Billion-dollar ideas have sprung from just listening in ordinary, everyday situations. For example, Bernard Silver was in a grocery store one day when he overheard the president of the store asking for help in automating his grocery checkout. The idea-light turned on in Bernard's head, and he went away and developed the barcode.

Apparently, the average doctor only listens to a patient for 14 seconds before interrupting (women say this is actually twice as long as most men). Dr. Jean Carruthers is one doctor who did listen to a patient and it paid off big time. Botox was being used to treat muscle spasms, and after Jean had injected it into a patient's eyelids, the patient asked her, "Why didn't you inject my brow?" Jean said, "Well I didn't think you were spasming there." And the patient said, "I know I'm not spasming there. It's just that every time you treat me there, I get this beautiful untroubled expression." That gave Jean the idea of using Botox to reduce wrinkles, which turned into a billion-dollar industry. No wonder Jean says, "So, you know, you've got to listen to your patients – number one." I would add, if you want to be good with ideas, make listening itself number one.

I like to listen. I have learned a great deal from listening carefully. Most people never listen.
Ernest Hemingway famous novelist and journalist

I just listen to everybody. Everybody has some kind of knowledge to impart. Listen and somewhere in there is a nugget of an idea.
Bruce Vilanch renowned comedy writer

Some people hear things and they don't pay attention, whereas I hear it and apply it. I look for linkages. Keep looking for linkages and connections.
Ted Stout founder & CEO, ROI Institute

I worked a long time in daycare and my stories came from really experiencing stuff with kids, and listening to them, and knowing what they like.
Robert Munsch celebrated children's author, over 20 million books sold

TO GET IDEAS BE CURIOUS

I am neither especially clever nor especially gifted.
I am only very, very curious.

Albert Einstein world's most-renowned physicist

Many people tell me that curiosity helped them succeed, and one of the great things about curiosity is it leads to ideas. The great scientist Albert Einstein was a very curious fellow. In fact, he came up with the big idea for his $E=mc^2$ Theory of Relativity thanks to his lesser-known Theory of Curiosity: "Never lose a holy curiosity."

Martha Stewart told me curiosity helped her come up with the ideas that created her homemaking empire: "I developed my curiosity. I've always had curiosity, but I think I've honed it now. I find it very important to success in any field." Curiosity led Bill Stumph to an idea for one of the world's most popular office chairs, the Aeron (which, by the way, I'm sitting in as I write this). Bill says, "I was always curious about this fundamental problem: how do you make something functional, and at the same time beautiful, and at the same time work in serial production?" Margaret MacMillan, author of the best-seller *Paris 1919: Six Months That Changed the World,* says, "Part of what drew me to the past was just curiosity, nosiness, wanting to know what it was like...I think we want to know why things are the way they are, and we want to know as much as possible."

Kids are naturally curious, and it was a childlike curiosity that led Louis Monier to the big idea of creating Alta Vista, one of the first great search engines for the web: "I always try to keep the point of view of a kid. I thought, 'What is the next interesting problem that needs to be solved, that would be fun solving?' I decided that searching the web was a good one, because I couldn't use any of the stuff that was available at the time to search the web." I'm like Louis, in that I work very hard to be curious and maintain a childlike mind. I think the exact word my wife uses to describe me is "immature." I keep telling her this is actually a good thing, and many successful people agree. Publisher Gerald Durnell says, "I do have a childlike curiosity that's insatiable."

Curiosity leads to ideas and success, but for some reason it gets a bad rap. We say, "Curiosity killed the cat." Little Red Riding Hood was warned not to be curious, and Curious George was always getting into trouble. Well, the truth is, if Little Red and George were really curious, chances are they'd also be very successful. So, encourage curiosity in yourself and others – oh yeah, and even cats.

Being really inquisitive and curious has helped me in my life. Be really curious and have an active, engaged relationship with the world.

Omar Wasow executive director, BlackPlanet.com

A big trait is curiosity. If you see something that's interesting, investigate it. Try and learn about it.

Don Tapscott technology consultant and author

Take advantage of curiosity. Maintain a childlike mind, a playfulness of spirit, openness. One of my differentiators is a childlike mind.

Steve Jurvetson renowned venture capitalist

I've always been very curious. I always had questions. Lots of questions.

Gail Percy anthropologist

I think a good CEO should be curious. Whether it's about the profit center or the product, you want to know because you're just so damn curious.

Bob Ferchat chairman, Bell Mobility

ASKING QUESTIONS LEADS TO IDEAS

The idea for the 3-door coupe came from one of our retailer's sons. He was 8 years old and **he asked, "Dad, why don't you have an easier way for me to get my stuff into the car?"**

Cynthia Trudell first woman in America to run a major auto company

Sometimes we hesitate to ask questions, because we're afraid we'll look dumb. But if you want to have great ideas, it's dumber not to ask questions. Richard Saul Wurman, a very creative designer, full of great ideas, says, "Questions drive all of my work." Scientist Robert H. Dennard says scientists are always questioning. Robert made the personal computer possible when he invented DRAM (Dynamic Random Access Memory), but he got his big ideas through DRAQ (Dynamic Random Access Questioning). In fact, asking questions is one thing humans can do much better than computers. As the great artist Picasso said, "Computers are useless. They can only give you answers."

Simple questions often spark ideas for great inventions. In the early days of photography, when it took forever to get pictures developed, George Land was walking on a beach and he took a picture. His daughter asked a simple question: "Why can't I see the picture right now?" That one question gave George the idea for instant pictures and he invented the Polaroid process. Gary Hamel, founder and chairman of Strategos, tells about another big idea that happened after another question was asked on a beach: "A guy is down in the Caribbean, and he works for Motorola. He's there with his wife, on an island so remote you can't get a cell signal out, and she turns to him and says, 'Honey, you work for a communications company. Why the hell can't I make a call?' And out of that comes the idea for point-to-point satellite communication all over the world."

On the previous page, Martha Stewart credited curiosity for her ideas, and part of that curiosity involves asking questions. Cindy Galbraigh, head of sales and licensing for TV Ontario, told me she ran into Martha at a trade show and was peppered with questions: "Martha was amazing. She asked me, 'What did you buy? Why didn't you buy this? What made you buy that?' She kept questioning me, but in a nice way. She wanted to know, and I was very impressed by that."

In school, they give gold stars more for answering questions than asking them. But when Isador Isaac Rabi got home from school, his mother would always say, "Did you ask any good questions today, Isaac?" That attitude helped Isador get the ultimate gold star, the Nobel Prize for physics. Have you asked any good questions today?

I think one of my biggest assets is that from the time I was a little kid, I asked a lot of questions. They used to call it being nosy. I prefer to call it inquisitive.

Gayle King TV host, *The Gayle King Show*

I'm best at solving complex problems. In truth, I don't actually solve the problems. All I do is ask a lot of questions that other people hadn't thought of asking. Ask lots of questions.

Elinor MacKinnon chief information officer, Blue Shield

Selling real estate is about asking questions. "Where do you live now? How many bedrooms do you need?"

Elli Davis top real estate agent

I ask a lot of questions. You listen, and that leads you to the next person, the next question, and you learn along the way. The answer, the path, the direction you need in your life will appear.

Leslie Westbrook marketing consultant

BORROW AN IDEA

THEN **BUILD** IT INTO A NEW IDEA

Don't be afraid to borrow and then modify. There's very little invented from scratch. **But be honest about where you got it.**

Wayne Schuurman president, Audio Advisor

When we run out of something, like milk, sometimes we'll borrow some from a neighbor. Well, when you run out of ideas, you can do the same thing – borrow someone else's idea, and then build it into a new idea of your own. Well, to be honest, some people don't call it borrowing, they call it copying. Pulitzer Prize-winning cartoonist and author Art Spiegelman says, "Most cartoonists learn their craft by copying other cartoonists." And in the newspaper industry, writing is actually referred to as "copy." How's that for honesty?

When I was young and idealistic I used to think copying was bad. But when I worked in advertising and design, I discovered only amateurs feel bad about copying. Professionals do it all the time. Creative people copy so much, creativity should really be called "copytivity." Some of the greats, like famous artist Picasso, actually come right out and admit they steal: "When there's anything to steal, I steal." But no matter what you call it – stealing, copying, mimicking, imitating, or inspiring – I prefer to think of it as borrowing, because eventually you give back when others come along and borrow your ideas.

Starting with somebody else's idea is just another way of charging up the creative battery in your head, sort of like jump-starting your car battery when it runs out of energy. Borrowing gets you going, and then – here's the important part – you need to BUILD what you've borrowed into a new idea. The idea for *West Side Story* was borrowed from *Romeo & Juliet* and then built into a musical format. Aesop borrowed ideas from Indian stories of 2000 years ago and built them into fables. Steve Jobs borrowed the idea for the computer mouse and GUI (Graphical User Interface) from Xerox and created the Apple Macintosh computer. Then Bill Gates borrowed what Steve did and built Windows for PCs. Each of these borrowed an idea and then built it into something great in its own right.

WARNING: Ripping-off someone else's idea and presenting it as your own is called plagiarism (although in Hollywood it's called an honest day's work). So, when you borrow, be sure to give credit where credit is due. The bottom line is, don't be afraid to borrow an idea and build on it. Who knows? Some day somebody might want to rip-off your idea. Then you'll know you've really succeeded.

Don't be afraid to borrow other people's ideas, but you should always attribute it to its source. Don't be afraid to say "I got a good idea from somebody."
David Zussman president, Public Policy Forum

I have no qualms about taking somebody else's great ideas and using them. My company Earthlink is no great idea. I just put it together better than anybody else.
Sky Dayton founder, Earthlink

We can't afford R and D, so we do R and C, which means Research and Copy.
Pannin Kitiparaporn Dreamworld Theme Park

I watched other people climb and tried to figure out what allowed them to be efficient. What was it they were doing? And I'd try to emulate that.
Laurie Skreslet first Canadian to summit Mount Everest

There's a lot of people that I steal from.
Macy Gray award-winning vocalist

TO GET IDEAS
MAKE CONNECTIONS

TAKE **ONE THING**

AND **CONNECT IT TO ANOTHER**

Make connections. Ask, how can this relate to that? Maybe if I join these two strange things together I'll get something completely new. That's human creativity.

Lindsay Sharp director, National Museum of Science and Industry, London

There's a myth you get somewhere in life because you know the right people and have connections. In reality, many people achieve success, not by having connections, but by making mental connections between different things. They see or hear one thing and connect it to something they already know or a problem they're trying to solve, and – BOING – the idea-light turns on and they have a new idea.

Douglas Adams was traveling through Europe with a book, *The Hitchhiker's Guide To Europe*. Then, one night as he looked up at the sky, his mind made a connection between the guidebook and the galaxies above him, and it sparked an idea for *The Hitchhiker's Guide To The Galaxy*. His idea turned into a radio play, best-selling book, and popular TV series. By looking up at the stars and making a connection, Douglas became a star himself.

3M scientist Art Fry also made a connection that changed his life. Art had a problem because the scraps of paper he used as bookmarks would keep falling out of his hymnbook in church, so poor Art was probably always singing the wrong hymn. Then one day he remembered a talk he'd heard by another 3M scientist about a new adhesive considered a failure because it didn't stick permanently. Art connected his bookmark problem with the low-stick adhesive, and got the idea for Post-it notes, those sticky pieces of paper that don't stick permanently. Post-it notes solved Art's problem, became a major product for 3M, and they're something I can't live without.

Beatles record producer George Martin says John Lennon was a master at connecting unrelated things and turning them into a song. Once, John took a newspaper headline he liked – "4,000 holes in Blackburn, Lancashire" – and started a song. Then he asked Paul, "Do you have anything we can put in the middle of this song?" Paul said he had another song, but it had nothing to do with what John was doing. John said, "It doesn't matter, we can stick 'em together," and "A Day in the Life" was born, my favorite Beatles song.

When you connect one and one, they don't just make 2, they make something new. As best-selling author Stephen King writes, "Two previously unrelated ideas come together and make something new under the sun." So keep looking for those connections, and it will help you connect with success.

> **Creativity is the power to connect the seemingly unconnected.**
> **William Plomer** novelist

> **I don't worry so much about discovering new information, but in connecting existing information in new ways.**
> **Richard Saul Wurman** designer, creator, TED conferences

> **If there's any one thing I love about writing more than the rest, it's that sudden flash of insight when you see how everything connects.**
> **Stephen King** best-selling author

> **You may have 2 ideas coming from separate directions and you put them together and you go, "Wow!"**
> **George Dyson** author and science historian

> **Creativity is about making a lot of quick connections – about the things you know, the things you've seen. The more you've seen, the more you've done, the easier it is to make that jump.**
> **Jerry Della Femina** influential advertising guru

TO GET **MANY IDEAS** MAKE **MANY MISTAKES**

I still remember my first day on the job in advertising. **The art director walked me over to the waste-paper basket and pointed to it and said, "Don't ever be afraid to use it."**

Steven Schwartz speaker and author *How To Make Hot Cold Calls*

We're usually taught mistakes are bad, and they are, but not all the time. When we need to come up with ideas, mistakes are actually good, because it's hard to come up with a great idea without first coming up with a lot of other ideas that really suck. So mistakes are really the seeds for creativity, and that's why Disney CEO Michael Eisner says it's okay to have films, TV shows, and plays that really flop, because it's the only way he'll get big hits. Filmmaker Robert Altman, who won an Oscar for his movie *M*A*S*H*, says *M*I*S*T*A*K*E*S* sometimes end up being the best idea: "I'm looking for mistakes. Shelley Duvall's skirt got caught when she slammed a car door in *Three Women*. I said, 'Great! Leave it in!'" I saw *Three Women*, and I thought that mistake was the most memorable moment in the film.

Many of us have a big fear of making mistakes, because we're taught from a young age NOT to make them. That becomes a big mental barrier when we're trying to come up with ideas. Illustrator Philip Burke told me the fear of making mistakes held him back at first, but he managed to get over it: "I now think it's okay to make mistakes, so I may start something, get halfway through, and just erase it all and start again. I learned if it's not working, wipe it out now. If it's still not working, wipe it out again. I might wipe out my entire cartoon 10 times." That willingness to take what he's done and coldly trash it, has made Philip a hot illustrator who is commissioned by the likes of *Rolling Stone* and *Vanity Fair* to do amazing portraits of Madonna and other stars.

I use the typical symbol of a light bulb over a person's head to show them getting an idea. But a trash can would also be a great symbol, because a whole bunch of ideas need to get trashed before we can get to that "Wow" idea. When immortal scientist Albert Einstein went to teach at Princeton and they asked him what he wanted for his office, he replied, "A desk, some pads and a pencil, and a large wastebasket – to hold all of my mistakes." Einstein realized the importance of mistakes and wasn't afraid to make them. In fact, his most famous formula, $E=mc^2$, didn't start out that way. In his manuscripts you can see where he first wrote $N= l/c^2$. He eventually realized his mistake and scribbled in $E=mc^2$. The rest, as they say, is history.

So, if you want an idea that goes down in history, churn out a lot more that go up in smoke. You've got to first produce garbage to end up with gold.

We often discover what will do, by finding out what will not do; and probably he who never made a mistake never made a discovery.

Samuel Smiles essayist, philosopher

In the beginning I made many mistakes. But I have tried to correct them and perfect them.

Geoffrey Beene fashion designer

It was when I found out I could make mistakes that I knew I was on to something.

Ornette Coleman jazz innovator

If you fail early and often, and persevere through it, that's often where you can make creative breakthroughs.

Steve Jurvetson respected venture capitalist

A word processor is one of the greatest inventions of all time. The minute the word processor came out I could make the world's biggest mistakes, then fix them later.

Terry Gilliam respected filmmaker, Monty Python member

MISTAKE → MISTAKE → IDEA

PLEASE MAKE MISTAKES

IDEA STAGE
MISTAKES ARE GOOD - THEY LEAD TO IDEAS

NO MISTAKES

IMPLEMENTATION STAGE
MISTAKES ARE BAD - CAN BE COSTLY OR EMBARRASSING

The previous page shows mistakes are good when we're coming up with ideas. But let's face it, there are times when mistakes are bad. So how do we know when it's okay to make mistakes and when it's not? Well, here's my take on it:

MISTAKES ARE GOOD IN THE IDEA STAGE. When we need ideas – whether it's to help us do a project, solve a problem, create a product, come up with a miracle cure, run faster, or whatever – mistakes are okay. Because only through a trail of mistakes, will we find the ideas we need.

MISTAKES ARE BAD IN IMPLEMENTATION STAGE. Once we have ideas and start implementing them, mistakes are no longer okay, because they can be costly, embarrassing, or dangerous. Mistakes are not okay if you're an airline pilot landing a plane, or a surgeon operating on a patient. As surgeon Douglas Dorner says, "The one thing you never want to say when you operate is, 'Whoops!'"

The trick is to know which stage you're in, at any moment, so you can give yourself permission to either make mistakes or not make them.

When chefs need ideas for a new recipe, they give themselves permission to mess up. Legendary chef Julia Child said, "I think of my strawberry soufflé. I did that at least 28 times before I finally conquered it." But when chefs move from creation to implementation and are serving dinners, it's not good when guests gag and have to be carried out on a stretcher.

When musicians are in idea mode, creating a song, they give themselves permission to bang out a lot of sour notes. I remember hearing a recording engineer telling about his experience working with U2 on a new song. He said at first the song sounded so bad he couldn't believe it was coming from one of the world's top bands. They just kept flubbing it, until it evolved into one of their biggest hits. But when musicians like U2 move from ideas to implementation and they're playing in front of a live audience, they do everything they can to make sure there are no mistakes.

When engineers are designing a bridge, their first ideas may flunk stress tests, and that's okay because it helps them get to the best design. But when they move to implementation, produce blueprints, and start construction, there's no tolerance for mistakes. One little lapse and the bridge could collapse.

Writers developing a book have initial drafts full of mistakes. My first draft of this book wasn't fit for human consumption, but it didn't bother me because only close friends got to read it and barf. But when the book moves into the production stage, all mistakes stop. It gets edited, my bad grammar gets cleaned up, and typos corrected. Otherwise, some sharp-eyed reader will send me nasty letters saying, "Hey, stupid, don't you know how to spel?" Then we'll have to scrap our entire production run of 10 books and, let me tell you, that gets costly.

In all these cases, it's like you flick a switch in your head. At first the switch is on one side and you say, "I'm in the idea stage. I can make mistakes, they're okay." Then you get to the production stage and you flick the mental switch to the other side and say, "No mistakes allowed." Learn to do that in your own mind and it will really help you switch on success.

WRITE DOWN IDEAS

BEFORE THEY FLY AWAY

If an idea comes up, I will always, always, stop and make a note wherever I am, even at dinner.

Issy Sharp founder, Four Seasons Hotels

I'm now going to let you in on one of the biggest secrets to coming up with ideas. It's something that will change your life! Are you ready? Okay, here it is: When you get an idea, write it down. That's it? Yes, that's it. I have pages and pages of successful people saying how important it is to jot down ideas the second you get them or they'll fly away, never to return.

Comedian Sinbad can memorize an hour-long stand-up comedy routine, but he told me that when he gets an idea, it will vanish in a flash unless he captures it: "I've had ideas and I'll call my secretary to tell her, and then go, 'Damn, I forgot the idea.' So now when I say something, I write it down. I'll be at dinner with somebody, and I'll just grab a napkin and start writing." Respected travel writer Pico Iyer says, "A discipline I have is that I take down a huge amount of notes then and there. I don't wait, even until the next day, because by the next day it's often forgotten. I don't trust myself to keep it in my head, or say, 'Well, maybe I'll do it tomorrow,' because it will never happen. You have to do it then and there."

Writing down ideas helped Bob Dylan become one of the greatest songwriters of his generation. David Hajdu, author of *Positively 4th Street,* writes, "Dylan has his antennae up all the time...he writes down phrases people say to him, or things he overhears in restaurants, then puts them in a box. Whenever he needs a song, he just reaches into the box and pulls something out." Instead of a box, Bob Ferchat, chairman of Bell Mobility, pulls ideas out of his briefcase: "I'll write ideas down on a slip of paper and throw them in my briefcase. They accumulate, then I add them to my research pile." Virgin Music/Airways founder Richard Branson always has a notebook by his side ready to capture ideas, and those notebooks now number in the hundreds.

John Nash, the brilliant mathematician featured in the book and movie *A Beautiful Mind,* always had a notebook handy and was ready to write when an idea struck. Well, maybe "write" isn't the correct word, since his scribbles were indecipherable to anybody but him. But, hey, those scribbles won him a Nobel Prize. So there's a tip: The important thing is the idea, not how neatly it's written. Focus on content, not looks.

The bottom line? If you want to move up to success, write down your ideas.

Write down the thoughts of the moment. Those that come unsought for are commonly the most valuable.

Francis Bacon philosopher

One secret to success I found the hard way is incredibly basic. Write everything down, leave nothing to memory. Memory gets you in trouble, memory ultimately betrays you.

Rick Pitino basketball coach

It's wise to write things down. I don't care how smart somebody is, in time memory fades. It's amazing what you can forget.

Peter Silverberg lawyer

We have scientists and Nobel Laureates go through our school and they write and sketch the whole time. So a very practical piece of advice I give kids is to always take notes. You should have a pad of paper where you're constantly jotting things down or making a little sketch. Keep your hand moving.

Michele Claeys
teacher, The Ross School

DO YOU COME UP WITH GREAT IDEAS, BUT ALWAYS FORGET THEM? THEN YOU NEED A P.E.N.

P.E.N.
Personal **E**conomical **N**otetaker

REVOLUTIONARY TECHNOLOGY

Introducing **P.E.N.**, the **P**ersonal **E**conomical **N**otetaker – an amazing device to help you capture those precious ideas. It's incredibly small and light, thinner than a computer mouse, and more compact than a cell phone. **P.E.N.** technology is all contained in one slim rod ergonomically designed to fit perfectly in your palm or pocket.

MAKES IT FAST, SIMPLE, AND CHEAP TO CAPTURE IDEAS

And get this: **P.E.N.** is completely cordless, requiring no batteries or electricity whatsoever, so it can be used absolutely anywhere. Wait, there's more. **P.E.N.**'s operating system is incredibly easy to program, because there isn't one. No 2-month training course required! And the best part? **P.E.N.** only costs pennies, not hundreds of dollars.

Get a P.E.N. today!
The world's best device to capture ideas before they slip away

SPIKE APPROVED

Now, don't get me wrong about technology. I'm a big computer user and this whole book was written on one. But my computer is never around when I'm walking down the street and I get a brainwave for somebody's birthday present, or I'm in a restaurant and hear a great idea for this book. So I adopted P.E.N. – Personal Economical Notetaker – technology years ago, and I always carry at least 2 back-up P.E.N.s, in case there's a system failure in one, like running out of ink.

Even successful high-tech people use low-tech P.E.N. and paper. Elinor MacKinnon, CIO in charge of all the computers at Blue Shield, says, "When I meet and talk with people, I always scribble on napkins, then file them at work." Why not use a computer? Because scribbling an idea on a napkin is faster than the world's fastest computer, if you include the time it takes to fire it up and type the idea in there.

Some of the world's greatest ideas see the light of day thanks to P.E.N.s and napkins. Stephen King was on a plane when he got the idea for his best-selling novel *Misery*: "I fell asleep on the plane and had a dream about a popular writer…who fell into the clutches of a psychotic fan living on a farm… I wrote it on an American Airlines cocktail napkin so I wouldn't forget it, then put it in my pocket." Legendary guitarist Jimi Hendrix jotted down ideas with his P.E.N. on anything handy, from napkins to the backs of envelopes. My colleague Thom Rockliff told me he was sitting with renowned musician Gordon Downie, lead singer and lyricist of The Tragically Hip. Gord didn't have any paper, so he was writing ideas on his hands and arms. There were so many ideas it looked like he was covered in tattoos.

It doesn't matter what you write on: hands, napkins, notebooks, envelopes, paper towels – I've even scribbled out many ideas on toilet paper (which some people say appropriately reflects the quality of my ideas). Now, I admit, I've finally gone high-tech and I carry a tiny digital recorder, which eliminates the need to carry paper and is a lot easier to use when running. In fact, the other day I was out for a run and I got this incredibly great idea. So, I whipped out my digital recorder – and the batteries were dead. Now I can't even remember what the great idea was, but I'm sure it would have changed the world. Sigh! Oh well, back to my good old P.E.N.

Even in this electronic age, and I'm in a high-tech company, I still write myself notes on little pieces of paper.
Jean Monty president, BCE

Even though I have a good memory, I still write everything down. "The faintest ink is better than the best memory."
Elli Davis top real estate agent

Don't you wish you could make your brain bigger? You can. Buy a notebook. I write things down. I take notes. Writing is part of your digestive process for ideas. When you put it in your notebook, you digest it to the next level.
Bob Rogers founder, BRC Imagination Arts

There are times on the weekend when I'm talking to my neighbor, and it all connects back to what I'm working on. So I take my little list out and write it down. It's amazing how many ideas come when you're in other settings.
David Zussman president, Public Policy Forum

HOW I GOT A BIG IDEA

There's no magic to coming up with ideas. It's just doing simple things, like the ones shown on these pages. How do I know? Because that's how I came up with a really big idea that won top international video awards. It started when my company was asked by a leading telecommunications corporation to produce a series of speeches and videos to be shown at a huge conference on the future of the telephone network. A lot was at stake for our clients, so our work had to be great. But my colleague Thom and I had a problem. How could we make ugly telephone switches and boring network diagrams interesting and understandable? We needed a great idea to bring the messages to life.

We **LISTENED** for weeks to dozens of technology experts fill us in on their ideas of the future phone network. We **ASKED QUESTIONS**, lots of dumb questions. We kept our eyes open and **OBSERVED** big things like the trends in the industry, and little things, like what our clients had on the walls of their offices. We read hundreds of research reports, magazines, books, and newspaper articles. We kept coming up with ideas and, even if they weren't great, we **WROTE EVERY IDEA DOWN**. But we still didn't have that big eureka idea. The deadline loomed, the pressure to produce increased, and we still needed a "WOW!"

Then one day we were on a flight to Atlanta, dead tired from working 20-hour days. I was staring out the window at the sky and Thom was telling me how optical fiber converted voice and data into electrons that could be sent through the phone network at high speed and – BOING – suddenly my mind **MADE A CONNECTION** between electrons and airplanes,

that **SPARKED AN IDEA**. I pictured us in a jumbo jet, but we were flying through fiber optics, and we weren't people, we were electrons that made up a phone call. I realized the whole story could be told from the perspective of electrons traveling inside the telephone network. We had our breakthrough idea! And we knew we could make it interesting, funny, and easy for the audience to understand.

I wrote the scripts, we dressed up actors as electrons, and then filmed them in jumbo jets and airports. While we were doing this I realized that 10 years earlier I'd seen a movie where people were dressed as sperm and were traveling on a plane. So maybe my subconscious mind **BORROWED AN IDEA** from an earlier time **AND BUILT IT INTO SOMETHING NEW.** All I know is the metaphor worked marvelously. The videos were a huge hit with audiences and won awards around the world for best corporate video and script.

I want to emphasize that I'm no creative genius. I'm just an ordinary guy. When I first started my career, I couldn't come up with a good idea if my life depended on it. But then I started working with people who were creative. I watched them and started copying the things they did, like problem solving, and listening, and observing, and trying to connect different things together, and writing ideas down. And slowly, over time, my ideas got better and better.

So take it from me, anybody can be creative. Just do the same things that all the successful people on these pages do, and great ideas will come to you, too.

IMPROVE

1. **PASSION**   2. **WORK**   3. **FOCUS**   4. **PUSH**

IMPROVE LEADS TO SUCCESS

IMPROVE
154 **SUCCESSFUL PEOPLE KEEP IMPROVING**

7 TIPS TO IMPROVE
156 **1. MAKE THINGS BETTER AND BETTER**
158 **2. GET REALLY GOOD AT WHAT YOU DO**
160 **3. AIM TO DO YOUR BEST**
162 **4. PRACTICE, PRACTICE, PRACTICE**
164 **5. KEEP REPEATING KEEP REPEATING**
166 **6. FOCUS ON STRENGTHS – FORGET WEAKNESSES**
168 **7. OUTSOURCE YOUR WEAKNESSES**

MY STORY
170 **MY ONE-WORD BUSINESS PLAN – IMPROVE**

5. **IDEAS**   6. **IMPROVE**   7. **SERVE**   8. **PERSIST**

KEEP
IMPROVING

At the end of the day you'd like to say,

"Gee, I improved in this way today."

Sherwin Nuland clinical professor of surgery, Yale

A common pattern among successful people is they're always on a mission to keep improving, whether it's their project, their product, their service or themselves. Improvement is so important that the corporate world even came up with a buzzword for it: Continuous Improvement. For example, FedEx founder Fred Smith says that FedEx's management system is "built on continuous quality improvement." In other words, they aim to keep getting "better and better, year after year."

Science and technology is driven by continuous improvement. Robert H. Dennard, the scientist who invented random access memory, making the personal computer possible, says scientists have a fundamental belief that anything can be improved. Yes, thanks to guys like him, the minute I buy a computer, within a couple of hours there'll be a new improved one that does twice as much for half the cost. And that's a good thing, or I'd still be writing on a clay tablet, instead of a silicon tablet that can store gazillions of words and images. Once in awhile I can even find some of them.

Athletics is all about continuous improvement, trying to knock even a fraction of a second off a record, or set new benchmarks. Basketball superstar Michael Jordan was an improvement machine. Chicago Bulls assistant coach John Bach says, "Michael had that rare capacity to be a genius who constantly wanted to upgrade his genius." Of course, improvement is as important in the classroom as it is on the basketball court. And I'm not talking about students improving. I'm talking about teachers improving. Professor Brian Little, voted most popular professor by students at Harvard, says, "You are always looking for what might be improved. Is there anybody bored over here? Have I missed doing this particular aspect of the presentation? Could I sort of tweak it a little bit next lecture?" Gee, I wish my teachers had taken whatever he's taking.

So, even though it's a corporate buzzword, I like the concept of Continuous Improvement, because that's what successful people keep doing, and it implies it never stops. And it doesn't stop. Pioneer fabric designer Jack Lenor Larson was in his 80s when I asked him what he wanted to do for the rest of his life, and he simply answered: "I want to keep on improving."

I have a willingness to improve and always learn.
Amy Tan, best-selling author, *The Joy Luck Club*

I never pick up an item without thinking of how I might improve it.
Thomas Edison inventor of the light bulb

In my mind, every day I'm trying to figure out how I can improve. I think that's important. You always have to strive to be better and to be more creative.
Sandra Ainsley renowned art gallery owner

People complain that I'm always changing things. Why can't I just leave them alone? But I can't do that. If I see it's not working perfectly, I want to adjust it a bit, rethink it a bit. Improve it.
Sam Sullivan quadriplegic, mayor of Vancouver

Attempt the impossible in order to improve your work.
Bette Davis film star

MAKE IT BETTER BETTER BETTER

You can always take what you have and **make it better.**

Ted Williams one of baseball's greatest hitters

Let's look at 7 tips to improve, and the first one is always try and make whatever you do better and better. Beatle Paul McCartney wrote a lyric about taking a sad song and making it better, and that describes Paul himself. He's one of the most successful songwriters, yet he says, "I'm still looking to write a great song." Successful up and coming singer/songwriter Hawksley Workman has the same attitude: "I'm always challenging myself to be better, to strive for some greatness. Why would you want to do anything else, no matter what you do?"

In the business world, General Electric CEO Jack Welch talked about, "A relentless, endless, company wide search for a better way to do everything we do." That attitude made GE a very successful huge company, and it also works for small companies. Richard Saul Wurman, creator of the very successful Access travel guides, told me: "Every time I did a guide book I tried to make it better. I mean, why do it if you can't do it better?"

In the film world, Robin Budd, who directs great animated films for folks like Disney, told me most animators continually strive to keep doing better and to out-do themselves: "I always try to do it better than I've ever done before, to push it just a little bit farther. Sometimes you'll see a scene up on the screen you thought would work really well, but you know it could be better, so you keep honing it and reworking it."

Instead of a movie screen, Onex CEO Gerry Schwartz sees the results of his hard work as numbers on a computer screen, and he's just as concerned about making them better and better. "We look at ourselves, and ask ourselves every day, how we can do better. Nobody here feels good about where we are." That itch to keep doing better doesn't necessarily mean being a perfectionist. Norman Lear, legendary producer of great TV shows like *All in the Family*, said to me, "I do strive to do better. But I'm not one of those people who's always unhappy if it isn't perfect."

It's like successful people have this voice in the back of their heads that keeps saying, "Come on, come on make it better." And that's a good thing, because success is like a staircase with many levels, and it's by getting better that we move from one level to the next. Oh, and sorry, there are no escalators.

I can't explain where it comes from, but I have this drive to keep doing better and better.
Suzy Favor Hamilton
3-time Olympian runner

I can't be satisfied with the way I am, the status quo. You have to keep improving, doing something better, more efficient, faster, getting more out of it.
David Gallo marine scientist, director, Woods Hole Oceanographic Institute

It's a lot of work, to try to get better...but you just can't quit.
Brian McLeod blind golf champion

Keep setting the threshold higher. So once you've done something, redo it. Don't sit back and say you've done it. Think about how you would do it better.
Maurizio Vecchione physicist, co-founder ModaCAD

GET REALLY REALLY
GOOD
AT WHAT YOU DO

The best chance you have to be successful is to **put your nose down in something and get damn good at it.**

Alex Garden game developer, CEO Relic Entertainment

Improvement is all about GOOD. As singer/songwriter Bruce Cockburn says, "Step one is to be as good as you can be, at whatever you pick to do. Obviously, if you are not good at it, nobody is going to be interested." Marketing guru Nancye Green likes to do things well. "Mastering things is important for its own sake. I believe that anything worth doing is worth doing well." And architect Susan Ruptash talks about doing great: "You always push for great in every aspect of what you do. You can't hit great every time, but you don't give up trying to do great next time."

Whether we call it good, great, excellent, magnificent, outstanding, top-notch, or doing things well, they're all degrees of GOOD. There's a lot of satisfaction we get from being good at what we do, and that helps fuel success. CNN reporter and author Meredith Bagby says, "There is something satisfying about being the good writer, the good speaker, the good mathematician. It's the self-satisfaction that you get after completing a project that you are proud of."

No matter what the job, doing good work brings respect from others. Famous filmmaker Norman Jewison told me about a man who sweeps the streets in his area: "Everybody respects him simply because he does a good job. He cares about what he does and he takes pride in the fact that his area of the street is cleaner than anybody else's." Unfortunately, not everybody wants to do a great job, but that just leaves more opportunity for those who do. Paul Bunt, who runs a successful traffic engineering company, says, "If you do something well you'll be rewarded. That alone will be enough to distinguish you, because there are so many people who don't seem to care."

Successful people do care, and often they care more about doing a good job than about fame or success. Oprah says the reason she has been so successful is that her goal wasn't success, it was doing good work. Marvin Hamlisch has won 3 Oscars for composing such great songs as "The Way We Were" but if you go to his apartment, you won't see the Oscars sitting there, because his priority isn't winning gold statues, it's doing good work. The moral of the story is don't focus on things like success, money, respect, or awards. Focus on doing really good work and all the other good stuff will come along automatically.

Be as good as you can be at what it is you are.
Murray McLaughlin singer/songwriter

A job worth doing, is worth doing well. If you're going to do something, do it well.
Douglas Dorner surgeon

Find something you're good at. Nothing makes people feel better about their daily lives than being good at what they do.
Geoffrey Cowan dean, USC

Somebody coming up and patting you on the back and saying, "Good job," is worth a lot more than the money.
Alan Way graphic designer

I definitely want to excel. Not for the sake of being better than someone else, but just because it's so satisfying to do something well. It's really tough to make it shine, but there is no other feeling like it. All the struggle is worth it for that moment of "Wow!"
Robin Budd animation film director

AIM TO DO YOUR
BEST

Even if you don't always make it!

I always wanted to be **the best I could be at whatever I did**. I didn't want to be the number one golfer in the world. I just **wanted to be as good as I could be**.

Greg Norman champion golfer

Another way to improve is to always try to do your best. Ian Craig, president of Nortel Networks Wireless Networks, said to me, "Every time I got a job, no matter what it was, I just did the best I could in that job. I never went into a job thinking, 'Gee, if I do great they're going to make me a supervisor.' You just do the best that you possibly can with the job at hand." Another wireless guy, Smart Wireless CEO Nez Hallett III, put it this way: "Whatever I do, I do it to the best of my ability. I don't like regrets, going back later and saying, 'Hey, I didn't give it my best shot.'"

Some people not only aim to do their best, they also want to be absolute best. Champion cyclist Lance Armstrong once said, "I want to be the best rider there is...I don't want to just be good at it, I want to be the best." And Lance became the best cyclist in the world 7 times. Virgin Records/Airlines CEO Richard Branson, says "Create the best. The best hotels and clubs and airlines never go bankrupt. The best always succeeds."

So, the question is, should you just aim to "do your best" or should you go all out and try to "be the best"? Like Lance and Richard, you can aim really high if it works for you. But often we have no control over the factors that lead to being number one and thinking about it can be a distraction. That's why many successful people simply aim to "do their best," and the irony is, many end up being the best anyway. Greg Zeschuk is a good example. He told me, "Instead of saying, 'I'm going to work to the goal of being the best video-game developer in the world,' you say, 'I'm just going to try and do my best.' Ultimately, we're just trying to do our best all the time." And by doing his best, Greg still became the world's best when Billboard named him "Game Developer of the Year."

Curling champ Colleen Jones didn't aim to be the best. She said, "I just want to play as well as I can on that day, and leave it with no regrets." Colleen still became the world's best, winning 2 world curling championships. One last example is actor Russell Crowe, who said to me, "You just want to do the best work you can do." And by always doing his best, Russell became the world's best, winning an Academy Award for Best Actor. The moral of the story is, don't worry about being the best, or shooting for the stars. Just aim to do your best and you could become a star anyway.

> **I wouldn't say I had a specific goal other than to just do the best I could do and I would succeed.**
> **David Cohen** renowned writer for *The Simpsons*

> **You strive to do your best, to be the best you can be all the time.**
> **Story Musgrave** 6-time space shuttle astronaut

> **You're constantly in search of excellence and that never stops. It's just trying to be your best.**
> **Issy Sharp** founder, Four Seasons Hotels and Resorts

> **Be the best you can. If you're going to be a surgeon entrusted with people's lives, you better work as hard as you possibly can and get it right.**
> **Douglas Dorner** vascular surgeon

> **Get out there and, whatever you are doing, do it to the best of your ability. No one can do more than that.**
> **John Wooden** legendary basketball coach

When people ask me about writing, I always say just **write, write, write** every day. Don't think about becoming a success, or finding a publisher. **Just do the practice.**

Pico Iyer respected travel writer

This tip to improve can be summed up in 3 words: practice, practice, practice. Getting better at anything is all about practice. When Lance Armstrong was asked how he won the world's ultimate cycling race, the Tour de France, for the 7th time, he simply said: "The difference is that my team practices 12 months of the year, not 3 or 4."

No matter what field you're in, the way you improve is by practicing over and over again. Vascular surgeon Douglas Dorner told me, "You need years and years of training and practice, so you know how to respond in a difficult situation. Training and practice are the big things, whatever we do." Even the study of stars and galaxies takes practice. Astrophysicist Jaymie Matthews says, "You've gotta keep practicing and you've gotta keep pushing yourself to practice."

It's easier to push yourself to practice if you actually enjoy the process. Classical guitarist Liona Boyd says, "I've always loved practicing so it's not a real chore." And no matter how good Liona gets, she says it still takes constant practice: "They say if you don't practice, the first day your hands know it, the 2nd day you know it, and the 3rd day your audience knows it."

I'm always trying to improve my writing – hey, who's that saying, "It's about time!" – so whenever I interview writers I always ask for advice. Award-winning playwright Eve Ensler told me it's all about practice: "If you want to be a writer, you have to write all the time. I write every day. I write everywhere I can. It's improving your instrument, it's teaching yourself how to do something better so words come easily, so you know how to put things together, so you can craft things in new ways. It just means practice, practice, practice. Everything's about practice." It worked for the Beatles. Paul McCartney says that when he and John Lennon were starting out they wrote a song every day. No matter what was happening, they wrote every day and that's how they got so good.

Practice is so important that some professions go as far as calling their business a "practice." My lawyer, doctor, dentist, and accountant all have "practices." But you know, since constant practice is the key to getting good at anything, maybe we should all call what we do our "practice."

> **You've got to practice. You've go to paint very, very hard, every day. And after a while it starts to look like something.**
> **Peter Max** renowned pop artist

> **I wasn't good at climbing when I started. It took a lot of practice.**
> **Laurie Skreslet** first Canadian to summit Mt. Everest

> **We learn by practice. Whether it means to learn to dance by practicing dancing or to learn to live by practicing living, the principles are the same.**
> **Martha Graham** famous dance teacher, choreographer

> **People don't realize, you have to practice until it hurts. That's what separates an athlete from an Olympian. They both have to practice, but the Olympian does it even when she's not feeling well.**
> **Steven Schwartz** author, *How to Make Hot Cold Calls*

DO REPS

REPETITION TO EXCESS PRODUCES SUCCESS

Repetition of action makes greatness. You've got to repeat what you do a lot. Repetition, every day.

Peter Max renowned pop artist

Improvement is all about practice, and practice is all about repetition – doing the same thing over and over again. When I go to the track for running workouts, the coach has us do repeats or REPS, which means we run flat out for one lap of the track then die – I mean rest – for 3 minutes, and then repeat it again 10 times. It's a killer workout, but reps improve speed and make you a faster runner.

Runners aren't the only athletes that do reps. Weight-lifters do them, and so do basketball players, except they call it shooting hoops. Legendary basketball coach John Wooden made reps the foundation of his training: "I created eight laws of learning...explanation, demonstration, imitation, repetition, repetition, repetition, repetition, and repetition." Cycling champion Lance Armstrong trained for the grueling Tour de France by doing grueling reps up steep hills. Lance writes, "There were something like 50 good, arduous climbs around Nice, solid inclines of ten miles or more. The trick was not to climb every once in a while, but to climb repeatedly."

Reps are associated with sports, but they're really the key to improvement in any area. By doing a lot of reps while training for space flights, Story Musgrave became the first astronaut to fly on 6 Space Shuttles, and cover 25 million miles in space: "I did more practice than I should have. People would haul me away from machines, saying, 'You're gonna wear it out!' I'd repeat exercises so many times the machines exceeded their limits and broke." Eve Ensler broke things too, except they were attendance records for her play, *The Vagina Monologues*. Eve says, "It's doing things over and over again. I did *The Monologues* for 5 years, night after night, after night, breaking through levels in myself, until I finally got to a place where I wanted to be."

Business people do reps. I mean, repeat a gazillion emails, memos, letters, and phone calls, and you find yourself eventually getting good at them. Repetition is so important that sales people are actually referred to as "sales reps." Okay, I admit it really stands for "representatives," but it should stand for "repetition" because that's the key to successful selling.

As you can see, reps are how people improve, no matter what field they're in. So I'd say REPS really stands for: Repetition to Excess Produces Success!

> I think of my strawberry souffle. I did that at least twenty-eight times before I finally conquered it.
> **Julia Child** famous chef

> Before I do a book, I'll tell stories for years, again and again and again and again. That's how they get good. That's the only way I know how to make stories good.
> **Robert Munsch** celebrated children's author

> To memorize plays I would read them out loud 5 times a day, every day and repeat and repeat. Even if I'd done a show 100 times, when I had a day off, I would still sit down alone in a room and repeat the whole show out loud.
> **Rick Mercer** award-winning comedian

> The most tiring – and yet the most rewarding – experiences are when you keep redoing it again and again, but what you end up with is actually the best thing.
> **Chip Kidd** acclaimed book designer

FOCUS ON YOUR STRENGTHS

FORGET ABOUT YOUR WEAKNESSES

There's no use trying to fix all our little weaknesses and idiosyncra-sies. **It's much better to say, "This is what I'm good at."**

Josef Penninger acclaimed medical geneticist

The 5th way to improve is to focus on your strengths and forget your weaknesses. Not everybody knows this little secret to success. In fact, over half the respondents in a recent survey said it was more important to work on your weaknesses than your strengths. When I read that, I thought, Gee, that's interesting. There's a lot of people putting effort into the wrong areas, because when I ask successful people the same question, they consistently say to go with your strengths and forget about your weaknesses. BCE president Jean Monty said to me, "Focus on the things you do well. If you're good at computers, and not football, don't try to be a football player. And don't be afraid to say you're weak in some areas, so you don't go down a rat hole trying to do something you know you won't be able to do very well." Of course, focusing on your strengths will mean you're really bad at a lot of other things. But who cares?

- J.K. Rowling's strength is writing great Harry Potter novels. Who cares if she was terrible at metalwork in school? J.K. says, "I was the worst in my class – just terrible...I did try, but I just could not do it."

- Lance Armstrong's strength in cycling made him a world champion. Who cares if he couldn't play ball? Lance says, "When it came to anything that involved moving from side to side, or hand-eye coordination – when it came to anything involving a ball, in fact – I was no good."

- U2 gave us great songs such as "With or Without You." Who cares if they couldn't play "We've Only Just Begun"? Bono says, "We were the worst wedding band on the planet."

- Quincy Jones' strength in composing music continues to drive him to count-less Grammy Awards. So who cares if he can't drive a car or a nail? Quincy says, "I couldn't drive a nail if my life depended on it."

Let's conclude with Erik Weihenmayer who focused on his strength in climbing, ignored his weakness of being totally blind, and climbed to the top of Mt. Everest, the world's highest mountain. Erik says, "I made a promise to myself. The things I could not do, I would let go; but the things I could do, I would learn to do well." The bottom line is you can be really bad at many things, as long as you're really good at one thing. So go with your strengths. Like Erik, that's how you'll climb to success.

You should understand your circle of competence, the thing that you're good at, and spend your time and energy there.
Bill Gates chairman, Microsoft

I know I'm not good at a lot of things. But what I'm good at is what I do.
Hawksley Workman singer/songwriter

Everybody is bad at a lot of things, but everybody has some unique thing they can be the worlds best at. And the trick is to find that unique thing.
Don Norman author, *The Way Things Work*

If I've learned anything, it's stick to what you do best.
Nez Hallett III CEO, Smart Wireless

In life, I gradually learned the things I was not good at, so I don't put myself in situations where I have to call on them. Instead, I go with the things that I do well.
Gary Burton Grammy award-winning vibraphonist

OUTSOURCE YOUR WEAKNESSES

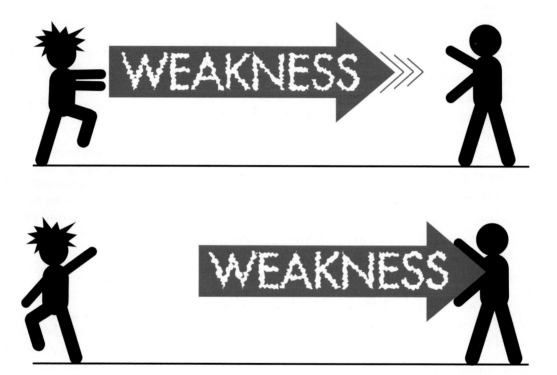

I think in order to be successful you have to **surround yourself with people who can take care of your weaknesses**.

Wayne Schuurman president, Audio Advisor

I just said it's important to focus on your strengths and forget your weaknesses. (Now comes the disclaimer.) The one time you can't forget a weakness is if it will be a big roadblock to your success in a particular area. No matter what field you're in, there are usually basic minimum standards that need to be met if you want to make it in that area. I mean, if you're dying to be a surgeon and you faint at the sight of blood, it'll be your patients who end up dying. So how do we handle success-blocking weaknesses? Successful people seem to have 2 strategies:

1. The first strategy is to work on the weakness and fix it. For example, one big weakness for many people is public speaking. BCE president Jean Monty told me, "I used to hate standing up and speaking in front of people, but if you want to lead a company, you've got to be able to speak in public. So I had no choice. It was a weakness, and I worked my ass off on it." I've seen Jean give great speeches to thousands of people, so by working hard on his weakness, he actually transformed it into a strength.

2. The second strategy is to borrow a trick from the corporate world and outsource your weakness. In other words, get somebody else to take care of it for you. For example, a company that's strong at product development, but weak in manufacturing, will often outsource their manufacturing and get another company to do it. Successful people do the same thing. Umbra co-founder Paul Rowan said to me, "I was artistic and I realized really quickly that I needed partners who were better organized and more business-minded, so I had business partners right from the beginning."

Ben and Jerry's co-founder Ben Cohen told me the reason he and Jerry really gelled (or ice creamed) was because they had strengths that compensated for each other's weaknesses: "Jerry is good at production and much more logical, and I'm the creative end of it. Jerry was doing production, and I was doing sales and marketing. He had no desire to do what I was doing, and I had no desire to do what he was doing."

So, the trick is to find somebody who's good at what you aren't and vice-versa. Then focus like crazy on your strengths. Now excuse me while I go and focus on my real strength – consuming enormous quantities of ice cream.

> **My great success has been because my partner was the wine maker and I'm the marketing and money guy. We had different strengths. We're like black and white.**
>
> **Donald Ziraldo** co-founder, Inniskillin Wines

> **I'm the creative force in the business and I employ sensible people to keep my feet on the ground.**
>
> **David Jensen** chief executive, Brooklands Executives recruitment

> **Some architects are fantastic conceptual thinkers, but need other people to run with their ideas. Good architectural partnerships let each person use their unique ability, rather than trying to do everything.**
>
> **Susan Ruptash** architect

> **Give me an operational person to match me, and I'll move mountains. I'm good at the big plan, but to actually make it work, I really need an operations person, and it took me awhile to figure that out.**
>
> **Lakshmi Pratury** director, American India Foundation

MY 1-WORD BUSINESS PLAN

IMPROVE

Successful people have this desire to keep improving themselves and their work, and I guess I'm no exception. It really bugs me if I think something I do isn't good enough. I've rewritten every page of this book and redrawn every graphic dozens of times, trying to improve it. I'll spend hours digging through my database to find a quote that makes the point just a little better than the one that's already there. There are people in my office whose job is to try and stop me from making changes. They keep saying, "It's good enough. Stop rewriting or we'll never get the book out." Sorry, I just can't stop myself.

I confess I haven't always had this overpowering desire to improve things and make them better. I remember one of my early assignments in college was to design a paper sculpture. Of course, I had more important things to do, like socialize, so I whipped off a quick design and left it on the professor's desk. In the back of my mind I knew it wasn't great, but I hoped it would squeak by. The next day, as I was passing by the display case exhibiting the best student work, I stopped dead in my tracks. There was my paper sculpture on display! As I stood there, thinking maybe it wasn't so bad after all, my classmates appeared, rolling on the floor with laughter. They'd swiped the key to the display case and placed my poor paper sculpture next to the really good work. I was humiliated, but it was a defining moment. I said to myself, "I'm never going to produce anything that bad again." Yes, the fear of ridicule is a great motivator.

From that moment on, I really tried to do good work. And "work" is the operative word, because I had to work my butt off to push my projects from mediocre to good. But, over time, I gradually improved and when a competition came along to create a new type of trophy, it was my design that took first place. And this time my work really did make it into the display case.

Suddenly, I discovered some of the benefits of doing great work, like the internal satisfaction and sense of self-worth. And there were also the external rewards, like the guys who laughed at me were now telling me what a great job I did. Suddenly, I was getting some respect. I also found if you do good work, then work comes to you. Instead of begging for a summer job, I was offered one. So, let's see… When I did bad work, I was ridiculed and laughed out of the room. When I did good work, I got satisfaction, respect, pats on the back, credibility, a job, and money. Hey, I was sold on the value of always trying to make things better.

From then on, improving myself and my work became my guiding light. Whatever I did, I just kept trying to make it better. When I started a company, I had no big goals or visions. I didn't even have a business plan. Wait, that's not true. Here's my business plan in one word: IMPROVE. When clients gave us a project, we put all our energy into doing good work and constant improvement. We figured if we did that, then things like success, awards, acknowledgement, and money would follow – and they did.

So I'd say, when you're sitting there, drawing up the business plan for your own life, consider this word for the cover: IMPROVE.

SERVE

1. **PASSION**   2. **WORK**   3. **FOCUS**   4. **PUSH**

SERVE LEADS TO SUCCESS

174   **SERVE SOMEBODY SOMETHING**

176   **WHO DO YOU SERVE? – 1.**

178   **WHO DO YOU SERVE? – 2.**

180   **WHAT VALUE DO YOU SERVE OTHERS?**

182   **1. SERVING OTHERS WILL GIVE YOU A RICH LIFE**

184   **2. SERVING OTHERS IS THE WAY YOU'LL GET RICH**

186   **TO GET RICH, DO WHAT YOU LOVE, PLUS SERVE OTHERS WHAT THEY LOVE**

188   **PEOPLE GET RICH BY SERVING OTHERS – NOT BY INVESTING OR GAMBLING**

8 SERVE TIPS

190   **1.   IT'S NOT ABOUT YOU. FOCUS ON THE PEOPLE YOU SERVE**

192   **2.   TO REACH THE TOP PUT OTHERS TOP OF MIND**

194   **3.   PUT YOURSELF IN OTHER PEOPLE'S SHOES**

196   **4.   SEE THE OTHER PERSON'S PERSPECTIVE**

198   **5A. LISTEN TO THE PEOPLE YOU SERVE**

200   **5B. LISTENING PAYS OFF**

202   **6.   BE ABLE TO SET YOUR EGO ASIDE**

204   **7.   SERVING DOESN'T MEAN SUCKING UP**

206   **8.   BEND OVER BACKWARDS TO HELP THE PEOPLE YOU SERVE**

5. **IDEAS**   6. **IMPROVE**   7. **SERVE**   8. **PERSIST**

SERVE SOMEBODY SOMETHING

I think success is to really see your life as serving. Period. We're here to do nothing else. Nothing else interests me, personally.

Eve Ensler award-winning author, performer

In this book we've talked a lot about you. You finding your passion, you working hard, you improving, you pushing yourself. Now, it's time to shift gears and, instead of looking inward, we need to look outward, because if you want to reach success and wealth, it's not about you. It's about serving other people.

Here's the awful truth: you won't achieve success by just being you. People don't care about you. They only care about how you can help them fix their problem, fix their plumbing, eliminate their pain, make them thinner, make them laugh, make them cry, make them comfortable, make their day, listen to them, give them inspiration, give them products, fill their stomachs, fill their soul, or fill a void in their lives. In other words, people only care about you serving them something that has some value, and helps them somehow.

The word SERVE is often misunderstood. Maybe it's because "servers" in restaurants say, "Hi, my name's Bobby and I'm your server." Then everytime you want something, Bobby can't be found. And when we hear "serve," the word that pops to mind is often "charity," for example, Mother Teresa serving the poor. Charity is important, but it's only one aspect of serving. As you'll see in this chapter, serving others is how most people get rich.

What I mean by SERVE is thinking about others, working on their behalf, and delivering something they want, need, or value, whether it's a service, a product, an experience, or a feeling. It's delivering the goods, and coming through for other people. And no matter what field you're in, serving is key to success. Four Seasons Hotels founder Issy Sharp told me that's what took him to the top: "Service was really what set the company on its course. The idea of acting more as a host, being friendly, accommodating, giving the customer service." I love this quote by award-winning author and performer Eve Ensler, so I'll use it twice: "I think success is to really see your life as serving. Period. We're here to do nothing else. Nothing else interests me, personally." Yes, as you'll see in this chapter, people succeed by serving others in some way, shape, or form.

So: 1. Who do you serve? 2. What do you serve them?

As an entrepreneur you are in the business of serving other people.

Omar Wasow executive director, BlackPlanet.com

I think I'm here to serve. I'm a messenger about communication, about ideas, and turning them into pop culture.

Paula Silver president, Columbia Pictures Marketing, *My Big Fat Greek Wedding*

I offer a service, and that's to clothe people.

Alexander McQueen fashion designer

This is all about serving. I'm out to serve humanity by delivering safe remedies that help them with their health issues. I'm out to serve the environment through efforts to protect it. And I'm out to serve indigenous, native people. I'm totally in a serve capacity. That's the whole deal. That's what drives me.

Chris Killam explorer-in-residence, Univ. of Massachusetts

WHO
DO YOU SERVE ?

SALESPEOPLE SERVE CUSTOMERS
DOCTORS SERVE PATIENTS
WRITERS SERVE READERS
ENTERTAINERS SERVE AUDIENCES
TEACHERS SERVE STUDENTS
ATHLETES SERVE SPECTATORS
ACTORS SERVE DIRECTORS
POLITICIANS SERVE VOTERS
PROFESSIONALS SERVE CLIENTS

Who do you serve? This is an important question, because success in any field means really knowing the people you serve, and they go by different names. If you're in business, you serve customers or clients. Writers serve readers, entertainers serve audiences, professional athletes serve their fans, pilots their passengers, doctors serve their patients, ministers their congregation, and the list goes on…

Whether you run a big business or a small one, success hinges on serving customers. As General Electric CEO Jack Welch said, "We want a company that focuses on nothing but serving customers…" AudioQuest CEO Bill Low puts it this way: "I am fanatically customer-oriented. My customers are audio dealers rather than consumers, but I give them both ultimate respect."

Professionals such as accountants, engineers, designers, and architects serve clients. Architect Susan Ruptash says, "We're not doing an artistic endeavor in isolation. It's a collaborative effort with a client, and serving the client is essential for us. If we're not giving the client what they think is appropriate and right, then, even if we think it's the greatest idea in the world, we've failed."

Another architect, William McDonough, said to me, "Everything I do is service." His buildings need to serve his clients who pay for them, as well as the people who work in them and those who walk by them on the street. William even serves the birds. He gave migrating birds a place to land and feed by building the biggest green roof in the world, on top of a Ford factory. And that ecological solution also served the accountants, saving $35 million over conventional engineering. So when people say his designs are for the birds, it's a good thing.

Entertainers may seem bigger than life on screen or stage, but what gives them life is serving their audience. *Simpsons* creator Matt Groening said to me, "The important relationship is with the audience, the people who actually watch the show, and that's what I always keep in mind." The audience is also on Barry Friedman's mind. He's one half of the Raspyni Brothers, an amazing juggling and comedy act: "We just keep thinking, 'Is the show good for the audience? Are they having a good time, are they getting their money's worth?'" And that attitude ensures the audience will get their moneys worth.

I believe in serving people. We're in the audio visual business. We're there to do a job for our clients.
Norbert Frischkorn
president, Frischkorn Audiovisual

When I tell stories, I try to keep the audience really happy. I'll do whatever I have to do, to make the story work for that audience.
Robert Munsch
celebrated children's author, over 20 million books sold

If you're not serving the customer, you'd better be serving someone who is.
Karl Albrecht billionaire founder of German discount chain

For me, accounting is just another way of serving a client. And that's what drives me.
John Rawle chief financial officer, University of Toronto

WHO DO YOU SERVE?

There's often one person you serve, whether it's a manager, supervisor, boss, foreman, big cheese, or head honcho. For executive assistant Nan Wilkens, it's Issy Sharp, head of Four Seasons Hotels and Resorts, and she serves him well. Nan told me, "In working to support an executive at this level, if he calls, you're there. You do whatever it takes."

Athletes serve their coach, their fans, and the spectators who watch them. Olympian figure skater Elizabeth Manley says, "I didn't want to disappoint people....You want to bring home gold. You want to make them proud of you." But what about an athlete like Ben Saunders? He's the youngest person to ever ski alone to the North Pole, and out there on the ice there are no spectators – and if there are, you don't want them, because they're polar bears. I figured Ben just served himself, until he told me, "What kept me going was the realization that this had some kind of value and was benefitting other people. I had hundreds of messages on our web site every day from cancer patients, paraplegics, war veterans, all saying, 'Wow! Keep going. You've inspired me to do something.' That made a huge difference, having some kind of purpose beyond myself, and knowing that every step was benefitting other people."

My wife Baiba is a civil servant, and, as much as I kid her about not being very civil to me, she works hard to serve the public with learning and courses delivered on-line, so people can access high quality education, no matter where they live. NASA whiz Dave Lavery also serves the taxpayers, and he says, "I chose to work as a federal government employee for NASA, rather than as a contractor making much more money. I guess I have a desire to work for the common good, rather than a dollar figure." Dave says the way he measures his own success is, "Have I helped deliver a quantum advance in knowledge to the American taxpayer?"

I'm determined that what I do works for the audience.
Lindsay Sharp museum director

I'm here to help the client. I really am at their service. It's those little details that make clients feel taken care of.
Theresa Brown VP, Washington Speakers Bureau

The truly great leaders throughout time were actually servants to something they considered greater than themselves, and people naturally followed them.
Kimberly King president, King & Associates Strategic Alliances

In addition to serving people, we can also serve a cause or mission. Wade Davis, explorer-in-residence with the National Geographic Society, says, "I've always felt motivated by a mission, whether it was to help stop the destruction of the rainforest, or to celebrate the levels of intuition of the Amazon Indians. I really feel that I've got a mission in life and it keeps me going." In the big picture you can serve an industry or profession. Aman Gupta, CEO of Imprimis Life, says, "I love the way health care shapes the world and, through it, I can make a little bit of a difference in the world."

United Nations undersecretary general for communications Sashi Tharoor serves humanity. "From a very young age, I always felt that it was important to try and make an impact for the better, either in one's own community, or through ideas, or through whatever gifts one could bring to improve the world." Google co-founder Larry Page told me he also wanted to serve humanity, but through technology: "I wanted to have a big impact...and I figured it would be good to do it through science and technology, because not many people were trying to do it that way." When Larry developed the Google search engine he did make a big impact, especially on my life, because now I can actually find stuff on the net.

In reality, we all serve numerous clients and success means understanding all their needs. Ronda Carnegie, advertising director for *The New Yorker* magazine says, "I serve the publisher of the magazine. I always say to him, 'It's your sandbox, I'm just playing in it.' Then I have to make sure that I live up to the readers' expectations. And I also serve all the advertisers and have to make them happy. So it's a lot of serving." But what about the people at the top of the food chain? They don't serve anybody, do they? Yes, even the President or Prime Minister of a country has to serve the voters, or next election they're out of a job. And the top dogs in companies, like Bill Gates, need to serve their boards of directors, shareholders, employees and, ultimately, customers, or they'll be in the doghouse.

Serving is so important that some businesses actually call themselves "service" businesses. But let's face it, no matter who you are, if you want to succeed, you need to think of yourself as being of service to somebody. Who do you serve?

To command is to serve, nothing more and nothing less.

André Malraux writer and politician

I'm serving society by helping people create new jobs. I'm in a non-profit foundation, and I use my business expertise to help people develop new products and businesses.

Satheesh Namasivayam program officer, The Lemelson Foundation

I serve the goals of the company I work for. It's Sony Image Works, but I joke with people that it's Sarnoff Image Works. It's my company, while I'm there.

Tim Sarnoff general manager, Sony Pictures Imageworks

As a younger person, I wasn't particularly socially conscious, but I stumbled into working with people with special needs, and found that you could make a huge contribution to society through the buildings you design.

Susan Ruptash architect, principal, Quadrangle Architects

WHAT VALUE?
DO YOU SERVE OTHERS?

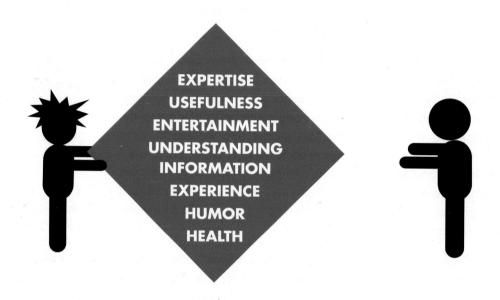

EXPERTISE
USEFULNESS
ENTERTAINMENT
UNDERSTANDING
INFORMATION
EXPERIENCE
HUMOR
HEALTH

If you can give value to people, then they'll give value back to you. You're not tricking them or talking them into doing something. You're creating something that they want and will use.

Jerry Hayes optometrist, founder of Hayes Marketing

Albert Einstein said, "Strive not to be a success, but rather to be of value." And being of value leads to success. So what value do you serve people? You can serve it through a skill, a service, a product, or an experience. Reggae star Jimmy Cliff says, "My way of serving is through music, so that's what I have to do."

Sometimes it helps to ask, "What's the real value I'm serving?" For example, you may be selling cars but, as Larry Burns, head of Research and Development for General Motors, says, "I'm serving people freedom, through transportation that will let you go where you want to, when you want to."

Expertise has value. Martha Stewart spent years becoming an expert on homemaking, and her expertise had high value for millions of women clamoring for tips to make a better home. Martha says, "I came to all these people with trusted information, useful information, valuable ideas, and products." There's that "valuable" word, and that's what made Martha a household name.

Understanding has value. Harry Rosen sells suits, but he says the value that built Harry Rosen Men's Clothing into a major retailer is understanding: "My personal formula for success is understanding the customer, being able to sense and communicate with each consumer, and show them clothing that's most appropriate." Arthur Benjamin is a professor of mathematics, and he helps students understand math: "I get paid to explain math to people. I love doing it, and it has value for others. I'm lucky being in a society that places value on explaining math to people."

Entertainment has value. People place high value on a good novel or thrilling movie that has them on the edge of their seats, and even one that makes them cry. Somebody said to me, "Danielle Steel writes such trashy novels. I don't know why people read them." Well, they may not be everybody's cup of tea, but those novels are serving millions of people with entertainment they value, and that's why Danielle has sold more books than any other living author.

Removing unwanted things has value, like pests or pain. Pest controllers remove people's mouse problems and dentists remove their mouth problems. Either way it has high value for people. (My apologies to pest controllers, for lumping you in with dentists.)

Information has value. But, you don't have to be in the news and magazine industries to serve information. Jerry Hayes was an optometrist, and he got tired of repeating the same information over and over to patients, so he wrote it out and printed some brochures that he could just give patients to read. Other optometrists started asking for the brochures, and suddenly Jerry had a whole new business. He says, "I discovered something I could sell to my own peers that added value for them."

Nez Hallett III, CEO of Smart Wireless, says: "The real secret to business is unlocking value. Go look for the value you can offer. Be vigilant at finding it every day and unlocking it, because that's really your competitive edge." I would add that unlocking value is the secret to success in any area, not just business. So, don't think, "What am I getting out of this?" Instead think, "What value am I serving others?" The higher the value, the higher you'll go.

SERVING OTHERS WILL GIVE YOU

HAPPINESS
SATISFACTION
APPRECIATION
CONTRIBUTION
ACKNOWLEDGEMENT

A RICH LIFE

You can have everything in life you want, if you will **just help enough other people get what they want.**

Zig Zigler speaker and author

Serving others is one of the most important things we can do to succeed, but we live in a ME, ME, ME world, and many of us are more into serving ourselves than others. So why bother helping other people at all? There are a couple of reasons and the first is, serving others will give you a rich life.

Having a rich life means being appreciated. William James, the father of modern psychology, wrote, "The deepest principle of human nature is the craving to be appreciated." And the way to get appreciated is to serve others something they appreciate. Top real estate agent Elli Davis does a great job for her clients and they show her their appreciation: "I like people to be really pleased with what I'm doing. When someone brings you a pot of flowers and says, "You did a really great job!" That's really nice. Or they write you a note and they're really happy."

Having a rich life means happiness. Physician Charles H. Burr once said, "Getters generally don't get happiness; givers get it." Missionary doctor Albert Schweitzer actually went as far as to say the only way to achieve happiness is by serving others: "I don't know what your destiny will be, but one thing I do know: the only ones among you who will be really happy are those who have sought and found how to serve." (Albert makes a great point, but, at the risk of sounding shallow, ice cream sometimes makes me happy too.)

Having a rich life means acknowledgement. I mean, being acknowledged beats being anonymous any day. We all want to feel that we matter in some way. Sherwin Nuland, clinical professor of surgery at Yale, says we form the image of ourselves by serving others: "It was a privilege to serve as a doctor. And serving is the greatest privilege of all, because it gives you a sense of yourself, and a self-image, to be able to do things for other people. The real rewards have to do with doing for others."

So, the great irony is that by serving others, we actually end up getting a whole bunch of stuff back, and it all adds up to a rich life. As poet Ralph Waldo Emerson said: "It is one of the most beautiful compensations of this life that no man can sincerely try to help another without helping himself."

> **I think the more you share and the more you put out there, the more comes back to you.**
> **Don Green** co-founder, Roots clothing

> **Serving other people serves me well. The more that I'm proud of what I do in my community, or the world, the happier I am. It adds meaning to my life.**
> **Daniel Schwartz** founder and CEO, Dynamica

> **The people who get the greatest pleasure out of life are those who believe that what they're doing is going to make a difference for other people - and it also helps them.**
> **Lindsay Sharp** museum director

> **I serve by working on charity projects with children. But I'm not doing it to be altruistic. I'm doing it because it makes me feel good. It's really very selfish, but it makes them happy also, so it's a win-win.**
> **Lakshmi Pratury** director, American India Foundation

SERVING OTHERS
IS THE ONLY WAY
YOU'LL GET RICH

STEP 1 **SERVE OTHERS** SOMETHING OF VALUE

STEP 2 **GET MONEY** IN RETURN

The second reason we should bother serving others is it's really the only way to make a lot of money. There's a myth that people get rich because of the 5-letter word called greed, but it's really because of the 5-letter word called SERVE. Now, I realize not everybody wants to get rich, and I'm sure you're one of those people. But in case you change your mind and do want a bit of money, here's the simple 2-step formula: 1. Serve others something of value. 2. Get money in return. It's so darn simple you have to wonder why so many people get it wrong and remain poor, or go broke in business. Could it be they put step 2 before step 1? They go after the money while forgetting the most important part – serving others.

Those who serve the most also receive the most, and that often includes money. Publisher and editor Edward Bok once said, "The making of money, the accumulation of material power, is not all there is to living…and the man who misses this truth misses the greatest joy and satisfaction that can come into his life – service to others." He's right, but the irony is Edward Bok became very rich through his service to others. The same goes for geneticist Craig Venter. When I talked to Craig, he was sailing around the world in his 95-foot yacht, doing a massive project to catalogue all the genes on earth. He said to me, "All the areas that I've tried to work in are areas that make a difference in people's lives: developing new medicines, new approaches to understanding disease. I think the purpose of science is to make a difference to people's lives." And making that difference in people's lives also made a difference in Craig's bank account – hence the 95 foot yacht.

So serving others will not only fill up your soul, it can also fill up your wallet. But remember, the rich ones, like Edward Bok and Craig Venter, really don't go after the money. They follow their passion and part of that passion is serving other people. It just so happens that one of the things they get in return is money. Studies show that most millionaires achieve their wealth by serving others something of value, whether they're doctors serving patients, entertainers serving audiences, retailers serving customers, or carpenters serving the building trade. There are 8 success factors, but if you want to achieve success plus wealth, SERVE is the big one.

You don't become a millionaire without serving other people. I mean, we can whine all we want about Bill Gates, but if we didn't want what he gave us, he would have failed. The fact is, people who succeed are people who serve needs.
Seth Godin author

You know, the money is a good thing. I like to earn a living. I need to pay bills like anybody else. But money's not what drives me. It's serving people that drives me. As it turns out, I make a great living.
Chris Kilham explorer-in-residence, University of Massachusetts

Be successful and the money will follow. Figure out what you need to do to be successful, and it's not chasing the money. It's making customers happy, and making your employees happy, and creating some value. If you can get everybody to win, then you win.
Nez Hallett III
CEO, Smart Wireless

THE **WAY** TO **WEALTH**
DO WHAT **YOU LOVE**

SERVE OTHERS WHAT **THEY LOVE**

Match what you love to do, with what people want. Financial rewards are the by-product of that.

Anthony Tjan senior partner, The Parthenon Group

In the Passion chapter I said to do what you love and the money will follow. That's true, but if you want to make a lot of money you can't just do what you love – you also need to serve others something they love.

Bill Gates loves computers and software and it brought him great wealth. But there are many people out there who love computers and they can barely pay the rent. The difference is, Bill didn't just serve himself, he served software to others that they loved, or needed. Oprah loves speaking to people and it has made her very rich. There are lots of other people out there who love to speak, even if they have nothing to say, but they're not rich. The difference is Oprah speaks about topics other people want to hear about and presents them in a way they can relate to.

It's pretty simple: 1. Do something you love. 2. Then serve it to others. If they also love it, they'll pay you for it. That's what happened to J.K. Rowling. She started out with nothing except the passion to write. But the key thing is she didn't just write for herself. She wrote for the Harry Potter in all of us. So kids love reading her books as much as she loves writing them. And that made her the richest woman in Britain.

I see many writers out there who are actively engaged in the first part, doing what you love. That's a good thing, but they'll stay poor unless they do the second part, doing what others love. Recently, I gave a summary of this book to a writer I know. He came back a few days later and said, "I could never figure out why I'm not making more money from my writing, but now I know. I love writing and I'm doing everything you say leads to success, except for one thing – I'm not serving others. I'm just writing for myself." He was right. I could see he was passionately wrapped up in his subject, but it was a subject most people wouldn't be interested in, so why would they want to spend their hard-earned money on his book?

I'm not saying everybody has to get rich. This writer is doing what he loves and getting a lot of satisfaction from it. But at the same time he feels there's something missing from his life – money! The trick is to take your passion and shape it into something others also love. Then you'll achieve the best of both worlds – love and money.

> **You don't make money doing something nobody wants.**
>
> **Ron Tarro**
> CEO, SDD Systems

> **I still, to this day, love to get up in the morning and go do what I do. It is really gratifying...And society does value what we do for a living. Physicians and surgeons are well-compensated.**
>
> **Douglas Dorner**
> vascular surgeon

> **Match what you love to do with what people want. Financial rewards are the by-product of that. Choose things you're really passionate about and excel at those. Then marry the market with your passion and capabilities. That's the magic formula that's worked for me – passion, capabilities, market.**
>
> **Anthony Tjan** senior partner, The Parthenon Group

MYTH

PEOPLE GET **RICH** BY **INVESTING** OR **GAMBLING**

INVEST
STOCK MARKET
GOLD
REAL ESTATE

GAMBLE
LOTTERY
CASINO
TRACK

REALITY

PEOPLE GET **RICH** BY **SERVING OTHERS**

THESE TOP BILLIONAIRES ALL GOT RICH BY
SERVING OTHERS SOMETHING OF VALUE

BILL **GATES**	SERVED	PC **SOFTWARE**
WARREN **BUFFETT**	SERVED	FINANCIAL **EXPERTISE**
THE **WALTONS**	SERVED	WAL-MART **DISCOUNTS**
LARRY **ELLISON**	SERVED	CORPORATE **SOFTWARE**
I. **KAMPRAD**	SERVED	IKEA **FURNITURE**
KEN **THOMSON**	SERVED	**NEWSPAPERS**
L. **BETTENCOURT**	SERVED	L'OREAL **COSMETICS**
MICHAEL **DELL**	SERVED	PERSONAL **COMPUTERS**
T & K **ALBRECHT**	SERVED	DISCOUNT **GROCERIES**
LI **KA-SHING**	SERVED	**ELECTRICITY/CELLULAR**
A. **SCHLECKER**	SERVED	**MEAT/DRUGSTORE** ITEMS
H. **YAMAUCH**	SERVED	NINTENDO **GAMES**

If you believe that people get rich by serving others, skip this page. But if you think people get rich by investing in the stock market or real estate, or they strike it rich by gambling or winning the lottery, then read on. I used to think investing and gambling brought wealth, but then I actually did get rich, and that's not how it happened. It's also not how the millionaires and billionaires I interviewed did it. The reality is, most people who have achieved wealth have done it by serving others something of value.

Have a look at the top billionaires on the opposite page. You'll notice they all got rich by serving something. Some serve low-cost products to many people. For example, Ikea founder Ingvar Kamprad became a billionaire by serving well-designed, inexpensive furniture to millions of people. Others serve fewer people something that costs a lot. Bill Gates, Michael Dell, and Larry Ellison all became billionaires by serving high-priced computers and software that also has high value for people. Only one, Warren Buffett, got rich through investing. But he wasn't an amateur investor trying to get rich quickly in the stock market. Investing is Warren's business and he serves other people, who give him their money to invest for them. So he, too, got rich by serving others. Same with gambling. The ones who strike it rich gambling are the people who own the casinos and serve the gamblers.

I'm not saying don't invest or gamble if you get a buzz out of it, just don't expect to get rich that way. Most wealthy people invest, but after they're already rich and can afford to lose. As the old joke goes – How do you become a millionaire? Start out a billionaire and buy stocks. I invest, but it's like a hobby and I've lost a lot of money doing it. On the other hand, I've made a lot of money by serving people. So have many others. You might be surprised that the couple running your local convenience stores are millionaires. They didn't get rich by winning the lottery, they did it by serving you lottery tickets and food when every other store was closed. Oh, they don't look like millionaires. They drive beat-up cars and dress down, because if you knew how much they made, you'd say, "I'm not shopping there. They're richer than me!"

The moral of the story is, take the time you'd spend investing or gambling, and use it to serve others something they value, then you really could become wealthy. Forget about striking it rich and think about serving it rich.

All lasting wealth comes from enriching others in some way.
Brian Tracy best-selling author

When people come to me and ask me what they should invest in, I tell them, "Invest in yourself, invest in your business." Don't go outside your area of expertise or your sphere of influence. If you do, you always end up losing.
Mickey Clagg CFO, Bob Howard Investments

Strive to make something good that people want and the money will follow. If you make a great product, people will embrace what you do, and at the end of the day, they'll buy it and you'll make money. Good companies are driven to make great products – profit comes later.
François Parenteau CEO, Defiance Capital, top independent analyst

FORGET ABOUT YOURSELF

FOCUS ON THE PEOPLE YOU SERVE

One of the first questions I ask a client is, "What are you trying to accomplish? How do I get you to where you're trying to go?" **Never mind where I want to go. I want to get you to where you want to go.**

Bob Rogers founder, BRC Imagination Arts

Serving others leads to a rich life – and riches. So the next few pages give some tips on how we can become better servers. And the first way is to forget about yourself and focus on the people you serve. Don't panic! I'm not saying forget about yourself all the time. I'm just saying that if you want to succeed, and maybe get rich, it doesn't do much good to dwell on yourself. It's far more useful, and fun, to be focused on your project, passion, client, or customer.

Issy Sharp didn't build Four Seasons Hotels into one of the world's great hotel chains by thinking about himself. He told me, "You always have to give customers what they want, rather than doing what you want." Even when Issy is doing high level negotiations, he focuses on the other person: "In any negotiation always, always, try to understand what the other person needs. I think you really have to be able to sit in the other chair and ask: How do I get that person what they need, as well as what I need?"

Whether it's a major hotel or a mini website, it pays to think of the person on the other end of the experience. Web design critic Jakob Nielsen says, "When people ask me for tips to design a good web site I say, 'Remember, you're not doing it for yourself, you're doing it for other people. What do other people think of it?'"

But, wait a minute! Don't artists just paint for themselves? Well, Ken Danby, one of the world's most recognized realist artists, says, "That's crap. Artists try to communicate to others. How long would I paint if I was marooned alone on an island? I don't think I'd paint very long. My motivation would dissipate in a big hurry." Legendary music producer Quincy Jones puts it a little more bluntly: "Any artist who says, I'm gonna write and play what I want, and I don't care if anybody likes it, is full of shit."

Yes, successful musicians are out to serve their audiences, so that famous song "I Did It MY Way" should really be "I Did It THEIR Way." Come on, let's all sing our new theme song. I'll lead. Okay? Here goes, "I did it THEIR waaaaaay…" What's that? You'd rather sing alone! Okay, I can take a hint. The bottom line is, if you want to succeed, it's better to be preoccupied serving others, than me-occupied serving yourself.

I don't do a presentation on what I think. I do it on what the audience wants to know.
John Caldwell president & CEO, CAE

It's no longer just about me. I think, "What can I do of value for other people?"
Sam Sullivan quadriplegic, mayor of Vancouver

What you're trying to do really is mirror what the client wants, not what you want.
Ann Turner founder, Profile Recruitment Consultants

I'm always thinking 2 or 3 steps ahead for a company, or a goal I'm trying to achieve, versus thinking about me.
Kevin Gilbert award-winning photojournalist, White House photographer

The best students that I have are the ones that feel life is not about them. My most successful student doesn't worry much about himself.
Douglas Jacobs pastor and professor

TO REACH THE TOP, PUT OTHERS TOP OF MIND

When I write a song **I'm thinking about the people who are going to be listening** to it.

Shania Twain singer/songwriter

Whether we just want moderate success or to go all the way the top, it means putting the people we serve top of mind. Warren Buffett made it to the top of the world's richest people list by keeping the owners of the companies he's going to invest in top of mind: "I tell everybody who works for our company…think like an owner."

Novelist Stephen King made it to the top of the best-sellers list by keeping his readers top of mind: "I think that every novelist has an ideal reader; that at various points during the composition of a story, the writer is thinking, 'I wonder what he/she will think when he/she reads this part?'" Shania Twain made it to the top of the music charts by keeping her listeners top of mind: "When I write a song, I'm thinking about the people who are going to be listening to it….People are going to go out and pay for the record, and I want my music to relate to their lives, not vice versa."

Umbra co-founder Paul Rowan says having a clear picture of customers in his head is what helped the company become a world leader in affordable, contemporary products for the home: "The customer is in our minds all the time. If she isn't satisfied, then we won't do well. The customer we have in mind is really an intelligent person, who doesn't have a big budget, but she likes value for her money, and she likes to buy good things. We really have to satisfy what she's looking for." In the technology world, Don Lindsay, manager of user interface for Apple Computer, says, "I think one of our strengths is we're able to put ourselves in the mind of the people who buy our products. Despite my 20 years of experience with computers, I'm able to sit here and look at something as if I'm a customer who's looking at the product for the first time, and doesn't understand it." (He must be talking about me.)

Another person in technology, Ian Craig, president of a Nortel Networks division, says, "I have customers on my mind all the time. You can't turn it off, so my personal life is very unbalanced. There are weekends where I can hardly sleep because I'm always thinking about some problem a customer is having." Hey, I never said thinking about the people you serve is always pleasant. I'm just saying it will make you successful. It not only made Ian very successful, it made him very rich. So when things got tough, at least he could cry all the way to the bank.

I'm thinking about customers all the time. It's only about customers, and everybody's a customer in the business world. It's as simple as that. And I think if you start with that attitude the business will come.

Joseph Ricciuti
National Practice Director,
Watson Wyatt Worldwide

I put myself in other people's thought patterns. I think, "Okay now, if I'm the other person, what is it they want to see? What's going to get them motivated? What are they going to take from this?"

Lisa Davis director of communications, AARP

I think of my readers all the time, day and night. When I was a kid, I'd read the newspaper and say to my mother, "In this story, the most important thing I want to know has been left out." And my mother would say, "Well, when you become a journalist, you can put it in." So, that's what I do.

Robert Fulford journalist

PUT YOURSELF IN OTHER PEOPLE'S SHOES

Putting yourself in other people's shoes is the secret to life.
I create solutions for other people, so I have to be able to get outside my skin and into theirs, or my solutions won't be successful.

Nancye Green founding partner, Donovan/Green branding, marketing

Sometimes when people ask me what led to my success, I say, "Shoes." They usually respond with, "Oh, you're in the shoe business?" I say, "No, but I'm pretty good at putting myself in other people's shoes." Okay, so it's a corny joke. But it's true. I have to put myself in my clients' and audiences' shoes, or the end result will be a flop.

Success in business really depends on putting yourself in the Birkenstocks, loafers, high heels, sneakers, or Doc Martens of your clients and customers. Ben and Jerry's ice cream co-founder Ben Cohen said to me, "I think I'm good at being able to put myself in the shoes of my consumer." He might have said their stomachs, since Ben comes up with their ice cream flavors.

Four Seasons Hotels founder Issy Sharp came up with many firsts by putting himself in his customers' shoes – and bathrobes: "There are dozens of things that we did, not because we thought as hotel managers, because we thought as customers. We were the first to put bathrobes in rooms, the first to put shampoo, bigger bars of soap, big soft towels, good showers. All these things were done as a result of thinking, 'This is what a customer might like.'"

When it comes to the medical profession, doctors are always poking around their patients' bodies, but vascular surgeon Douglas Dorner told me you also have to put yourself in their place: "As a patient, you're sick, you're scared, you're frightened. As a surgeon, I think you have to put yourself in that patient's shoes and give them explanations they can understand. I think it's terribly important."

Another person who thinks it's important is David Zussman, president of the Public Policy Forum: "I know a lot of very smart people who have not made an impact, where others less talented have. I think, in large part, it's because the talented people are concentrating on themselves and success requires putting yourself in somebody else's shoes. I think successful people are always saying, 'Oh, yeah, I see where you're coming from.'"

So if you want to be successful, put yourself in other people's shoes. Yeah, I know some shoes are really smelly so it can be kind of unpleasant. But, if you don't do it, your chances of success will really stink.

Putting yourself in other people's shoes is highly underrated. In a service business like public relations you really have to put yourself in your client's shoes.
Jessica Switzer president, Switzer Communications

I've known talented musicians who were not very good at putting themselves in other people's shoes, and they did not become very successful.
Gary Burton Grammy award-winning musician

Even people you may violently disagree with, you stretch your mind to walk a little bit in their shoes and stand where they stand.
Gerald Durnell CEO, ProTech Publishing

I've led a fairly full life and lived a lot of different situations, both personal and business. That experience helps me put myself in other people's shoes.
Bob Ferchat chairman, Bell Mobility

SEE THE OTHER PERSON'S PERSPECTIVE

If there is one secret of success, it lies in the ability to get the other person's point of view, and **see things from that person's angle, as well as from your own.**

Henry Ford first to mass-produce automobiles

Many people say a secret to success is being able to see things from the other person's perspective. Journalist Walt Mossberg says that's what led to the success of his technology column in *The Wall Street Journal*: "I can always put things in the perspective of a regular person. I imagine the reader to be a smart person, who has neither the time nor interest to figure out the inner workings of these computers, but really wants to know."

Russell Campbell, president of ABN AMRO Asset Management Canada, says, "Being sensitive to other people, I think, is my primary skill. You need to be able to relate to other people, and see where they're coming from, then build a bridge between yourself and them." Ian Craig, president of Nortel Networks Wireless and Carrier Solutions, says he puts everything in the perspective of his customer: "What's their measurement for the success of their business? Share price going up, number of new customers, or how quickly their network is up and running? Then I gear myself to making them successful."

Animals may have a slightly different perspective than people, which is why show jumping champion Ian Miller says, "You have to see life through the eyes of the horse. That's the real trick." And that ability helped Ian win back-to-back World Cup showjumping titles.

I don't know much about horses, but I once learned to see things from a cat's perspective. I was a junior assistant in a large photography studio and one of my assignments was to take a photo of a cat for a pet food package. I found the right cat and then dropped it right in the middle of the huge photo studio, prepared to take the perfect shot. Except the cat took off like a shot. So there I was, frantically chasing this cat around the studio, crashing into lights and diving under tables trying to get a picture, like the coyote chasing the roadrunner. I was ready to shoot the damn cat with a gun instead of a camera, when one of the old pro photographers called me over and said, "Think like a cat." "Huh?" "If you were thrown into this strange environment, with all the commotion, wouldn't you be jittery?" So I got everyone out of the studio, made it dark and quiet, and put out a nice dish of cat food. Within 5 minutes, the cat nibbled the food, licked its paw, and I got a great shot. The moral of the story? If you don't want fur to fly, see the perspective from other's eyes.

View your own product with the customer's eyes.
Jean Monty CEO, BCE

We don't live on this planet alone. If we can see things through other people's eyes, we're apt to be more successful.
Lisa Davis director of communications, AARP

I always think from the customers' perspective and imagine what their experience is like. Then I try and construct something that makes it ideal for them and solves all of their problems.
Gord Lownds founder, Sleep Country

It's all about taking the perspective of other people, understanding their needs, and translating that into technical and business requirements.
Eve Shalley senior VP, Intrasphere

LISTEN
TO THE PEOPLE YOU SERVE

We provide a technical service but **what gives us an edge is listening**. You need to understand what people really want rather than what you think they want.

Paul Bunt founder, Bunt and Associates Engineering

How do you serve people well? By listening to them. Ears are very important, but mouths make more noise, and get more airplay, so everybody thinks they're the critical thing. However, successful people will tell you it's more important to have big ears than a big mouth. Linda Keeler says listening is what helped her become general manager of Sony Pictures: "I kept my mouth shut and my ears opened and I listened."

Even people who may appear to have big mouths stress the importance of listening. Lawyer Peter Silverberg says, "A lot of people may think that a lawyer has to be good at talking, but I think listening is a really important facet of being a lawyer. It takes a lot of effort and a lot of concentration." You'd think that real estate agents would need to talk a lot in order to sell houses, but top agent Elli Davis told me, "You just listen. Keep your mouth shut and listen." Yes, contrary to popular belief, sales is about listening as much as talking. BCE chief executive Jean Monty said, "If you go into a monologue with a customer, you won't make many sales. Go to a customer and listen to their needs, and then say, 'Okay, here's how my product will satisfy your needs.' So empathy and listening are basic skills of sales."

In the world of movies, we picture film directors talking to the crew through their megaphones. But when Drew Barrymore was a kid acting in the movie *E.T.*, she said it was listening that made Steven Spielberg a good director: "He's a great listener, and as a child to be listened to, it's the greatest gift in the world, because adults always want to get back to their adult conversation, and he's not like that."

The other day, a friend of mine said he was going to take a public speaking course. Personally, I thought that's the last thing he needs. He already talks too much. What he really needs is a public listening course. I mean, the guy never listens to anybody. He totally monopolizes conversations, and it's impossible for anybody else to get a word in edgewise, which could explain why he can't hold down a job. So, in an effort to help, I told him what I thought. It didn't do much good. He didn't listen to me. Maybe I'll just slip a note under his door with the words of Calvin Coolidge, 30th President of the United States: "No man ever listened himself out of a job."

I like to listen. I have learned a great deal from listening carefully. Most people never listen.
Ernest Hemingway
famous author

As a publicist, you talk a lot, but I find listening is very, very important.
Kevin Pennant publicist

My specialty is that I'm a good listener. It's an acquired skill. My dad once told me, "The good Lord blessed you with 2 ears and 1 mouth, so listen twice as much as you speak."
Elliot Wahle
VP and general manager, Toys R Us, Times Square

I only wish I could find an institute that teaches people how to listen. Business people need to listen at least as much as they need to talk. Too many people fail to realize that real communication goes in both directions.
Lee Iacocca CEO, Chrysler

LISTENING
PAY$
OFF

We were awarded a **million-dollar contract because we listened.**

Richard St. John

Listening leads to success, and it also leads to money. In fact, there's a whole profession of people out there who make a lot of money just by listening. They're called psychiatrists. They're also known as shrinks, because that's what happens to your wallet after they listen to you.

In a sense, we're all professional listeners, no matter what field we're in, because it really pays to listen to the people you serve. In business that means clients and customers. As Wayne Schuurman, president of Audio Advisor, told me, "Listen to your customers or you go out of business." And John F. Smith, former CEO of General Motors, once said, "We listened to what our customers wanted and acted on what they said. Good things happen when you pay attention."

I couldn't agree more. My company won a million-dollar contract because we listened. It was when we were asked to do a proposal for a product launch and our client said, "Tell us how you'll handle the launch, but don't give us any creative, since you aren't yet familiar with our products." Later when we were doing the proposal, we were tempted to impress him with some zippy creative ideas, knowing that's exactly what our competitors would produce. But when we re-listened to the recording we'd made of the meeting, he definitely said, "Don't give us any creative." So we didn't, and we figured we'd never win. But when he called with his decision he said, "You were the only ones who listened. So congratulations, you win the contract." By the way, as an aid to listening, we record all important client meetings and conversations, then re-listen to them and take accurate notes. Doing that, you soon realize it's amazing what you missed the first time: "Oh, she said $18,000, not $80,000.

Many people don't listen because it's hard work. I was reminded of this the other night at dinner when my wife suddenly blurted out, "You're not listening!" I shot back, "Hey, I'm a professional, who has mastered the art of listening through hundreds of interviews." She responded, "Okay, tell me what I just said." My mind was blank. I had spent all day intently listening to clients and just couldn't stay tuned anymore. It really does take a lot of effort to listen – but not nearly as much effort as trying to make up with your spouse for not listening. Take it from me, it pays to listen.

We listen directly to our customers. We cut out the middleman.
Michael Dell
founder, Dell Computers

I take all calls from customers even if I'm in a meeting. There is no filtering system before they get to me.
Harry Rosen chairman, Harry Rosen men's clothing

Customers usually tell you what they want if you listen hard enough.
Rick Moran
VP, Cisco Systems

I would say that listening to the other person's emotions may be the most important thing I've learned in 20 years of business.
Heath Herber
Herber Company

Listening is important in a service business. You have to really focus on what somebody is saying to really hear them.
Jessica Switzer president, Switzer Communications

BIG EGO MAKES A POOR SERVER

SET ASIDE EGO AND FOCUS ON OTHERS

You want to **make sure that your ego doesn't get in the way** of your own success.

Joseph MacInnis physician, deep sea explorer, author

There's a myth that successful people have big egos. I can't say if they do or don't, but I do know they have the ability to set aside their egos. And that's a good thing, because big egos make poor servers. Ego is all about serving yourself not others.

In my interviews with more than 500 very successful people, I haven't seen a single visible display of ego. No arrogance, no boasting, even with people who have every right to toot their own horn. In fact, from my experience, the bigger the name, the smaller the apparent ego, and the more concerned they seem to be with helping others. A few examples:

I saw Quincy Jones, legendary music composer and winner of 26 Grammy Awards, walking across a hotel lobby. I rushed up to him and said, "Quincy, can I get an interview?" His handlers quickly stepped in: "Sorry, Mr. Jones can't speak with you right now." Then Quincy spoke up: "Wait a minute. I want to talk to this guy." He sat down with me and gave me his undivided attention for 20 minutes while his handlers paced back and forth, because he probably had to be somewhere more important.

Another time, I was standing interviewing Hollywood legend Norman Lear, creator of great TV shows like *All in the Family* and *The Jeffersons*. He was in his 70s, but he rushed away and brought back a chair to make me more comfortable. He didn't seem to care about his own comfort.

During the coffee break at a conference, my colleague Thom and I were surveying the crowd, when he said to me, "Aren't you gonna interview Martha?" There was Martha Stewart, standing right in front of me,

but I didn't recognize her because she wasn't being the TV Martha. She was being the real Martha, without make-up, fancy clothes, or entourage. She was by herself, talking on her cell phone. I nervously went up and said, "Martha, can I get an interview?" She put the cell phone down and said, "Of course, what would you like to know?" No third-degree like: "Who are you?" or "Who's your publisher?" Those are the first questions I'm usually asked when I try to go through a public relations department to get an interview, and since I'm not a famous journalist writing for *Time*, they don't give me the time of day. I always get rejected. But if I can get to the big names themselves they usually say, "Sure, how can I help?"

One last example is Warren Buffett, one of the top 2 richest people on the planet. I haven't interviewed Warren, but he said something at an annual meeting we wanted to use in this book, so we sent a request to use the quote to his company Berkshire Hathaway. Then we waited to see if they'd let us use it, and if it would cost us anything. Well, when their fax came back, I nearly fell off my chair. Who signed our little permission form? None other than Warren Buffett himself. I couldn't believe it. He may be the richest man in the world, but his ego isn't so big that he can't take time to deal with the little details, or the little people like us. And the best part? He said we could use his quote for free!

The moral of the story is, there's a myth that nice guys finish last. But from my experience, I'd say it's the nice guys who finish first. And a lot of it has to do with being able to put their egos aside and serve other people in many little ways.

SERVING
DOESN'T MEAN
SUCKING UP

There's service and then there's slavery.

Michael Stadtlander world-renowned chef

Some people have the wrong impression of SERVE. They think serving means being subservient. It doesn't. The relationship between a server and the person being served is equal, a partnership, a win-win.

I always put my clients first, but that doesn't mean I'm subservient or suck up to them. In fact, sucking up is one of my personal weaknesses. I'm just not great at it. It's like giving compliments. If my wife's new outfit sucks, I'm sorry, but I just can't fake it and say it looks great. I have to be honest and suffer the consequences. In the same way, I was never a yes-man to bosses or clients. If a client came up with a great idea I'd say so, but if the idea sucked I'd also say so. Clients must have appreciated the honesty because they kept coming back.

Not sucking up actually won me work, according to one of our former clients: "I remember when we were trying to decide whether to give our business to you or your competitor. Your competitor dressed to the hilt in a slick suit. He served us fresh ground coffee in fine china in his fancy boardroom. But he was always sucking up to my boss, and even took him sailing. It was like I didn't exist. He never even looked at me. So I said to my boss, 'I don't want to work with that man.' He said 'Okay, fine.' And we chose to work with you. You were the opposite. You were understated. You came dressed in jeans and hadn't slept because you'd been up all night editing. And instead of fine china you served us fruit juice in cans. But you earned our trust because you didn't put on a façade and you treated us both with respect."

Fruit juice in a can – not even a glass! Gee, I didn't think I was that bad at schmoozing. I can barely spell schmooze, let alone do it. But I wasn't as bad as one of my suppliers who'd yell at his clients, including me, and on occasion even throw chairs at us. You'd think the guy wouldn't last 5 minutes in business, yet he outlived all his competitors and became a multi-millionaire. Because, other than busting a few chairs, he also busted his buns to serve his clients, and he always came through for us. We put up with his eccentricities because he did such a great job.

The moral of the story is, serving doesn't mean sucking up. If you serve people something they really value, you can even throw chairs at them instead of compliments – although it's not a strategy I'd recommend.

Xerox's Barry Rand was right on target when he warned his people that if you have a yes-man working for you, one of you is redundant.

Colin Powell
U.S. Secretary of State

I respect customers, but I won't bow down to them. I remember we were bidding for a contract with a customer and I beat him at golf. I said, "It was good to beat you out there today, but I have a feeling we might have lost the contract." He said, "Far from it, you've won it. You played hard to win and I like that."

Ian Craig
president, Wireless and Carrier Solutions, Nortel Networks

I don't really "schmooze." I think it's nice to be friendly, but I'm not phony. I've never done parties. I don't send birthday cards. My service, my work, should be the gift.

Elli Davis top real estate agent

BEND OVER BACKWARDS

TO HELP THE PEOPLE YOU SERVE

I drive myself crazy over the needs of our clients. I care about the quality of our service.

Jessica Switzer president, Switzer Communications

The last serve tip is to bend over backwards to help the people you serve. That's what successful people like animation film director Robin Budd do: "I serve the client and the client's problem, and to do that I will put myself out. I'll go without sleep. I'll be away from my family."

Personally, I'm not a very flexible person. I mean, I can't even touch my toes. But I will bend over backwards to do whatever it takes to serve my clients. One of the big factors that has helped my company succeed for over 25 years, is just being willing to focus all our energy on helping clients, rather than spending a lot of time on ourselves. We care about clients and their projects, and we're out to assist their success. We like the pat on the back and to hear, "Good job." Clients always come first, we come second, and we'll do just about anything for them – put our personal lives on hold, cancel vacations, forget sleep, and even forget personal hygiene.

An example is one time when business partner Thom Rockliff and I were working out of town, producing a huge product launch. We were staying in a hotel, except we were so focused on our client's project we never went back to the hotel. We'd just flop down on the client's office floor and sleep for 20 minutes then get back up and keep working. This went on for days. Eventually I noticed other people in the office starting to hold their noses when they came around me, so I figured I'd better clean up. I went back to the hotel, only to discover they'd cleaned out my room. They said they thought I was dead. I assured them I was very much alive. I only smelled like I was dead. Thom would actually ship his clothes by FedEx to his mother, who would wash them and ship them back, so at least he was clean.

We were so intent on making the project successful, we didn't want to spend a minute on ourselves. But the interesting thing is, by forgetting about ourselves and focusing 100% on making our clients successful, we also became successful. As Ralph Waldo Emerson said, "It is one of the most beautiful compensations of this life that no man can sincerely help another without helping himself." Based on my experience, I'd say he's right.

Oh, and I also discovered, in the grand scheme of things, the people you serve don't care if you stink, as long as what you serve them doesn't.

We bust our ass for our clients.
Jack Diamond
renowned architect

I try to make it as easy as possible for my clients.
Elli Davis top real estate agent

I know what women want, and I know what they need, and I'm gonna make sure they get it.
Isaac Mizrahi
fashion designer

You always have to give customers what they want, rather than being an artist who does what you want.
Issy Sharp founder, chairman, Four Seasons Hotels

What you're trying to do, really, is mirror what the client wants, not necessarily what you want. You have to know what they want.
Ann Turner founder, Profile Recruitment Consultants

PERSIST

1. **PASSION**   2. **WORK**   3. **FOCUS**   4. **PUSH**

PERSIST LEADS TO SUCCESS

210   **BE PREPARED TO PERSIST, PERSEVERE, ENDURE, STICK-TO-IT, HANG IN THERE**

SECTION 1: PERSIST THROUGH TIME

212   **SUCCESS IS DISTANT GRATIFICATION – NOT INSTANT GRATIFICATION**

214   **IT TAKES MANY PEOPLE 10 YEARS TO SUCCEED**

216   **THERE'S NO SUCH THING AS OVERNIGHT SUCCESS**

SECTION 2: PERSIST THROUGH FAILURE

218   **BE PREPARED TO FAIL – ALL SUCCESSFUL PEOPLE DO**

220   **REMEMBER THAT FAILURE IS FERTILIZER FOR SUCCESS**

222   **MAKE FAILURE YOUR SCHOOL – NOT YOUR FUNERAL**

224   **TO SUCCEED A LOT YOU'VE GOTTA FAIL A LOT**

226   **SUCCESSFUL PEOPLE MAKE LOTS OF MISTAKES**

228   **MORE MISTAKES = MORE SUCCESS**

SECTION 3: PERSIST THROUGH CRAP

230   **PERSIST THROUGH CRAP**

232   CRITICISM - **FILTER OUT DESTRUCTIVE CRITICISM**

234   CRITICISM - **USE CONSTRUCTIVE CRITICISM TO IMPROVE**

236   CRITICISM - **BE PREPARED FOR FRANK CRITICISM**

238   REJECTION - **SUCCESSFUL PEOPLE GET REJECTED BUT KEEP ON GOING**

240   REJECTION - **THINK OF REJECTION AS A BADGE OF HONOR**

242   ASSHOLES - **PERSIST** THROUGH **ASSHOLES**

244   PREJUDICE - **PERSIST** THROUGH **PREJUDICE**

SECTION 4: 9 WAYS TO PERSIST

248   **1A. TAKE SMALL STEPS RATHER THAN BIG LEAPS**

250   **1B. SMALL STEPS ARE JUST EASIER**

252   **2. DEVELOP QUITOPHOBIA – A BIG FEAR OF QUITTING**

254   **3. NEVER GIVE UP**

256   **4. DEVELOP BOUNCE-ABILITY   JUST KEEP BOUNCING BACK**

258   **5. BE TOO STUBBORN TO QUIT**

260   **6. BE SHORT-TERM IMPATIENT & LONG-TERM PATIENT**

262   **7. DON'T LOOK BACK**

264   **8. GO FOR LONG-TERM BALANCE – NOT DAILY BALANCE**

266   **9. USE RFM – RELENTLESS FORWARD MOTION**

5. **IDEAS**　　6. **IMPROVE**　　7. **SERVE**　　8. **PERSIST**

Persistence is the number one reason for our success.

Joe Kraus co-founder, Excite

PERSIST BE PREPARED TO PERSIST, PERSEVERE, ENDURE, STICK-TO-IT, HANG IN THERE

Once more, let me say that *The Top 8 Success Factors* are not in any particular order, since they're all important. But I thought it would be appropriate to make the Persist chapter the last one, since persistence is all about lasting. Many people attribute their success to simply outlasting others. James Baker, CEO of the FX Palo Alto Laboratory, says, "The head of one of our divisions once told me the only reason he was in his job was just that he outlasted everyone else. Persistence counts for an awful lot." Robert Ward, Universal Studios senior VP of design, told me, "You really have to be prepared to persist because it won't be easy and there will be failure. You need to pick yourself up, stay on course and continue down that path."

The most successful people are often the most persistent people. Emmy Award-winning news anchor Forrest Sawyer says, "I have persistence to a fault. My friends say I'm like a dog with a bone. I get smacked in the nose and I just keep plugging along, and plugging along, and eventually it works." Greenpeace co-founder Robert Hunter told me he discovered the importance of persistence in one of his first jobs as a traveling salesman selling encyclopedias door-to-door: "You had to be persistent because 50 doors would slam, but the 51st would open. I'd say that helped me doing journalism more than anything I was taught."

You know something is important when we have a lot of words for it. Apparently, the Inuit have a dozen words for snow, because it's so important to them. (It's not important to me, so I only have two words for it – damn snow.) But PERSISTENCE must be important, since we have so many words for it: Perseverance, Tenacity, Lasting, Endurance, Relentless, Stamina, Staying power, Stick to it, Hang in there, Determination, Doggedness... They all mean the ability to keep going through the failure, pain, rejection, criticism, negativity, and crap we encounter – not to mention all the bad things.

This chapter is the last of the *Top 8 Success Factors*, which means you're probably tired of reading. It's also the longest chapter in the book, so just when you want to cozy up to a nice, easy, little chapter, here's this huge one you have to slog through. Ha! Isn't that just so appropriate, that you have to persist to get through the Persist chapter? Well, just do what so many successful people do and hang in there, stick-to-it, keep going, and don't give up. Think of it as a persistence practice for the real world.

Persistence is critical. We're absolutely persistent.

William McDonough acclaimed architect

Be ferociously persistent... It's persistence that makes you great, it's persistence that allows you to reach your dreams.

Rick Pitino renowned basketball coach

It's being determined to persist. Being prepared to want to get there, regardless of the obstacles, and however difficult things seem.

Ann Turner founder, Profile Recruitment Consultants

Let me tell you the secret that has led to my goal. My strength lies solely in my tenacity.

Louis Pasteur discovered the germ theory of disease

I think one trait for success is perseverance. You just keep going at it and being tenacious. Don't let stumbling blocks get in the way. Try to learn from them, and not get defeated by them.

Steve Davis CEO, Corbis

PERSIST – SECTION 1.
PERSIST THROUGH TIME

Success for me was spending over a decade in complete obscurity…My writing time was ten at night until three in the morning. I did that for over ten years.

David Baldacci best-selling fiction writer

In this age of instant gratification, success is something that's very gratifying, but far from instant. Achieving anything worthwhile never comes easily or quickly, which means a big thing we need to persist through is time.

Dean Kamen, renowned inventor of innovative products like the Segway Human Transporter, told me all his projects take much longer than he ever thinks they will, but he just keeps going: "Persistence is my middle name. I'm like a cockroach. You can step on them and step on them, but you just can't kill them." Biomedical researcher Ulrich Trechsel said to me, "Perseverance is very, very important. I just finished a study where the idea was actually there in a very short time, but it took 5 years to do it and get the results."

Renowned graphic novelist Seth says, "Doing a long comic narrative has started to feel like climbing a mountain. So much effort is involved. The hardest part is working on something for years that you have become so close to that you can't even tell anymore if it's any good." Grammy Award-winning vibraphonist Gary Burton says, "It takes many years to reach a point of proficiency, and for me it was about 20 years, working at it pretty intently." Yes, becoming good at what we do doesn't happen overnight. Daniel Gilbert, professor of psychology at Harvard, told me: "You can't be a neurosurgeon or a good artist tomorrow, no matter how much you want to. It takes commitment and persistence over extended periods of time. But if the goal is really right for you, then working towards it is actually fun. I mean, you're not going, 'This is really hard. Someday I'll be good.' You're going, 'Wow, it's amazing. I'm better than I was yesterday.'"

Many people don't realize success takes time, so they pack it in much too soon. Best-selling author Seth Godin says, "The way a bricklayer builds a wall is one brick at a time. He doesn't lay a few bricks, and say, 'Oh, it's not working,' and give up. And the problem is, too many people say, 'If I don't have it workin' in a week, I've gotta give up.'"

The bottom line is, success means distant gratification, not instant gratification. So be prepared to hang in there and persist for a long time. As screenwriter Wilson Mizner once said, "Life's a tough proposition, and the first hundred years are the hardest."

Behind every successful man there's a lot of unsuccessful years.
Bob Brown environmentalist, Australian senator

Diamonds are nothing more than chunks of coal that stuck to their jobs.
Malcolm Forbes founder, *Forbes* magazine

It took me half my life to realize that I could do things and to realize the facilities that I did have.
Don McKellar actor, writer, director

Progress…is comparatively slow. Great results cannot be achieved at once; and we must be satisfied to advance in life as we walk, step by step.
Samuel Smiles author and reformer

If you hang in there long enough, the tide turns. Don't expect immediate success. Hang in there, but enjoy it.
Sinbad comedian

SUCCESS TAKES 10 YEARS

Dancers to develop
Surgeons to be trained
Surfers to ride big waves
Running champions to develop
Tom Wolfe to write *A Man in Full*
BlackBerry to be developed by RIM
Einstein to develop Theory of Relativity
Christina Aguilera to become well-known
Lance Armstrong to win the Tour de France
Linda Evangelista to do her first *Vogue* cover
Spielberg to feel ready to make *Schindler's List*
Microsoft to market a good version of Windows
Columbus to raise the money for his epic voyage
Mozart to produce an acknowledged masterpiece
Spike to leave big corporation and start own business

I don't know how to break this to you gently, so I'll just say it. Success takes 10 years. Sorry! I know a decade seems like an eternity, but the number 10 just keeps showing up, over and over again, in my research.

- Famous modern dance teacher and choreographer Martha Graham says it takes 10 years to make a dancer.
- One study found that it takes an average of 10.2 years for running champions to develop. (I've been at it for 30 years and I'm still waiting for the championship part.)
- Ken Bradshaw says it takes at least 10 years for a surfer to be able to ride those monster waves we see on TV, and he should know since he holds the world record for surfing the largest wave.
- Surgeon Douglas Dorner did 4 years of medical school and then 6 years of general surgery training: "So, 10 years plus an additional year of vascular surgery training before I could hang out my shingle." (After all that time you'd think they'd give doctors aluminum siding instead of a shingle.)

In addition to careers, the 10 year journey also applies to many projects.

- Albert Einstein took 10 years to publish his Theory of Relativity.
- It took Microsoft almost 10 years to get a successful version of Windows.
- Steven Spielberg had the rights to *Schindler's List* for 10 years before he felt ready to make the movie that won him an Oscar for "Best Director."
- Before starting my own company I worked at a big corporation for 10 years. Well, to be precise, it was actually 9.92 years. I left a month before getting my 10 year company pin. But that decade of experience was the foundation for my success, so I ended up getting something much better than a pin. I earned a membership in the 10 Year Success Club.

Yes, success takes time. I'm not telling you this to depress you. I'm doing it so you won't get depressed when you think you'll whip something off in a few months, and here you are years later still working on it. Now when that happens you can say, "Oh yeah, there's that 10 year thing." But, by then, you'll be so far down the road you won't want to quit. You'll just hang in there, keep going, and wake up one day to realize you, too, are a member of the 10 Year Success Club.

BlackBerry didn't happen overnight. There was over 10 years of research and experimentation before the 'overnight' success.
Mark Guibert VP Marketing, Research In Motion

Success took me at least 10 years. I mean, I started working on cartooning when I was 15, and didn't get a *Vanity Fair* contract until I was 25.
Philip Burke renowned commercial artist

You toil a long time before you start to see any success. We worked really hard and were pretty successful within the first 10 years.
Brian Curtner principal, Quadrangle Architects

For the first 10 years they called us the small people, the fly-by-night. And all the people who used to say those things about us are now gone. It took 10 years to build it up.
Nez Hallett III CEO, Smart Wireless

THERE'S **NO OVERNIGHT SUCCESS**

Actually, **I'm an overnight success.** But **it took 20 years**.

Monty Hall TV game show host

We call ourselves "**The 30 year overnight success.**"

Ron Rice founder, Hawaiian Tropic

The Loch Ness Monster, Bigfoot, Sasquatch, and UFOs are all things people claim to have seen, but there isn't much evidence they really exist. In the interests of science, I would like to add one more to the list – the Overnight Success. In my own research of more than 500 people, plus combing through thousands of other success stories, I have yet to find a single example of true overnight success.

Oh, sure, some people appear to rush to the top. Christina Aguilera was 8 when she sang the National Anthem before a live audience of 50,000 people, but it wasn't until a decade later, at 18, that she became well-known. Other singers such as Britney Spears and Celine Dion have similar stories. Michael Jackson started singing at the age of 4. It wasn't until 10 years later that he had his first major solo hit, "Got To Be There," and it was another 10 years before he released *Thriller,* one of the most commercially successful albums of all time. The myth of overnight success is nothing new. Mozart had his first public appearance at age 6, so we think he was an overnight success, but it took him another 10 years before he produced an acknowledged masterpiece.

So, when you see those little brats on TV, who seem to be overnight successes, don't forget that, on the road to success, they got their beginners permits when they were still in diapers. As actor/singer Jennifer Lopez says, "It hasn't been overnight. There's no such thing as overnight in this business." (Although, in Hollywood there is overnight marriage.)

At one point in my research, I thought I did find one example of real overnight success. Sky Dayton was quite young when he founded Earthlink and sold it for a gazzilion dollars, so the first thing I said to him was, "Sky, you're an overnight success…" But he quickly corrected me: "Earthlink didn't happen instantly. Before that I had a window washing business, a candy store, a couple of coffee houses, a computer graphics company. It was baby steps."

So, I'm still on the search for the elusive Overnight Success. If you find one, send over a photo and I'll put it in my display case, along with those blurry photos of the Loch Ness Monster, Bigfoot, Sasquatch, UFOs, and the teenager who actually listened to his parents.

Success did not happen overnight for me. I had to work very, very hard. It was not overnight.

Dawn Lepore chief information officer, Charles Schwab

I started the agency when I was 29 and I worked for somebody else before that, so it took awhile, and it was a big awhile. It was an overnight success we spent 15 years working on.

Jay Chiat co-founder Chiat/Day advertising

In the beginning I was chief cook and bottle washer, a one-man sales force…. Now, 41 years later, we're an 'overnight success.' Actually, it's what happens with a lot of hard work.

David Oreck founder, Oreck Vacuum Cleaners

It doesn't happen instantly and I think people need to realize that. Don't be discouraged just because it takes awhile. Realize there are steps, so you may not get there right away.

David Carson top graphic designer

I failed my way to success.

Thomas Edison invented or refined the light bulb, phonograph, stock ticker, typewriter, motion pictures

Wouldn't it be nice if there were "Failure Ahead" signs on the road to success? Then we'd know what was coming and could avoid it. But life's not like that. We're cruising along just fine, heading towards success and suddenly – YEOW – the road drops and we plunge straight down a steep hill, and end up splattered against a sign that reads, "Welcome to Failure." In spite of the efforts of the Failure Marketing Board to improve its image, it's still a place nobody wants to visit. But all successful people do fail, and if you want to succeed you'll probably end up there, too. As doctor and deep-sea explorer Joseph MacInnis says, "Failures are just a kind of road map. Everybody who is successful looks at a trail of failures. It's part of the deal."

Every successful person I've talked to says they failed in one way or another, and that also goes for people I didn't talk to. Abraham Lincoln failed in business twice, had a nervous breakdown and was defeated in politics 8 times. He kept persisting and ended up president of the United States. Einstein, the world's most famous scientist, failed an exam that would have allowed him to study for a diploma as an electrical engineer. The great painter Paul Gauguin was a failed stockbroker. Winston Churchill failed grammar in primary school, plus his army entrance exam, not once but twice, and still became British Prime Minister. No wonder he said, "Success is the ability to go from failure to failure without losing your enthusiasm."

François Parenteau says that when he started in the investment business "I did pretty bad, initially. I did about as good as a skydiver who jumps out of the plane and forgets to strap on his parachute. So, I came crashing down." But François picked himself up, and has since been named top independent analyst by *Business Week*. Of course, nobody wakes up in the morning and says, "I think I'll fail today." But it happens and, when it does, the trick is to just keep going and persist through it. Direct marketing guru Joseph Sugarman says, "I failed at practically everything I tried, but I never gave up. I just knew that one of these days I'd make it if I just hung in there."

So, when you slide downhill into the town of Failure, pick yourself up, get out of town, and keep going. Don't think of failure as the end of the road. Think of it as a little detour on your way to a much better place called Success.

At first I had more failure than success.
Oliver Stone Academy Award-winning filmmaker

I came in dead last in the field of 111 riders. I crossed the finish line almost a half-hour behind the winner, and as I churned up the last hill, the Spanish crowd began to laugh and hiss at me.
Lance Armstrong cyclist 7-time Tour de France winner

I'm not afraid to fail. I think that's a very important element of success. A lot of people see an opportunity but they never act on it, because the fear of failure is too big for them.
Jerry Hayes optometrist, founder, Hayes Marketing

Failing doesn't stop you. Quitting stops you. Persevere and don't be afraid to fail. You can afford to fail over and over again, because there will always be many, many more opportunities to succeed.
Gerry Schwartz CEO, Onex

Failure is **fertilizer** for success

That's why it feels like **shit**

The person interested in success has to learn to **view failure as a healthy, inevitable part of the process** of getting to the top.

Dr. Joyce Brothers renowned psychologist

If you're discouraged about failing, it helps to know that failure can actually lead to success. As renowned author and educator Dale Carnegie once said, "Develop success from failures. Discouragement and failure are two of the surest stepping stones to success." When famous inventor Thomas Edison failed, he said, "I am not discouraged, because every wrong attempt discarded is another step forward."

The thing is, by pointing out the wrong way, failure can actually steer us towards the right way, or a new way. I mean, Columbus set off in search of the East Indies continent, but, typical guy, got his directions wrong. However he did find a new, or slightly used, continent called America, so the failure led to a success. Plus it gave men renewed confidence they could do just fine, thank you, without asking for directions.

Poet John Keats said, "Don't be discouraged by a failure. It can be a positive experience. Failure is, in a sense, the highway to success, in as much as every discovery of what is false leads us to seek earnestly after what is true." And that really holds true in the field of science. Medical geneticist Josef Penninger said to me, "We have a lot of failures. About 90% of the time we are wrong. We work doggedly in the lab for 2 years making genetically-modified mice, and often nothing happens. But all you need is to be right once, and it makes a difference – a big difference." Josef's failures have led him to some discoveries that will make a big difference in people's lives, like uncovering the master gene for osteoporosis and finding a protein that stops the growth of colon cancer tumors.

Sometimes you're the only person who knows you failed, but not so for Dave Lavery, the NASA whiz who sends robots to Mars. Dave says, "We have very, very public failures. Everybody on the planet knows that we screwed up. You're disappointed, you're hurt, you're humiliated. But, when you fail you don't stop. You say, okay, I've learned what not to do. Now I'll figure out how to do it right. Persistence is part of the process."

So when you're feeling really down because you've failed at something, remember the words of basketball coach Rick Pitino who said, "Failure is only fertilizer for future success." And I would add, "That's why it feels like shit."

I failed my way right to the top.
Paul Haggis film director, writer, *Million Dollar Baby*

Don't think of it as failure. Think of it as time-released success.
Robert Orben speechwriter for Presidents Nixon and Ford

My advice to anybody who wants to be creative is to get into something that will fail. I've failed at a lot of things in my life and I hope to fail at a lot more.
Jerry Della Femina one of the 100 most influential people in advertising

Failure just tells me where I am in the process. It doesn't mean I've failed; it just means I've got a longer way to go. Okay, that didn't work, so what else do I need to come up with?
Ronda Carnegie advertising director, *The New Yorker*

DON'T CRASH AND BURN – CRASH AND LEARN

MAKE **FAILURE** YOUR **SCHOOL**

NOT YOUR **FUNERAL**

You want failure to be an opportunity to learn and not a block to your forward motion.

Bruce Cockburn singer, songwriter

Failure can be heartbreaking. And when it happens you have a choice. You can let it be your school or your funeral. It's your school if you learn from it and move on. It's your funeral if you become devastated and let it stop you in your tracks. Ben Saunders became the youngest person to ski solo to the North Pole, but he told me his first try was a disaster: "My first expedition was, in so many ways, the biggest failure of my entire life. We didn't get anywhere near the Pole, and came back in massive debt. I was mentally ruined and convinced that I'd failed. But, if I hadn't gone through that first expedition, I wouldn't be where I am now. So replace the word failure with learning – that's what it's all about."

David Fairchild said, "Don't look down on failure. I have learned many fascinating things by my failures, things which are as interesting as the successes." Since David was a world famous botanist (I feel a pun coming on) he actually flowered from failure (sorry). Moving from botany to technology, Cisco Systems VP Rick Moran says, "You learn something from failure. If you go into something that you thought you could do and you find out that you can't, learn a little bit about it, forgive yourself for having done it, and get the hell out."

Movies often fail at the box office, but animation film director Robin Budd says the learning still pays off: "You can't get too hung-up about failures because they teach you many things. Failure is something that I am terribly afraid of, but it is a big part of the whole process." Comedian Sinbad adds: "Enjoy the fall off the horse. Enjoy the not being able to drive a car, or the fact that you're not that good with a camera yet. That's when you learn the most."

As much as we hate failure, it can be a much better school than success. Sure, success feels good, but when we succeed we just say, "Wow!" It's only when we fail that we ask, "Why?" Bell Mobility chairman Bob Ferchat says, "Successes reward you and pat you on the back, but they don't really teach you very much. Failure is where you learn, and understand why it happened, and what you did wrong. Successes are just rewards for continuing to fail." So, if you're feeling really down from all the failures and flubs you're making, think of them as your school, not your funeral. Don't crash and burn – crash and learn.

> **Failure is success if we learn from it.**
> **Malcolm Forbes**, publisher

> **The times I have experienced failure have been the most growing for me, had the most important impact. Success is wonderful but failure is when you really meet yourself and ask, "Who am I?"**
> **Cynthia Trudell** first woman to head an auto manufacturing division

> **Life is filled with lots of failures along the way. I fail every day. It's part of the growth process, part of learning, and one should not be discouraged by failure.**
> **David Zussman** president, Public Policy Forum

> **Remember the two benefits of failure. First, if you do fail, you learn what doesn't work; and second, the failure gives you the opportunity to try a new approach.**
> **Roger von Oech** creativity expert and author

TO **SUCCEED** A **LOT**
FAIL A LOT

I've missed more than 9,000 shots in my career. I've lost almost 300 games...**I've failed over and over and over again in my life. And that is why I succeed.**

Michael Jordan basketball superstar

If you're not as successful as you'd like to be, maybe you're just not failing enough. Remember that while Babe Ruth had the most success in terms of home runs, he also had the most failures in terms of strikeouts. Rower Silken Lauman says when she started rowing she tipped the boat over more than anyone else: "The first time I started rowing I tipped 21 times. Just to put it in perspective, most people tip maybe once or twice in their entire career. This is how my summer went: Splash! Crawl back into the boat. Splash! Crawl back into the boat. Splash! Crawl back into the boat." Yet all those failures helped turn Silken into a world-champion rower.

Quantity counts. There often seems to be a correlation between the number of times people fail and the number of times they succeed. It's almost like successful people collect "Frequent Failure Points" – sort of like Frequent Flyer Points, where the more you fly, the more points you get towards a free ticket. With Frequent Failure Points, the more you fail the more points you get towards success. Real estate agent Elli Davis has lots of Frequent Failure Points. She says, "I was going through old files the other day and I can't tell you how many times I did not get the deal. People say, 'Oh, Elli, she gets everything!' And I say, 'You should see what I don't get.' It's a numbers game. I get a lot because I do a lot." And that's helped take Elli to the top of her field.

Google co-founder Sergey Brin said to me, "You have to fail many times to succeed once." When he said that, my immediate response was, "Wait a minute. Google isn't exactly a failure. It's a super colossal success." To which Sergey responded, "Google didn't fail but we have many projects that do fail. Not all projects work out." It's comforting to know that even the big guys rack up their share of Frequent Failure Points, same as the little guys. In my company we learned long ago that to succeed a lot you've got to fail a lot, so when we're trying to come up with ideas for an ad campaign, a video, or even where to have lunch, we'll generate dozens of ideas. All of them will fail and get tossed in the garbage, except for one. And that's okay, because one good idea is all we need.

So if you'd like to have more successes, have more failures. Start earning your own Frequent Failure Points today. They could be your ticket to success.

Ninety-nine times, the conclusion is false. The hundredth time I am right.
Albert Einstein
immortal physicist

You miss 100% of the shots you don't take.
Wayne Gretzky
superstar hockey player

My coach at Purdue, Piggy Lambert, constantly reminded us: "The team that makes the most mistakes will probably win."
John Wooden
legendary basketball coach

My life drawing teacher said, "You have thousands of bad drawings in you. Why don't you get them out so you can get to the good one?"
Robin Budd
animation film director

I believe in a lot of failures, and failing quickly. That way you don't spend too much money, waste too much time, and you can move on to the next thing.
Russell Campbell
president, ABN AMRO Canada

PERSIST THROUGH MISTAKES

FLUBS
FLOPS
GOOFS
ERRORS
SNAFUS
GAFFES
SLIP-UPS
TRIP-UPS
FUMBLES
MESS-UPS
FOUL-UPS
BLUNDERS
STUMBLES
BLOOPERS
SCREW-UPS
BOO-BOOS

There are days when **I've made the same mistake 14 times**, and I say, 'Do I have any sense?'

Oprah Winfrey top talk show host

At first I was going to lump mistakes in with failures, since mistakes are sort of mini-failures. However, I figured they really deserve their own section, because so many successful people say they continually make flubs, errors, boo-boos, blunders, bloopers, goofs, gaffes, and snafus. They muck-up, screw-up, mess-up, slip-up, trip-up, and foul-up; not to mention flop, fumble, and stumble. But they just keep persisting through it all.

Mistakes are smaller than failures, but some big names make them. Michael Jordan was a basketball superstar, but he still fumbled a lot: "People expect their heroes to be flawless, never to make mistakes...And no one can do that. No one never makes mistakes, and no one always does everything right..." Anita Roddick, famous founder of the Body Shop, says she's made lots of mistakes over the years. Her advice is similar to many successful people who say to admit it and then do something about it: "When you make a mistake, you have to face up to the fact and take immediate steps to change course."

Kevin Eubank, Mississippi Parent of the Year and construction firm owner, said to me, "Everyone makes mistakes. It's how you handle those mistakes. Those that learn from their mistakes are the ones who are the most successful. Those that don't learn are the ones that are not in business anymore." Yes, mistakes are all about learning. Intel chairman Andy Grove says, "You must understand your mistakes. Study the hell out of them."

According to famous corporate management guru Peter Drucker, mistakes are the best teachers: "You don't learn things out of books, you learn things by getting your hands dirty. You learn things by making the stupid mistakes." (I've tried to make smart mistakes, but they don't seem to be any better.) Buckminster Fuller, futurist and inventor of the geodesic dome, said, "Whatever humans have learned had to be learned as a consequence only of trial and error experience. Humans have learned only through mistakes." So I'd say, even if they don't go to college, successful people still earn an MM degree: A Master of Mistakes.

The bottom line? 1. It's okay to make mistakes. 2. Try to correct them as soon as possible. 3. The worst mistake you can make is not learning from a mistake.

I hope you understand that business is a series of trial-and-error. It's not a great science. Mistakes are made. It's just moving the ball forward....
Jack Welch
CEO, General Electric

You've got to learn to accept the fool in you as well as the part that's got it goin' on.
Tyra Banks supermodel

If I'm a good football coach, it's because of my mistakes. I try to learn from them.
Steve Spurrier football star

I started from scratch and made every possible error that you can make. I just continued to move forward.
Nez Hallett III
CEO, Smart Wireless

I came to realize that basically all learning is trial and error at one level or another. Every mutation is a mistake.
Daniel Dennett director, Cognitive Studies, Tufts University

MAKE MORE

MISSEDTAKES

MISTAAKES

MISSTAKES

MISTACKES

MISTAEKS

MISTAKES

Make mistakes more often is one of my favorite adages, because **I learn from making mistakes**. And I've done a lot of dumb things that I've learned from.

Austin Hill co-founder, Zero-Knowledge Systems

Are you feeling bad about all the stupid mistakes you're making? Well, cheer up, it could be a sign you're on your way to success. As actor Joan Collins said, "Show me a person who has never made a mistake and I'll show you somebody who has never achieved much." And the opposite is also true. Show me a person who is making a lot of mistakes and I'll show you somebody who is probably achieving a lot. Lindsay Sharp is a good example. He said to me, "After 10 years, a project we worked on was very successful even though we made every conceivable mistake in the book." But all those mistakes helped Lindsay become a renowned museum director in charge of 4 London museums.

Jessica Switzer does public relations for technology companies, and she says technology innovations are built on a foundation of mistakes: "In technology, you've got to get out there and make the mistakes. If you stand still, you die. Action is what it's all about." Paul Rowan told me that making many mistakes helped his company, Umbra, become a leader in the design of affordable, contemporary products for the home: "People always talk about their successes, but I talk about how I made mistakes and how I turned them into success. When you're doing innovative products you're bound to make a lot of mistakes, because you're going places that people haven't gone before, with either the manufacturing technique, or the materials, or the forms, so you're bound to make some mistakes along the way. I think that's really the key to our success."

Daniel Dennett, famous philosopher and director of the Center for Cognitive Studies at Tufts University, said to me, "Make more mistakes, make better mistakes, more sophisticated mistakes. Be willing to make mistakes in public and admit them. Try to get over your embarrassment and your anger and your shame and, instead, adopt an attitude of curiosity about your own mistakes." (I can see this one's gonna take a lot of practice.)

The thing is, each wrong way leads us to the right way, so each mistake we make is like a compass, but instead of pointing to true north, it's pointing us towards true success. So if you're not achieving the success you want, maybe you need to make more boo-boos, blunders, and bloopers. How many mistakes have you made today? Sorry, that's not enough.

It was when I found out I could make mistakes that I knew I was on to something.
Ornette Coleman
renowned jazz innovator

Experience is just another name for a bunch of mistakes.
Bob Ferchat
Chairman, Bell Mobility

Mistakes are not failures of character or ability; they are often just another way of doing things.
Pamela Wallin respected broadcaster, diplomat

No man ever became great or good except through many and great mistakes.
William E. Gladstone
British Prime Minister

It's been a series of disasters. Trial and error. And now I'm really starting to know what I'm doing.
François Parenteau
CEO, Defiance Capital, named top independent analyst

PERSIST – SECTION 3.
PERSIST THROUGH CRAP
Criticism Rejection Assholes Prejudice

PERSIST THROUGH **CRITICISM**

A successful person is one who can **lay a firm foundation with the bricks that others throw** at him or her.

David Brinkley famous TV journalist who helped shape TV news

On the road to success we need to persist through a lot of CRAP, which, I think, stands for Criticism, Rejection, Assholes and Prejudice. Let's start with Criticism. It's something we all have to put up with, but it helps to remember that, throughout history, some of the most successful people have also been the most criticized.

- Mozart, one of the greatest composers, still had to put up with criticism from Emperor Ferdinand: "Far too noisy, my dear Mozart. Far too many notes."
- Elvis Presley was told after auditioning, "Stick to driving a truck, because you'll never make it as a singer."
- Even the Beatles were roundly criticized by Decca Records: "We don't like their sound, and guitar music is on the way out."

Gee, I'd say, if you don't like criticism, don't get into the music business. Of course, it's easy to escape criticism. Just lock yourself away and don't say anything or do anything. Unfortunately, that approach means there's something else you also escape – success. So, the trick is to hang in there through criticism and not let it destroy you. It should be the critics who are destroyed, not you. When you're feeling hurt from criticism, set your timer for 5 minutes. When the bell rings, stop feeling sorry for yourself and get on with it. If a day has passed and you're still hurting, eat a tub of ice cream. You'll feel much better – at least until you're criticized for gaining weight.

Remember, it helps to get criticism earlier rather than later, preferably before dawn when the critics are still asleep. The sooner you get feedback, or criticism, the better. It's easier to change something after spending a day on it, than after spending a month on it. Also keep in mind that critics are not all created equal. Some are created from bad chemical reactions. So know which criticism to reject and which to respect. It helps to be your own worst critic, so you've already thought of all the negatives, and either changed them or decided they're not so bad after all. Darlene Lim, science whiz kid and post-doctoral fellow at NASA, says, "I am my own worst critic. Maybe that's what pushes me. You keep beating yourself up." But Darlene, don't beat yourself up too much. That's the job of the real critics.

The bottom line? If you're being criticized, congratulations! You're on your way to success. Now let's look at how to persist through it.

In spite of bad reviews, in spite of people attacking you for your beliefs, you just have to get up every morning and keep going.
Eve Ensler award-winning author, performer

When I started to sing like myself, as opposed to imitating Nat Cole...I got a lot of criticism for it.
Ray Charles pioneering pianist and soul singer

I could take it, but my wife hates it, my mother hates it, the whole family hates it when people are so critical of me.
Michael Jordan basketball superstar

Honest criticism is hard to take, particularly from a relative, a friend, an acquaintance, or a stranger.
Franklin P. Jones

You're never as good as everyone tells you when you win, and you're never as bad as they say when you lose.
Lou Holtz famous football coach

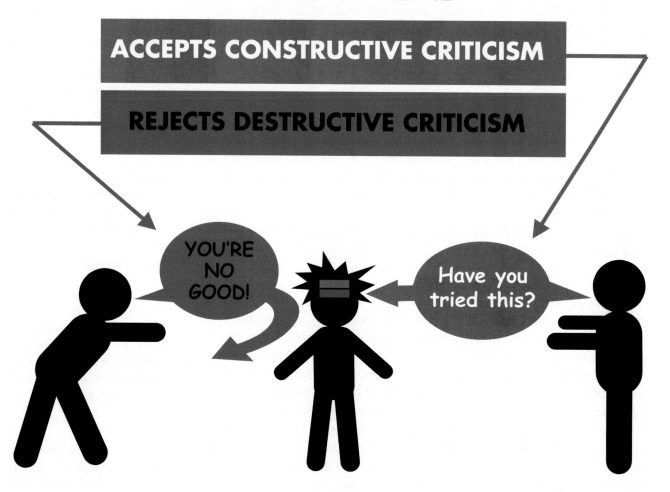

Something that can help you persist through criticism is to develop a Criticism Filter in your head. Then when you get criticized, your Filter quickly scans the criticism and decides whether to accept it or ignore it. "Hey, why can't I just ignore all criticism?" Because, as you'll see on the next page, some criticism is actually constructive. The kind we want to ignore is destructive criticism. You know, the negative flak that does nothing but put you down or tear you apart. It serves no real purpose, except to make the critic feel good, and it's a waste of time to listen to it. So develop a strong Criticism Filter and it will make sure destructive criticism goes in one ear and out the other, bypassing sensitive parts of your head, like tear glands.

Comedian Rick Mercer developed a strong Criticism Filter that helped him ignore all the flak encountered in show business. He told me, "I've had some brutal, brutal criticism. When I did my first one-man show, a critic said on the radio, 'Dear Rick Mercer, you should never set foot on the stage again. Your show is an abysmal disaster.' He just ripped me apart. Luckily, I was 18 and very cheeky, so it didn't affect me. It could have easily driven other people from the stage, and they would never go back." By ignoring the criticism Rick went on to great success. And he didn't take criticism personally, which is another key to ignoring destructive criticism. As Anatomical Travelogue CEO Alexander Tsiaras says, "I'm totally insensitive, I take nothing personally." Same with Diane Bean, senior VP of business development at Manulife: "I don't like criticism, but I don't take it super-personally. You can't think it's a conspiracy and get paranoid." So make sure your Criticism Filter is very impersonal – sort of like a tax auditor.

The only catch to ignoring bad criticism is you also have to ignore good praise. Famous music producer Quincy Jones says, "If you start to guzzle all the praise and adulation, then when they say you're shit, you have to swallow all that too." When director Steven Spielberg was shooting *The Color Purple*, Oprah rushed up to him, very excited, holding a copy of *Time* magazine with him on the cover. Steven told Oprah to put it away. He doesn't read about himself, because if he believes the good he also has to believe the bad. So, when you're developing your own Criticism Filter, make sure it filters out the applause, as well as the destructive criticism. Sorry!

Don't pay any attention to what they write about you. Just measure it in inches.
Andy Warhol one of the most famous 20th-century artists

Sometimes you have to think, "I can't pay attention to what people are saying, I've got to keep moving, I've got to do this."
Lisa Davis director of communications, AARP

The famous saying about reviews is, if you believe the good ones, you'll believe the bad ones. It's better to look at 'em after you've finished the run.
Rip Torn actor

What people think doesn't really bother me. I don't look for other's approval, because if you're looking for their approval, it's just as easy for them to criticize you. So whatever way they do it, it's control over what you're going to do.
Ann Turner founder, Profile Recruitment Consultants

USE **CRITICISM** TO

Sometimes the criticism is correct. Sometimes you need to say, "Maybe I am wrong and I need to course-correct here."

Lise Buyer renowned Wall Street investment banker

We've seen how it helps to develop a Criticism Filter in your head, so you can filter out criticism that's destructive. But a more important function of your Criticism Filter is to accept criticism that is actually constructive and will help you improve. As famous British Prime Minister Winston Churchill once said: "Criticism may not be agreeable, but it is necessary. It fulfils the same function as pain in the human body. It calls attention to an unhealthy state of things." Successful people are always trying to improve, and listening to constructive criticism is one way to do it. For example, FedEx founder Fred Smith says he sees criticism by customers as a good opportunity to improve operations and make FedEx a better company.

Of course, when you're getting flak, it's not always easy to think of it as constructive. The other day my colleague Thom wandered by my desk and asked, "How's it going?" I said, "Great!" and gave him the first draft of this criticism section. Then what did he do? He started criticizing it: "It's convoluted. You've got too many quotes, blah, blah, blah..." Of course, I reacted like any enlightened, new age person would – I wanted to strangle him. Instead, I stormed out of the office to get a coffee, and as I walked along, I heard this little voice in my Criticism Filter say, "Maybe Thom's right?" So, I thought about what he said, and in most cases he was right. Damn! But it didn't take me long to make some fixes and improve the section. Often, hidden away in what seems like flak, there's a spark of improvement. And that's the real purpose of criticism. It's not about clobbering or crushing – it's about correcting.

Accepting criticism helped James Watson and Francis Crick make their huge discovery of the structure of DNA. James told me he showed one of their ideas to a chemist and was immediately criticized: "He said, 'It's wrong, you've got the hydrogen atoms in the wrong place.' I'd just put them down like they were in the books. The next day, I thought he might be right, so I changed locations [of the atoms] and we knew we were right. It all happened in about 2 hours, from nothing to bing! And we knew it was big." Big is an understatement, since it won James and Francis the Nobel Prize and led to the DNA analysis we see on all those crime investigation TV shows.

Sometimes listening to a little criticism can lead to big success.

If you give me constructive criticism, I'll make the change right away. But if you're just negative for the sake of being negative, I don't want to hear about it.

Steven Schwartz author, *How to Make Hot Cold Calls*

If you are serious about improvement, be brutally honest with yourself.

Greg Norman champion golfer

I've been doing this for so long, I'm not as fazed by, "Sorry, we don't like it. Start over."

Chip Kidd acclaimed book designer

Time and time again I was told that I would never make the film on time and never make it on budget. That kind of criticism tends to turn me into a great big motor of efficiency.

Richard E. Grant actor, filmmaker

WARNING FRANK CRITICISM

People don't always have time to stop and think about how to make their criticism sound constructive, even if it is. That's why a guy named Frank invented "Frank Criticism," which gets right to the point without being nice about it. You may encounter Frank Criticism in the business world, because people are often in a hurry, with a lot on their minds, like where to eat lunch, so they don't always have time to phrase things nicely. Once when General Electric CEO Jack Welch was critiquing a storyboard their ad agency had just done, he simply threw it on the floor and said, "We don't like it! It doesn't work!" Actually Jack was being nice. He didn't jump up and down on it.

In spite of appearances, Frank Criticism is not always destructive. It's just the way it's presented that's destructive. The criticism itself may actually be constructive and help us improve. Terry Gilliam told me it was Frank Criticism that helped the Monty Python group produce such wonderful TV shows: "The great thing about the group is that we were ruthless with each other. If an idea sucked we said it sucked. We respected each other enough to do that. I know they say, 'Oh, make sure you don't put somebody down.' But put 'em down. People are incredibly strong and resilient. You want to encourage people, but if they're not producing good work, then you slap 'em."

I first discovered Frank Criticism in kindergarten when our teacher, Mrs. Singer, had us draw an outdoor scene and I drew a line across the top of the page to represent the sky. Another kid, probably named Frank, looked at my drawing and said, "Are you ever stupid. There's no line in the sky!" (Good thing this kid wasn't in kindergarten with Picasso: "Hey Picasso, you idiot, you gotta put the guy's nose on his face,

not on his shoulder.") At first I was hurt, but then I went outside and looked up and realized, "Gee, he's right. There is no line in the sky." So he gave me new insight, and I gave him a black eye.

Fast forward about a decade to when I was in art college studying design. (I didn't show them my kindergarten drawing or they never would have let me in.) Professor Charlie had us design a new screwdriver, and I spent weeks coming up with what I thought was the world's best screwdriver.

Presentation day arrived. I rushed to class and placed my creation proudly on the judging table. Charlie walked along eyeing all the screwdrivers, then suddenly stopped and picked up mine. Yes! I was elated. He was obviously going to use my masterpiece as an example of breakthrough design. Which, in a way, is what happened. Charlie hurled my precious screwdriver against the wall and it broke into a million pieces. My heart sank. I was devastated. But after I put a contract out on Charlie's life, I realized maybe, just maybe, my design wasn't as brilliant as I thought it was, and I came up with a much-improved design.

I don't recommend the shatter approach to criticism. Simply saying, "It's not good enough. Make it better," would have worked just fine. But I must admit that, after watching Charlie shatter my screwdriver, there's not much any critic can say to shatter me. Which was probably the point of the exercise.

The moral of the story is, get used to dealing with criticism. There are a lot of Franks and Charlies out there in the real world.

PERSIST THROUGH
REJECTION

...I think you have to develop a kind of resistance to rejection, and to the disappointments that are sure to come your way.

Gregory Peck celebrated film star

The R in CRAP stands for Rejection. No matter how you look at it, rejection is just a painful kick in the butt. And don't expect to be rejected only one time. If you were only thrown out the door once, it would be called ejection. It's called re-jection because it happens repeatedly. Joe Kraus told me that when he and his buddies started Excite, persisting through all the rejection was the number one reason for their success: "We've been rejected and told no so many times that, to us, it's just like the starting gun of a race. So when you get rejected the first time, it's really when the starting gun goes off."

There's a long list of people who were rejected over and over again and still achieved incredible success. It's hard to believe cycling champion Lance Armstrong was ever rejected, but it happened when he was starting out: "No one wanted me. No European teams wanted me, and corporate America didn't want me." Ruth Handler was rejected when executives at the Mattel toy company laughed at her idea for a doll, but she ignored them and created Barbie, the world's most popular doll. Debbi Fields had a great idea for cookies, but was rejected with these words: "A cookie store is a bad idea. Besides, the market research reports say America likes crispy cookies, not soft and chewy cookies like you make." Debbi persisted and ended up making a lot of dough.

When Issy Sharp had the idea of building a new type of motor hotel, he drove straight into rejection: "For years I knocked on doors, and had flat-out rejection, with people saying, 'Kid, you don't know what you're talking about. You don't even know anything about the business. Why would you even think you can do it?' But that didn't deter me, because I just saw and felt something that I thought would work." Issy persisted and took Four Seasons Hotels to the top of the hotel market. Ed Robertson says when the Barenaked Ladies started out, they were also thrown out: "We were rejected by all the record companies and told we would never get a record deal. But music made us really happy and we had fun doing it, so we just kept doing it." And their persistence led to sales of well over 10 million records.

So remember, when you get rejected, you're going to get dejected, but the important thing is to also get injected with the determination to persist. (Especially through cheesy rhymes.)

When I went to see publishers with the first *Day in The Life* idea, I got laughed out of every office.

Rick Smolan creator of the best-selling *Day in the Life* books

My professor, who was the chairman of the pre-medical panel of the college, said I didn't have what it took to be a good doctor and he would see to it that I never went to medical school. I cried.

Ken Woodrow M.D., Professor of Psychiatry, Stanford

There'll be weeks when, boom, boom, boom, boom – 4 things get rejected. And you just think, "Well, the hell with this. I've got to get another job." It can get discouraging but, inevitably, it turns around.

Chip Kidd acclaimed book cover designer

Unless I'm getting rejected, I'm not pushing the boundaries enough. Perseverance is important.

Lakshmi Pratury director, American India Foundation

I have 175 rejection slips in my files. I keep them around to remind me that if you give up at any point, nobody in the world cares that you're not succeeding, except you. So you have to really want it. **You have to keep at it, and if you do, nobody can stop you.**

Robert J. Sawyer best-selling science fiction writer

Many successful people have an interesting strategy to persist through rejection. They treat their rejections like badges of honor, sort of like war veterans wearing their medals. The rejection slips show what they've been through and act as a reminder to keep persevering. It helped best-selling novelist Stephen King keep persisting when he first started writing and was trying to get his stories published. They were rejected over and over, but instead of throwing the rejection slips out, he pounded a nail in the wall above his bed and stuck them on it. He writes, "By the time I was fourteen...the nail in my wall would no longer support the weight of the rejection slips impaled upon it. I replaced the nail with a spike and went on writing." I love that story.

A lot of successful people can tell you exactly how many rejection badges they have, especially writers. Seth Godin says, "When I got into the book business, I got 950 rejection letters before I sold my first book." Author Steven Schwartz told me, "I was rejected 49 times before I was hired by an ad agency." The first Dr. Seuss book was rejected by 43 publishers. John Grisham's first book was rejected by over 30 publishers. All these writers kept their pens moving and keyboards clicking, and went on to become best-selling authors.

Some people frame their rejection slips and proudly display them for all to see. One lawyer-turned-writer was rejected by publishers hundreds of times. Then, after he achieved great success, he wallpapered his huge 20' by 20' bathroom in his mansion with all the rejection slips. Then he could sit there and laugh at all the people who said his writing was crap.

To be honest, I've never been good with rejection. However, I'm getting better thanks to the continual rejection I face every time I ask somebody for an interview for this book. Most of the time people are happy to help, but I've also been flat-out rejected. The interesting thing is, the more I get rejected the less it destroys me the next time. Practice, practice, practice. And I've found the fear of rejection is usually worse than the rejection itself. One rejection that really stands out is Matt Groening, creator of *The Simpsons*. He rejected me – get this – 4 years in a row. Every year I'd see him at a conference and ask for an interview, and every year he'd refuse. But I kept asking, and finally he said yes. Matt gave me a great interview, as well as my own personal drawing of Bart Simpson. It's hanging on my wall as a constant reminder that persistence really does pay off.

Y'know, every major studio and agent turned down my scripts. I still have a collage of the rejection letters on the wall in my office.
Edward Burns
writer, director, actor

I began to see this pattern time and time again in Quincy's life...with each rejection he'd come back stronger and stronger.
Peggy Lipton
Quincy Jones' first wife

My wife claims I warm up only upon rejection... Rejection inspires me. The impossibility of something gives me delight.
Richard Saul Wurman
information architect

In the ad business, your success is based on the opinions of people who have absolutely no respect for you. The way we dealt with that was, if our work got rejected, we'd go back and try to top it. We'd try to do it better.
Jay Chiat co-founder Chiat/Day advertising agency

I must say that in all my years in business most of the people I encountered were very nice, agreeable, considerate, courteous, helpful, friendly people. But there were times when I came face-to-face with – let me see, how do I say this nicely? – real Assholes. To be honest, I never actually refer to anybody as an asshole, but, I'm sorry, there's just no better word to describe the behavior of some people.

These are people who are confrontational, throw temper tantrums, blame everybody but themselves, have egos that are out of control, and heap verbal abuse on everybody. When you're rolling along the road to success, you'll not only run into lots of potholes, you'll also run into lots of Assholes, so be prepared for an encounter. Fortunately they are few and far between, but they're out there, waiting for you to drop in.

Scientific estimates vary on the exact number of Assholes in the world, but representatives of this species are found everywhere. Some common varieties include:

- Bad-tempered, grumpy, abrasive

- Cruel, brutal, intimidating

- Lying, greedy, ruthless

- Rude, mean, unkind, condescending

- Self-centered, arrogant, egotistical

On this last point, recent scientific data indicates that the mysterious human organ called the ego is actually located inside the rectum, which could explain the preponderance of egotistical Assholes. Like it or not, we all have lapses of Assholeness at some point in our lives. According to unreliable sources, like my wife, I too have been one at times. They're even found amongst some parents and friends. You may love 'em, but they're still Assholes.

Assholes can be all sugar and spice and nice one minute, then suddenly blow up the next. They won't listen to you. They'll discount you. They'll make you feel like crap. You are the scum of the earth. They'll verbally abuse you, and not just in private. They seem to get great pleasure by heaping abuse on you in public, while others stand nervously by, wondering where to look.

How do you survive an encounter with an Asshole? First, remember not to take it personally. It's not about you. They treat everybody the same. You have no control over them. The only thing you have control over is how you react to them. There's nothing you can ever say or do that will get through to them, or have any effect, because, bless their hearts, they are thoroughly contemptible, detestable people.

Avoid the temptation to fight back at an Asshole. By fighting back you could inadvertently become one yourself. Instead, stay calm and don't pay any attention to them. They hate it when you stay calm. What they really want is a reaction out of you, and by not reacting, you suck the power right out of them. So be cool, persevere and hang in there.

The thing to remember is that, in the long run, you'll be the one to come out on top. Because Assholes, by their very nature, always end up on the bottom.

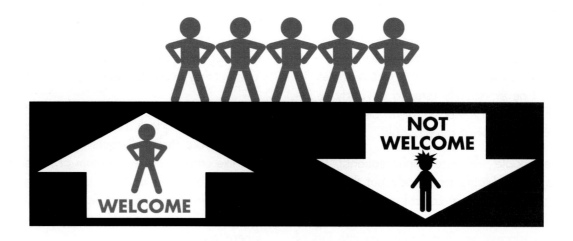

PERSIST THROUGH PREJUDICE

As a child, every time I encountered prejudice...I would feel it down to my core...I would go home and sit on my bed and weep and weep...the tears streaming down my face.

Bessie Delany second black female dentist in New York

The P in CRAP stands for prejudice. And let me just say that I'm really no expert on the subject. I mean, growing up a white guy in North America is sort of like having a prejudice-free pass. Since I'm part of the majority, I don't have to spend a lot of time and energy fighting the injustices that so many other people encounter. But I've come across enough prejudice to know that it stinks.

Back in the hippie days of the 60s, I was one of the first guys in my area to have long hair. One night, a friend and I were walking his dog and we decided to go into a restaurant for a bite. As we sat down, the dog jumped up on a chair, and I could see the waitress giving us the evil eye. I said to my friend, "Dogs aren't allowed in restaurants. She's gonna throw us out." Sure enough, the waitress stomped over and scowled, "You'll have to leave." I said to my friend, "See, I told you dogs aren't allowed." The waitress looked at me and said – and this is absolutely true – "The dog can stay. But your hair is too long. You have to leave."

At that moment I had the sinking feeling in the pit of my stomach you get when you realize somebody rejects you just because you're different. Imagine what it's like to experience that every day of your life. We quietly left the restaurant, as I steamed over the unfairness of it all. I mean, the waitress really should have made the dog leave first – it's hair was much longer than mine.

Prejudice is all about being judged mainly on looks, rather than facts or personal experience. And it's often based on being different. You can be different because you have different hair, different clothes, different accent, different skin color, different race, different religion, or different gender. You can be different because, in a group, you're the youngest or the oldest; the tallest or the shortest; the thinnest or the fattest; the worst-looking or the best-looking; the poorest or even the richest.

Being different is a factor that helps many people succeed. The downside is that it also makes them a magnet for prejudice. But they just keep persisting through it, and many actually turn it around and use prejudice as a driving force. Editor and author Peter C. Newman said to me, "I'm Jewish, and there's still a lot of anti-Semitism. So you have to work twice as hard to get half the recognition." Many women echo the same thought. Actor Margot Kidder once said, "Being a career woman is harder than being a career man. You've got to look like a lady, act like a man, and work like a dog."

Black music and fashion entrepreneur Russell Simmons has run into prejudice in predominantly white Hollywood, and he says a lot of it is due to being uninformed and unaware of other cultures: "White Hollywood executives....just assume black people don't know anything, because they don't know any black people. What you're dealing with is not aggressive racism, but cultural ignorance."

The bottom line is that, on the road to success there's a good chance you'll encounter prejudice in one form or another. You have no control over it and you may have to work a lot harder to detour around it Just don't let it stop you. Persist through it.

PERSIST – SECTION 4.
9 WAYS TO PERSIST

9 WAYS TO PERSIST

9 WAYS TO PERSIST

248   **1A.**   **TAKE SMALL STEPS RATHER THAN BIG LEAPS**

250   **1B.**   **SMALL STEPS ARE JUST EASIER**

252   **2.**   **DEVELOP QUITOPHOBIA – A BIG FEAR OF QUITTING**

254   **3.**   **NEVER, NEVER, NEVER GIVE UP**

256   **4.**   **DEVELOP BOUNCE-ABILITY**

258   **5.**   **BE TOO STUBBORN TO QUIT**

260   **6.**   **BE SHORT-TERM IMPATIENT & LONG-TERM PATIENT**

262   **7.**   **DON'T LOOK BACK**

264   **8.**   **PERSIST THROUGH THE UNBALANCED TIMES**

266   **9.**   **USE RFM – RELENTLESS FORWARD MOTION**

TAKE SMALL STEPS

MYTH	REALITY
SUCCESSFUL PEOPLE TAKE **BIG LEAPS**	THEY TAKE **MANY SMALL STEPS**

I've learned that **if I just put one foot in front of the other, things will work out well**. And I believe that.

Gord Lownds founder, Sleep Country

It's not always easy to persist, so let's look at 9 ways that can help us keep going. And the first way is to take Small Steps. Oh, sure, there's a myth that successful people take big leaps in life, but the reality is most successful people just take it one step at a time. And even those who took the occasional big leap say a lot of little steps led up to it. The truth is, we reach success in much the same way a baby learns to walk, by stumbling along and taking small steps. Adobe Systems CEO John Warnock said to me, "One of the important things in life is to look down at your feet and take the next step and then the next step. Don't focus on things too far away, but make sure your direction is right and take one step at a time."

Forrest Sawyer told me small steps took him from unknown radio announcer to famous TV news anchor: "I started with 1-minute pieces, and then I would do 3-minute pieces, and I would keep doing them until I got them right. And then I did 10-minute and 13-minute pieces." Small steps took Peter Cochrane from a childhood of poverty to the chief technologist position at British Telecom: "I thought it would be wonderful if I could get a technician's qualification. Then I thought it would be wonderful if I got a Bachelor's degree. Then a Master's degree, then a Ph.D., then a D.Sc. One step at a time."

Anatomical Travelogue CEO Alexander Tsiaras, a pioneer in the field of medical-imaging technology, points out that many small steps can make it seem like you've taken a huge leap: "People say to me, 'Oh, you guys made a quantum leap from the technology you had last year.' I say, 'No, we didn't. Our algorithms got a little cleaner, CPUs got a little cheaper, memory a little bigger. If you add up the incremental advances in every one of them it looks like you've made a quantum leap. But it's actually many small steps.'"

So you don't need to take big leaps in order to succeed. You also don't need to have a big vision. Issy Sharp told me that when he started Four Seasons Hotels he had no vision: "I didn't do this to build a business. I did it to build one hotel. That was it. I wasn't even thinking of doing it again. It was very much baby steps." And with that approach, Issy built Four Seasons into one of the world's great hotel chains. The moral of the story is don't underestimate the power of small steps. As Neil Armstrong said when he set foot on the moon, "That's one small step for man; one giant leap for mankind."

In an early interview...a radio talk-show host asked me how I wrote. My reply: "One word at a time."

Stephen King best-selling novelist

Success is taking something on and achieving it in small intervals.

Lakshmi Pratury director, American India Foundation

I always had this dream to design every artifact in the world and if I just did one at a time, eventually I'd get there.

Karim Rashid acclaimed product designer

Some people are always hanging back, hanging back, because they want to do it in one big step. Do it by iterations.

Moses Znaimer president, City TV

I think I've worked with everybody in music for the last 50 years. And I don't know how it happened. You know, you just walk up there, you do one thing, you put one foot in front of the other, and you hope you get through.

Quincy Jones Grammy Award-winning music producer

SMALL STEPS ARE JUST EASIER

Life is hard by the yard,
but **by the inch it's a cinch**.
Quincy Jones, famous music producer

The great thing about small steps is they not only make it easier to persist, they make it easier to get going in the first place. As Mark Twain said long ago, "The secret of getting ahead is getting started. The secret of getting started is breaking your complex overwhelming tasks into small manageable tasks, and then starting on the first one."

Violinist Adrian Anantawan told me the same approach works for him: "I never hold myself to any promises. I say, 'Well, I'll just start it. I don't have to do a lot and I have nothing to lose.' But then you start it and you go, 'Well, I've already started it, so maybe I'll do a bit more, and then a bit more.' And then I just keep on going." That approach has helped Adrian create beautiful music, in spite of being born without a right hand.

Graham Hawkes holds the world record for the deepest solo ocean dive, and he also builds those cool submersibles that take divers to the bottom of the sea. Graham told me it's complex technology, but small steps keep the problems from sinking him: "I build these submersibles and if I really understood how long, and how much money and effort it would take, I'd never start. Where's the money coming from? Will it work? Will people want it? So, you have to fool yourself into not looking at all the problems. Just focus on the next step."

By all means set huge goals and dream big, if it works for you. But then keep the dreams and goals in the back of your mind and concentrate on the step you're taking now. That was mountain climber Laurie Skreslet's advice to my wife Baiba and me, as he guided us up Aconcagua, the highest mountain on the American continent. At one point, when I looked up at the peak and thought, "Oh, I'm never gonna get there," Laurie said, "Don't look at the top. It's a distraction. Just stay focused on your next step." He also added, "It's easier to take small steps. If you're going to be a good climber you start with the basics and get them down really well before you start to try the harder and harder stuff. I know people who have gone right to the hard stuff in their first 2 years of climbing and failed miserably." That one-step-at-a-time approach took Laurie to the top of Everest, the world's highest mountain.

Climbing the stairway to success is like climbing a mountain. They haven't installed escalators yet. Sorry, there's no easy way up. So just keep putting one foot in front of the other, and remember that little steps lead to big success.

Nothing is particularly hard if you divide it into small jobs.

Henry Ford automobile pioneer

If you get overwhelmed by the largeness of something, break it down into manageable components and start doing those.

Eve Shalley VP, Intrasphere

Make sure you don't make the task too daunting. If I take a briefcase full of work home, it will sit there. But if I take 2 things home, I'll do them.

John Caldwell president, CAE

The secret to realizing any long-term ambition is achieving dozens of short-term goals.

Rick Pitino basketball coach

When you're running a race, do it in segments and break it down into manageable pieces you know you can do. I qualified for the Olympic team by just approaching each competitor ahead of me as the next guy that I'd try and catch.

Jeff Galloway, training expert, columnist, Olympian

QUITOPHOBIA
AN INTENSE FEAR OF QUITTING

It's always too soon to quit.

Steve Spurrier football star and coach

There's a lot of fear out there. I mean I just read a list of phobias, and there were the usual ones like Acrophobia (fear of heights) and my personal favorite Ophidiophobia (fear of snakes). But would you believe there are over 500 other phobias? There's even Phobophobia (a fear of phobias). One poor little letter of the alphabet that doesn't seem to have a phobia is Q. So, in the name of science, I'd like to coin the world's first "Q" phobia – Quitophobia, an intense fear of quitting. I've discovered that many of the world's most successful people have severe cases of Quitophobia, which is actually a good thing, because it helps them persist and succeed.

You can tell Oprah has Quitophobia when she says, "I couldn't bear to think of myself as a quitter." And CNN founder Ted Turner, when he says, "Why do you think my own racing yacht is named Tenacious?...Because I never quit. I've got a bunch of flags on my boat, but there ain't no white flags. I don't surrender. That's the story of my life."

Refusing to quit helped Ted win the ultimate sailing trophy, the America's Cup. It also helped Lance Armstrong win the ultimate cycling trophy, the Tour de France, 7 times. He picked up Quitophobia from his mother who always told him, "Son, you never quit." Early in his career, Lance was competing in a triathlon, ran out of energy and was about to pack it in. His mother found him on the course and reminded him that he couldn't quit. So Lance walked to the finish line.

It's not that successful people don't think of quitting. Ben Saunders told me he thought of it when he was skiing 800 miles to the North Pole: "There was a whiteout for days where I couldn't see anything, and that's the closest I came to going completely nuts. At times, I would fall over and be disappointed that I hadn't fractured my wrist or broken my ankle, so I could get picked up and flown home with my pride intact." But Quitophobia kept Ben skiing all the way to the North Pole, and to become the youngest person to do it.

The bottom line is you don't necessarily need to be the smartest one, or the funniest one, or the best one. You just need to be the last one standing. And you get there by not quitting. So if you must have a phobia, I'd say forget heights, snakes, and the other 500 phobias, and go for Quitophobia.

I'm tenacious. I don't give up just because it's hard. The important thing is the stick-to-it-ness, so hang in there.

Bill Joy chief scientist, Sun Microsystems

In my line of work perseverance often makes up for a lack of brilliance. Just stick-with-it-ness.

Howard Weaver editorial page editor, *Sacramento Bee*

I was a very good cyclist and runner, but it was because I just didn't quit. It was as simple as that.

Dave Irvine-Halliday founder, Light Up the World Foundation

There's only one thing that can guarantee our failure, and that's if we quit.

Craig Breedlove 5-time world land speed record holder

Age wrinkles the body. Quitting wrinkles the soul.

Douglas MacArthur famous World War II General

NEVER NEVER

The 3rd way to persist is to take the advice of British Prime Minister Winston Churchill and "Never, never, never give up." Many successful people tell me a big reason for their success is, when the going gets tough, they just keep going. Deana Brown, CEO of Powerful Media, said to me, "It's a question of persistence. If I am successful, it is just based on the sheer fact that I don't give up. There are going to be things that are put in your way and they are surmountable. If you can't go over them, go around them. If you can't go around them, go under them. It's really that simple. I just don't give up."

Top real estate agent Elli Davis says, "Some days I have really rotten days. Everything goes wrong. Every phone call is a bad phone call. Everybody has bad things happen to them, and I think the most successful people are the ones who don't give up. The whole thing is just not giving up." Cobalt Entertainment CEO Steve Schklair says, "Every project and every great idea has a million setbacks. If you quit at the first setback or the 50th setback, then you won't succeed. If you don't ever give up you will eventually win. Never, ever, give up – ever."

Of course, when the going gets tough, the tough are tempted to give up. Like the other day, when I was hammering away at this chapter and it really wasn't going well. I had a couple of interviews set up with famous people who cancelled at the last minute. I couldn't get the quotes organized, my writing was even worse than usual. Finally, out of sheer frustration, I shut down the computer and started to walk away. Then it hit me: "I'm about to give up on the persist chapter. Is that ironic or what?" So I did what so many successful people say to do – I didn't quit. I fired up the old computer and just kept going. (I hate it when I have to follow my own advice.)

Inside of a ring or out, ain't nothing wrong with going down. It's staying down that's wrong.

Muhammad Ali 3-time world boxing champion

I just never give up. If it doesn't work one way, you try it another way. And you never give up.

Diane Bean VP business development, Manulife

Keep fighting. Never ever give up. That would be my favorite motto.

Donald Trump famous real estate developer, celebrity

My greatest point is my persistence. I never give up in a match. However down I am, I fight until the last ball.

Bjorn Borg 5-time Wimbledon tennis champion

NEVER GIVE UP

Frustration isn't the only reason we're tempted to give up. Don Norman, author of *The Way Things Work,* says things don't work so well when he hits those tedious parts of the job: "I write a lot of books and usually at some point I say, 'Why am I doing this? I hate it.' But you have to keep going, 'cause it's worth it in the end. That's true of all projects. There's always a part in the project that is dull and tedious, but essential. I just plow through it and take it step by step every day."

True North Records president Bernie Finkelstein also says, "I've learned to stick to it. Most people that succeed in the music business have one common trait and that is they knew how to stick to their plan, whether they had a plan or not. Just don't give up."

The problem with giving up is you could pack it in when success is just around the corner. Electronic Data Systems founder H. Ross Perot says, "Most people give up just when they're about to achieve success. They quit on the one-yard line. They give up at the last minute of the game, one foot from a winning touchdown." Sleep Country founder Gord Lownds adds: "A lot of people give up. They have an ideal vision of something and they get to 80% and then the last 20% is just too difficult to do, and so they either ignore it or they walk away. Focus on that last 20% even if it's really difficult. Don't give up. Go the extra mile. It's the willpower and the determination and not giving up that makes the difference between success and failure."

Adopt the "Never give up" strategy and you just might live as long as Sister Esther Boor, who was 106 when she said, "Sometimes I feel like I'm 150, but I just made up my mind I'm not going to give up." Amen.

Our greatest weakness lies in giving up. The most certain way to succeed is to always try just one more time.

Thomas Edison famous for hundreds of inventions

My parents were Holocaust survivors and my father told me 2 things: Don't be afraid and never give up.

Jeanne Beker host, producer, Fashion Television

Sometimes you want to quit. But you build character through perseverance.

Oliver Stone Academy Award-winning filmmaker

How you respond to the challenge in the second half will determine what you become after the game, whether you are a winner or a loser.

Lou Holtz renowned NCAA college football head coach

DEVELOP
BOUNCE-ABILITY

FAILURE	MISTAKES
CRITICISM	REJECTION
NEGATIVITY	PREJUDICE

The test of success is not what you do when you are on top. **Success is how high you bounce when you hit bottom.**

George Patton U.S. General, World War II

Recent medical data, which I can't seem to find right now, shows that successful people have a couple of abnormal skin conditions that help them persist through adversity. One of these is unusually thick skin. Wall Street investment banker Lise Buyer confirms this when she says, "A thick skin has helped me. You need resilience, because you will smack into some walls." Ouch! To lessen the damage suffered when hitting those walls, many successful people develop rubber-like skin that enables them to keep bouncing back from adversity. Singer/songwriter Naomi Judd said to me, "I think resiliency and flexibility are key. It's like my grandchild's toys, Weebles Wobbles. They don't stay down. I call it bounce back ability. You have to have that, 'cause life is going to continually kick you in the teeth."

Bounce-ability means you're resilient, so after being bent, pounded, stretched, and torn to shreds, you can spring back to your original shape and recover quickly. Dawn Lepore, CIO of Charles Schwab, says, "Resilience is important. You do have to be able to roll with the punches. If you're striving for something, things are not always going to go your way, and if at the first setback you say, 'It's never going to work anyway,' or you fall apart and don't believe in yourself, then you're not going to get very far."

When you get knocked down, how long do you stay down before you bounce back? I used to be devastated by failure, criticism, or rejection and mope around for days making myself even more miserable. I wish I'd talked to famous co-founder of Chiat/Day advertising Jay Chiat years ago, because he knows how to spring back quickly: "Everybody's gotta have failures. The point is how long are you going to remain depressed? If it's a week, you really have a problem. With me, it's about an hour-and-a-half max and then I get on with it. The ability to handle your failure and continue on, without getting depressed or diverted, is important."

Medical research scientist Eva Vertes says, "When I do not succeed it makes me angry. But it's not something where I get down and I can't get up again. It's, okay that failed, so let's do it again better, and let's succeed this time. It's being persistent." The bottom line is develop bounce-ability, so when you hit bottom you'll spring back into shape quickly. After all, it's much more fun to bounce than crash.

I don't fret. I don't crash. I land lightly and then I go off again. I bounce.
William McDonough
renowned architect

Failure stinks. I don't take it that well, but I tend not to let it get me down. The setbacks set you back, but I always bounce back.
Steve Jurvetson
renowned venture capitalist

I'm not very good with failure, but I would rate myself very high on being able to bounce back from failure. I give myself an "A" for resilience. I don't stay down for more than a couple of hours, not weeks or months.
Jessica Switzer president, Switzer Communications

The critical point is not how many times we don't succeed. The critical point is getting up quickly every time we falter. Because the faster we get up, the faster we can try again. The faster we're going to eventually succeed.
Silken Laumann
world champion sculler

BE TOO **STUBBORN** TO QUIT

A certain degree of stubbornness is really good.
Not blind stubbornness, but just saying, "I'm going to go for it.
I'm going to keep on going."

Patricia Seemann M.D., CEO of Sphere Advisors

Another way to persist is to be really stubborn. Now, I know stubbornness is sometimes seen as a bad thing, but when it comes to persisting it's not so bad, because it helps us hang in there when we're really tempted to quit. Renowned criminologist Kim Rossmo says, "I think stubbornness is a big one. You're never going to have a straightforward path, so you need to be able to handle the problems and the setbacks, and just keep going. I think tenacity is a really big part of it." Moving from the crime lab to the science lab, medical geneticist Josef Penninger says, "I think the most important thing is to be very stubborn. For one year, we had no idea of what was going on, but we just kept going at it and going at it and digging, digging, and we found some beautiful new principles of how pain is perceived. So you have to be very stubborn and many people are not willing to do this. It's not even believing in yourself. It's being stubborn and staying at it."

Musician/composer Wendy Watson told me that being stubborn helped her persist through financial setbacks: "Stubborn, my mother calls me. I do not give up. Once, when we were owed money, I was polite for 6 months, but when they just wouldn't pay I marched down to their offices with a good book and wouldn't leave until they paid me. I sat there and read for at least 6 hours – almost finished the book."

Being stubborn is a big thing that helps me through those 26-mile (42 kilometer) marathon runs – especially the last 6 excruciatingly painful miles. By then my legs are carrying picket signs and threatening to go on strike – "That's it, we're outta here." There's always a huge debate between the smart part of my brain and the stubborn part. The smart part keeps saying, "Hey, there's no logical reason in the world to keep running." It's right, but the stubborn part isn't logical and it says, "I refuse to give up." Stubborn usually wins over logic and that's the only reason I finish. Journalist Michael Wolff told me he uses the same kind of persistence strategy: "I think it's a matter of not accepting logic. The logic is that you probably cannot do it, so you may as well give up. Intelligent, well-balanced people probably give up. And I seem not to have that kind of logic."

So, whether you're running a marathon or jogging through the marathon of life, develop a good case of stubbornness. It'll keep you keepin' on.

I had that stubborn streak, the Irish in me I guess.
Gregory Peck Oscar-winning actor, *To Kill a Mockingbird*

I suspect one thing you need, whether you like it or not, is stubbornness. Because if you care about something, and you're willing to work hard at it, you also have to be willing to keep working hard at it.
Jennifer Mather renowned psychologist, animal behaviorist

It gives me great pleasure indeed to see the stubbornness of an incorrigible nonconformist warmly acclaimed.
Albert Einstein world's most renowned physicist

Hope begins in the dark, the stubborn hope that if you just show up and try to do the right thing, the dawn will come. You wait and watch and work: you don't give up.
Anne Lamot author

BE **IMPATIENTLY PATIENT**

BE SHORT-TERM **IMPATIENT** TO GET THINGS DONE	BE LONG-TERM **PATIENT** TO PERSIST FOR YEARS

DAILY	**YEARLY**

I'd win the impatience contest hands-down. Successful people are always in a hurry. **But you have to have the patience to stay at it and make it happen.** Perseverance is one of my strengths. I just don't give up.

Bob Ferchat chairman, Bell Mobility

The 6th way to persist is to be impatiently patient. Which means, on a day-to-day basis, be impatient to get things done. On the other hand, have the patience to persist for a long time. Successful people want to get things done now, not tomorrow, but they're also willing to hang in there until they succeed, no matter how long it takes.

Medical geneticist Josef Penninger said to me, "I'm very impatient. I want things done. Be restless. You can never be satisfied." Yet he also said, "We work doggedly in the lab for 2 years making genetically-modified mice, and often nothing happens." So Josef has the patience to hang in there, and that combo of short-term impatience and long-term patience helped him make some big genetic discoveries.

When I asked Ben & Jerry's co-founder Ben Cohen what he was good at he said, "I'm good at not sitting still." He's very impatient to get things done, but he also had the long-term patience to hang in there and make Ben & Jerry's a leader in its field. Famous playwright Neil Simon told me he was impatient, and when I asked him if he also had patience he said, "The first play I wrote took 3 years, so that's patience."

Being impatiently patient means that successful people tend to overestimate what they can get done short-term, and underestimate what they can achieve long-term. Nortel president Dave House says, "I find when people set 30-day or 90-day goals, they usually don't score very well. They think they can get more done in the short-term than they really can. But when they look at a year, 5 years, 10 years, they are usually amazed at how much they got done in that period of time. I have far, far exceeded the goals I set as a teenager and in my 20s." Many successful people echo the same thought. Comedian Steve Martin says he achieved much more than he ever thought he would, starting out as a stand-up comedian and also becoming an accomplished actor and writer. Henry Kravis, co-founder of KKR, the world's biggest buy-out firm, says he, too, far surpassed his early goals.

So, if you're short-term impatient, that's a good thing. Be restless and use that energy to keep you moving forward. Just make sure you also have the opposite side – the patience to persist and hang in there over the long haul.

I'm impatient. I get bored easily. It's very hard for me to sit still. Yet I can be very patient for something that I want.

Lisa Nugent co-founder, ReVerb

I'm a very impatient person. I don't have much of a future as a Zen monk.

Michael Schrage author, MIT Media Lab fellow

I'm very impatient, and rather intolerant of people who aren't impatient when things need to be done. I like to move fast. Sometimes you piss people off, so it's slightly dangerous to be impatient.

James Watson Nobel Prize, co-discoverer of DNA structure

I hate waiting. I want to get things done and move on to the next thing. My doctor said to take up yoga. I said, "I sit on planes a lot. That's as close as I get to yoga."

Francis Kay founder, marathon-photo.com

I've been on this script for 7 years. You've just got to be patient and hang in there until it's completed.

Russell Crowe Academy Award-winning actor

FAILURE
MISTAKE
FAILURE
FAILURE
MISTAKE
MISTAKE
FAILURE
FAILURE

DON'T
LOOK BACK

Promise to forget the mistakes of the past
and press on to greater achievements in the future.

John Wooden legendary basketball coach

If successful people were cars, they'd have very small rear-view mirrors. In fact, the great architect Frank Lloyd Wright had the rear window taken out of his Lincoln Continental because he said, "I never look behind." I don't recommend the don't-look-back strategy when you're driving, but I do recommend it when you're driving through life, because not looking back is one way successful people persist through all the failures, mistakes, and crap they encounter. Psychiatrist Ken Woodrow is one of many successful people who tell me: "Don't look back. Just keep moving." Acclaimed violinist Adrian Anantawan says, "In failures or discouragement, I never look back. I look back at what I've learned from them, but not the failures themselves. I look ahead at what I should do next."

Chicago Bulls basketball coach Phil Jackson, who coached Michael Jordan during his championship years, said Michael never looked back: "When he fails, he doesn't dwell on the failure part if it. He visualizes himself doing it successfully the next time." Real estate superstar Elli Davis told me she has the same attitude when it comes to selling houses: "Sometimes I've worked on a listing for 6 months. I've done everything, torn my hair out with it, and I lose the listing. Someone else gets it. It does upset me, but I don't dwell on it, because negativity will really get you down. You won't be able to get up the next morning and smile and go out and do it again. I try to see the good in spite of the disappointment, and just go on to the next one."

Bob Rogers, founder of BRC Imagination Arts, says, "You can't take failure personally. Sometimes you fail because there isn't anything wrong with you, but because the situation wasn't right. If you beat yourself up about it, then it really could be damaging, but it won't be caused by the event; it'll be caused by you." So how do we not take failure personally? I'd recommend developing a really bad memory: "Failure? What failure?" General Motors founder William Durant said, "Forget past mistakes. Forget failures. Forget everything except what you're going to do now and do it."

So, to persist through to success: 1. Have a really small rear-view mirror. 2. Don't look back. 3. Develop a terrible memory. It's not a formula that will help you pass a driving test, but it will help you persist through the failures and mistakes on your drive towards success.

> **I have bad performances all the time but you can't sit and dwell on them. Instead of thinking, "I am so bad!" you think, "What am I going to fix next time?"**
> **Naida Cole** award-winning classical pianist

> **I always look forward. I don't look back. What's gone is gone. Just keep moving forward.**
> **Sandra Ainsley** renowned art gallery owner

> **You must put that failure behind you and start to move forward. You cannot continue to linger in the failure...Yes you've failed, but now the question is very simple and direct: What are you going to do about it?**
> **Rick Pitino** basketball coach

> **Never take failure personally. In jobs and business, it usually has to do with a lot of things. It may not be your own fault and it's not that personal. You've gotta just shrug it off.**
> **Jay Chiat** co-founder Chiat Day advertising agency

UNBALANCED

PERSIST THROUGH UNBALANCED TIMES

We're always searching for balance in our lives. But in order to succeed at anything, we really need to focus on it, pour tons of time and energy into it, and give it all we've got. This means the personal side of life – like family, friends, leisure, entertainment, hobbies, sleep, sex, and even ice cream (oh no!) — get put on hold for awhile, and there's zippo balance.

The thing is, it's hard to be successful and balanced at the same time. How do I know? Because so many successful people tell me they're not balanced, at least when they're achieving success. Architect Susan Ruptash says, "When I was starting out I wasn't balanced, but I didn't see it as a bad thing. I was doing exactly what I wanted to do, which was pour every ounce of my energy into my work. So I wasn't balanced but it didn't matter. I could do things like read books later in life." Austin Hill is co-founder of a company called Zero-Knowledge Systems, but it could just as well be called Zero-Balance Systems: "I am absolutely not balanced. I don't believe you can really follow your passions by being balanced and objective and restrained. Those words just don't go with chasing your passion."

Successful people love what they do and have fun doing it. They're WorkaFrolics, not workaholics. But, there's often this nagging voice in their

> **I'm still trying to figure out how to balance my personal life.**
>
> **Omar Wasow** executive director, BlackPlanet.com

> **I've met a lot of great people and basically they're imbalanced. And that's why they are great.**
>
> **Kevin Kelly** founding executive editor, *Wired* magazine

> **I'm not balanced. I can't wait for Monday morning to come, so I can go back to work.**
>
> **Norbert Frischkorn** president, Frischkorn Audiovisual

heads saying, "I really should be more balanced." And that's not the only voice you hear when there's a chorus of friends and family reminding you to "Get a life." At times like that it can be tough to maintain your dedication and commitment to work that you're passionate about and believe in. So here's 3 tips to help persist through the unbalanced times:

1. Remember that being unbalanced is necessary for success, so don't feel guilty about it. Know that you will get balanced later, just not right now.

2. Don't try to achieve balance through moderation. Dave Lavery, the NASA whiz who sends robots to Mars, is typical of many successful people when he says, "You should do everything in excess. Find your passion. Find out what excites you and turns you on, then jump in with both feet. Do everything the best you possibly can with all of your energy, all of your focus, all of your being. Moderation is for monks."

3. Achieve balance over time, rather than on a daily or weekly basis. For periods of time, become totally unbalanced on the work side. Then shift gears and plunge yourself totally into your personal life, and become just as unbalanced on that side. Averaged out over time, you achieve balance. Dave Lavery says he may not see his family for a couple of weeks, but when he gets home, "I become obsessively super-dad and that balances it out." Catherine Mohr, product engineering manager for Aerovironment, says, "I'll work my butt off for 5 months and then go to Alaska kayaking for a month."

It took years for George Lucas to achieve balance. At first he was totally focused on creating great films like *Star Wars*, so his personal life was zip. George says, "I basically, just completely, was living [film] 24-hours-a-day, 7-days-a-week. That's all I thought about, that's all I did. I'd be working all day, all night...It was a great life." George achieved great success, then stopped filmmaking, and focused entirely on his family life, adopting 2 kids. So, at any one time, he was totally focused on either his work life, or his personal life, but averaged out over the long-term the two strike a balance.

The moral of the story is, you don't have to be balanced on a daily or weekly basis to achieve balance. Do it over time and you get the best of both worlds — success plus balance.

> **If you had asked me 10 years ago if I had balance in my life, I would have said absolutely not! I was trying to achieve my career, so that got top priority.**
>
> **Dawn Lepore** Chief Information Officer, Charles Schwab

> **If you're trying to do something that requires dedication and focus, you can't say, "I'm going to be balanced." Sometimes you just can't have a life, because the music comes first.**
>
> **Naida Cole** award-winning classical pianist

> **[My wife and I] didn't do anything. We didn't go anywhere. We just ate, and then went back to bed, so I could get up in the morning and train again.**
>
> **Lance Armstrong** world-champion cyclist

> **We can't succeed in this competitive society without super, super focus, and super hard work. But then you go and just hang out with your kids. So you get a balance.**
>
> **Steve Davis** CEO, Corbis

RELENTLESS FORWARD MOTION

RFM

You persist even when there doesn't seem to be any hope. **I say to myself, "I'm going to get there and I don't care if it kills me. I'm going to do it."** And sometimes it very nearly does kill you.

Ann Turner founder, Profile Recruitment Consultants

Our last example of ways to persist is to use RFM – Relentless Forward Motion. It's a term used by those crazy, I mean persistent, people in the sport of ultra-marathoning. This is extreme running, and I mean extreme, where runners race over 100 miles in a single day. And they don't always pick a nice, cool, scenic place to run. They pick scorching, desolate places like the Sahara Desert or Death Valley. So, just finishing takes incredible persistence. And the key is Relentless Forward Motion. They just keep moving forward no matter how bad the conditions, or how awful they feel.

Pam Reed used RFM to become the first woman to win the Badwater 135 mile run across Death Valley. Other runners stopped for a rest, massage or quick bite, but Pam only stopped once to shake what she thought was a rock out of her shoe. It turned out to be a huge blood blister, so she popped it and kept on running. Pam said, "I don't stop unless I have to throw up. And I never did." (Gee, I throw up just thinking about it.)

RFM isn't found only in ultra-marathoning. Successful people in all fields seem to have it. You can tell Nortel president Dave House has Relentless Forward Motion when he says, "When you decide you want to do something, just keep at it. Pursue it relentlessly. I kept working at it. I just worked real hard. I kept at it and I didn't let up. I worked weekends. I worked nights. Persistence always wins in the end. Just keep going in a direction." Michael Stadtlander, who is rated one of the world's top-10 chefs, has RFM. I attended an outdoor feast for 200 people at his farm and, as he was cooking up a storm, I asked him what led to his success: "You have to be persistent. You cannot just give up. If you fall down, you have to get up again, and keep on going until you get what you want. You cannot give up."

Sphere Advisors CEO Patricia Seemann works with many top executives in America and Europe and she says: "I sometimes wonder if energy and perseverance aren't the key differentiating factors. The CEOs I work with are just the last men and women standing. When everybody else has given up they just keep on going." So when you're passing through a rough stretch, and you're tempted to pack it in, I'd suggest keeping these 3 letters in the back of your mind: RFM. No matter what happens, just keep moving forward relentlessly. You'll be surprised at how far it'll take you.

Nothing happens until something moves.
Albert Einstein world's most renowned physicist

Success seems to be connected with action. Successful people keep moving. They make mistakes, but they don't quit.
Conrad Hilton founder, Hilton Hotels

My motto was always to keep swinging. Whether I was in a slump or feeling badly or having trouble off the field, the only thing to do was keep swinging.
Hank Aaron baseball home run record setter

The way to improve is to keep trying through the down times. Keep trying and keep banging on the door until it opens.
Nick Bollettieri tennis guru

Its good to move because if you stand still too long, people will come over and hang a coat on you.
Leslie Nielsen actor

THERE YOU HAVE IT
THE TOP 8 SUCCESS FACTORS

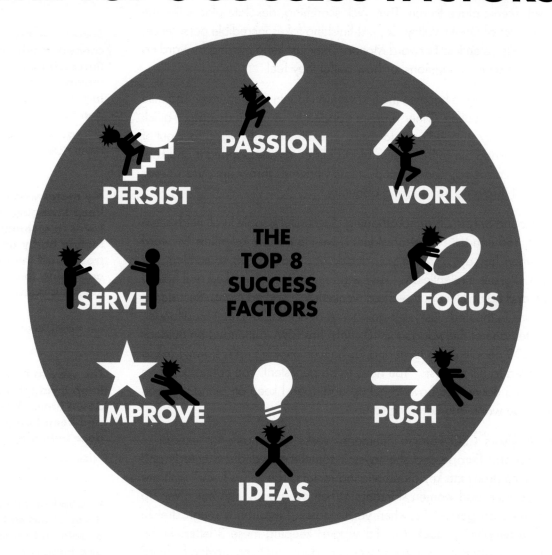

PASSION

WORK

PERSIST

SERVE

THE
TOP 8
SUCCESS
FACTORS

FOCUS

IMPROVE

IDEAS

PUSH

THE TOP 8 SUCCESS FACTORS
ARE THE CORE FOR SUCCESS

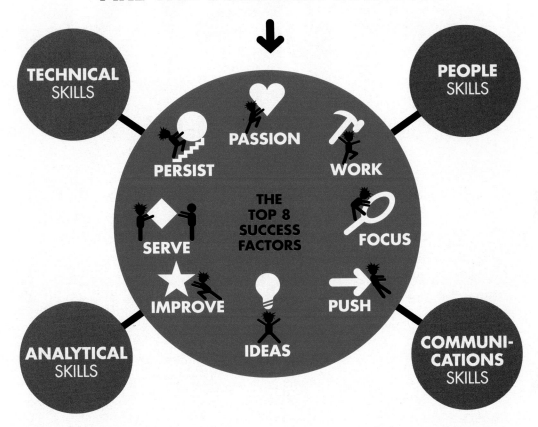

This book is about the *Top 8 Success Factors*. However, I'm not saying they're the only things you need to succeed. Depending on the field you're in, there are other things that are essential. I mean, if you're a surgeon or car mechanic it helps if you know how to wield a scalpel or wrench.

If you're a writer, you need to develop communications skills (although I seem to have survived without them). My point is, there are other things you pile on top, but you've gotta have these big 8, no matter what field you're in. These are the real deal, the fundamentals, the foundations for success.

SECTION B

So, now we know what really leads to success – *The Top 8 Success Factors.* But, when I started giving talks about the content in this book, I'd sometimes get to the end of the presentation and a person in the audience might say something like, "Successful people are just really smart," or "If you're good looking you've got it made," or, "Success is all due to luck."

Well, based on my research, smarts, looks, and luck don't lead to success. And, if we believe they do, we'll never get around to doing the things that really will make us successful – *The Top 8 Success Factors.*

So the purpose of this section of the book is to debunk the myths that smarts, looks, and luck lead to success. And while we're at it, I'll throw in one additional myth that needs to cleared up – The Reach the Top and Stop myth.

DEBUNKING THE SUCCESS MYTHS

MYTH #1   **SMARTS** LEAD TO SUCCESS

MYTH #2   **LOOKS** LEAD TO SUCCESS

MYTH #3   **LUCK** LEADS TO SUCCESS

MYTH #4   **REACH** THE **TOP** AND **STOP**

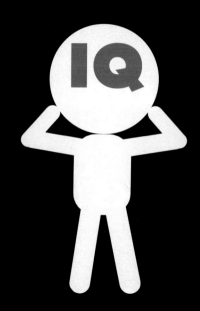

MYTH #1

SMARTS LEAD TO SUCCESS

274   **YOU DON'T HAVE TO BE SUPER SMART TO SUCCEED**

276   **YOU DON'T HAVE TO BE AN "A" STUDENT TO SUCCEED**

278   **LITTLE MARKS DON'T HAVE TO STOP BIG SUCCESS**

280   **EVEN IF YOU'RE NOT SMART, STAY IN SCHOOL**

282   **WORK WINS OVER SMARTS**

284   **PERSISTENCE WINS OVER SMARTS**

286   **IQ SHOULD REALLY STAND FOR IDEA QUOTIENT**

288   **LEARNING DISORDERS DON'T STOP SUCCESS**

290   **IF YOU'RE SMART, PLAY DUMB**

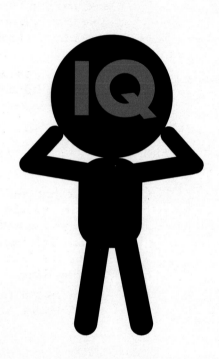

MYTH

SUCCESSFUL PEOPLE **ARE SUPER SMART**

REALITY

MANY **AIN'T** SUPER SMART

When you're a rocket scientist, people tend to assume that you're automatically a genius, which isn't true. **I'm not an idiot, but I'm not a super-genius either.**

Jaymie Matthews astrophysicist, mission scientist for MOST space telescope

There's a myth that being smart is the ticket to success. Of course, there are a lot of smart, successful people out there. But what surprised me was the high number of successful people who say they aren't that smart. In fact, when many were young, they were told they weren't smart enough to succeed. J.K. Rowling wasn't exactly told, she was shown: "We were seated according to the teacher's perception of our brightness, and after ten minutes she put me in the *dim* row." I'd say it was the teacher who was dim, since J.K. became a best-selling author, with her Harry Potter books selling millions.

Ken Woodrow told me, "The chairman of the pre-medical panel at college said that I didn't have what it took to be a good doctor and he would see to it that I never went to medical school. I cried." Interesting how Ken is now an M.D. and professor of psychiatry, at Stanford no less. Then there's Dave Lavery, who was told he was no rocket scientist, yet he actually became one. "When I was an undergraduate getting my degree in computer science, a professor said, 'Get out of computer science. This is obviously not your calling. Go do something else.' Twelve years later I was running the artificial intelligence research program for NASA." We think of scientists as the brainy ones, but on these pages you'll see Nobel Prize winning scientists, like James Watson, co-discoverer of DNA structure, saying they're not that smart. Nobel Prize-winning physicist Richard Feynman writes, "I was always a little behind. Everybody seemed to be smart, and I didn't feel I was keeping up." Physicist Greg Olsen says, "I'm an average guy. I'm not a genius. I didn't come from privileged people. I didn't go to the best of schools. I just fought my way up." A long way up, I might add, since Greg succeeded well enough to spend the $20 million for a ticket to go up on a space flight.

Robert J. Sternberg is an authority on human intelligence and, get this, he says he isn't even intelligent: "I bombed IQ tests when I was a kid." He adds this was actually a good thing "Because I learned in elementary school that if I was going to succeed, it wasn't going to be because of my IQ." He's right. In over 500 interviews I conducted, not one person, whether they were smart or not, said that being intellectually or academically smart was a reason for their success. So, if you're not the smartest, it doesn't mean you can't succeed. And if you are smart, it's no guarantee you will succeed. There is no IQ test on the real road to success.

> I don't believe you need to be that smart to be successful. I'm certainly not that smart. I can't even remember my own zip code. You don't need to be an MBA, and you don't need to be a CFA, and you don't need to be able to crunch numbers better than a Cray computer.
>
> **François Parenteau** CEO, Defiance Capital, named top independent analyst

> It's not that you're brighter than someone else. You know something that someone else doesn't know, and that's really the vital thing.
>
> **James Watson** co-discoverer of DNA structure, Nobel Prize

> Because of my work on Alzheimer's I've had people say, "Oh Eva, you're a genius!" But I'm not a genius. It's not brilliance that gets you somewhere.
>
> **Eva Vertes** scientist

THESE STUDENTS CAN SUCCEED

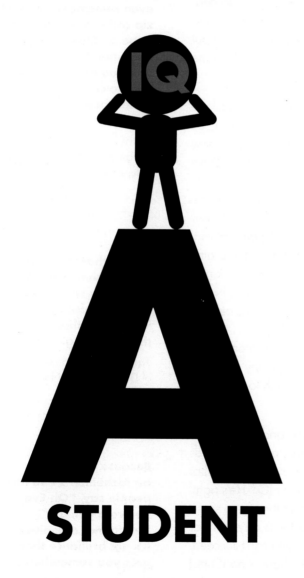

THESE STUDENTS CAN ALSO SUCCEED

Education is very important. Successful people never stop learning. And being able to get top marks is a great achievement in itself, so if you're an "A" student, be proud of it. These days, you'll need top marks to get into many courses. But what if you're trying really hard and you're still not making those "A" grades? Well, you can still go places. In my research I discovered that many successful people were not the smartest ones in the classroom. The letter that keeps popping up isn't A, it's C.

- Linda Keeler, VP and general manager of Sony Pictures: "I got C's all through high school."
- Nez Hallett III, CEO, Smart Wireless: "I graduated from high school with a C average, and from college with a C minus average."
- Star Wars creator George Lucas: "I was an average student. You know, I was a C, sometimes a C minus student. I was definitely an underachiever."
- Evangelist Billy Graham was a C student in high school.
- Fred Smith got a C at Yale University on his paper that described the concept for Federal Express overnight delivery (I'd say his professor should get an F).

If you look at the reams of other successful people who got a C-grade average, then I'd say C really stands for fully Capable. Hey, I even talked to professors who weren't great students in high school. Daniel Gilbert said, "I'm a professor of psychology at Harvard University, and a high school dropout. I think my proudest achievement is that I am listed between Dizzy Gillespie and Glen Campbell on the world's most famous high school dropouts website. I never did get a high school diploma." Leonard Susskind, a professor at Stanford and one of the world's top physicists, says, "I was a very bad student. Inner city, South Bronx, and just out on the streets all the time." Leonard flunked every course in college, except physics, but he was so good at that, his profs convinced Cornell to accept him as a graduate student. So he's a Ph.D. with no bachelor's degree.

The bottom line is, stay in school and try to get good grades. However, if you're just a C student, you can still achieve great success. After all, the word SUCCESS has two C's and no A's.

I was told that writing was my worst skill. I scored in the 400s on the SAT in the verbal areas. That's out of 800. So it's not indicative that I would ever make my living out of the artful arrangement of words.
Amy Tan best-selling novelist

I was a high school drop-out. I was bored and I didn't have good grades. Then I figured out what I wanted to do, went to college, and I was very focused.
Lee Smolin
theoretical physicist

I've been successful in business, and I'm not even a university graduate. I barely graduated high school.
Sandra Ainsley
renowned art gallery owner

My father was born in the backwoods, and he started out poorer than dirt. My mother taught him how to read and write, and he became a successful businessman and president of 2 large companies.
Sandy Hillmer VP, Knoll

SUCCESS

↑

LITTLE MARKS DON'T STOP **BIG** SUCCESS

CANDIDATE'S EXAMINATION RECORD	
Grade XII Courses	Percentages
Standard	
English (a)..32. ⎫	..6.6...
English (b). 34.. ⎬	
Algebra.....3.6. ⎫	.8.1....
Co-ordinate Geom & Trig. 45. ⎬	
Latin.............	‾
French...........	5.8...
German..........	‾
Physics...........	
Chemistry.........	..6.0...
Biology............	68...
Geology..........	‾
History............	62
Modern World Problems........	‾

NEED A GOOD LAUGH? HERE'S MY ACTUAL 12th GRADE REPORT CARD

As more evidence that little marks don't have to stop big success, I present myself. I'm living proof that you don't have to be a top student to succeed. They should stuff me and put me in a museum as an example of "Ignoramus Successus." Then kids who aren't doing well at school can look at me and go, "Gee, if that guy can succeed, I can too!"

I'd actually forgotten how dismal I was in school until one day when I was sorting through my father's old papers and I discovered my 12th grade report card. Dad must have saved it for those times when he needed a good laugh. And when I saw it, I chuckled. On the opposite page is my report card, in all its magnificent glory. As you can see, I was no Einstein. These days I probably wouldn't even make it into college.

I'm obviously not smart, yet, as I may have mentioned a zillion times, I have achieved success and wealth. I used to feel guilty that I got somewhere in spite of not being bright, like I was a freak of nature, the one lemming that didn't fall off the cliff. But now I discover I'm not alone. In *The Millionaire Mind*, Thomas Stanley says that most millionaires – not just some, but most – weren't top students, didn't get high marks on tests, and teachers thought they'd never go anywhere. Gee, now I feel better. I'm a member of "The Dumb Millionaires Club."

Even though I didn't do well in high school, I still went to college to study design, and, after a slow start, got good marks because I loved it. But I didn't end up with a degree, just a diploma in design. I don't have an MBA or a PHD. Or is it Phd? No wait, maybe it's Ph.D. (Guess you have to be one to know how to spell it.) Yet, it's interesting that I achieved more success in the real world, no matter how you measure it, than many of the people I know who have those degrees.

I'm not bragging, and I'm not saying school isn't important. I'm just saying you also need to do other things to succeed. I didn't let the fact that I wasn't an "A" student, or go to the top schools, stop me. I knew I had other strengths, although they were invisible at the time. Finally I found my calling, followed *The Top 8 Success Factors*, and achieved success. And now, when I look back at the low numbers on my report card, I really don't feel bad, because the numbers on my bank statement are much higher.

I was never an A student. Never. Everything that involved science, I got Ds, Cs and Fs. Ironically, I had a much harder time in school than I do in life, because my skill set is better fitted for life.

Ken Woodrow M.D., professor of psychiatry, Stanford

It still puzzles me today as to why I was not successful in school, because I was trying. But, for whatever reason, it didn't compute. Maybe I had a learning problem. Maybe it put a chip on my shoulder and I knew I needed to do better in my second act.

François Parenteau CEO, Defiance Capital, top independent analyst

We wanted to get Ph.D.s, but we dropped out of school [to start Google]. I'd worked for this guy who had gotten an MBA, and he said, "Oh, you don't really need an MBA. It's not that worthwhile for starting your own company. You should just go do it."

Larry Page co-founder, Google

STAY IN SCHOOL

SUCCESSFUL PEOPLE MAY **NOT** BE THE **SMARTEST**

BUT MOST STILL **GO THROUGH COLLEGE**

The best thing my parents did for me was say, "Hey, we don't care how long it takes, **we don't care what grades you get, we just want that piece of paper at the end."**

Nez Hallett III CEO, Smart Wireless

Smarts don't lead to success, but just because you're not wild about school or doing well at it, doesn't mean you should slack off or drop out. Many successful people didn't like school, were not top students, and were often tempted to drop out, but they still hung in there and struggled through. Nick Foster said to me, "There are those of us who just can't stand institutionalized learning. I never did very well in school. I was the annoying kid who really didn't want to play the game, but actually loved the learning." Nick hung in there, all the way through to a Ph.D., and it paid off when he won an Academy Award for computer-generated special effects in movies.

I was like Nick. No, not the Ph.D. or Academy Award part, the not liking school part. I remember sitting in high school trying to learn subjects I wasn't interested in, being taught by teachers who couldn't care less, (or worse, teachers who beat me if I gave the wrong answer), and staring out the window wishing I wasn't there. I'm sure some teachers also wished I wasn't there. But I hung in there and struggled through college, and I'm glad I did.

The thing is, even if you're not the smartest and you don't ace the exams, you pick up other things in college, besides a date. Like the ability to WORK and PERSIST. Those are some of the most valuable skills you learn, even though they're not on the curriculum. A study that tracked Harvard sophomores and disadvantaged inner-city youths for 60 years, discovered one of the key things education provided was the ability to persist. Kevin Eubank, Mississippi Parent of the Year and construction firm owner, says, "College shows that you've got the ability to hold out for 4 years to get a degree. It means a lot to an employer, that you're willing to stick to it, to make that commitment, to get that degree." Yes, college is like running a marathon. For most of us, it's not how we place at the finish that matters, it's just finishing that matters.

Successful people always keep learning, whether they're in school or not, and the nice thing about college is that it makes learning a lot more convenient than trying to do it on your own. It's like somebody preparing dinner for you. All you've gotta do is eat it. Yes, there will be times when it's hard to digest, and you won't always like it, or do well, but just hang in there and keep going. As the great British Prime Minister Winston Churchill said, "Personally, I'm always ready to learn, although I do not always like being taught."

The door to freedom is education…
Oprah Winfrey top talk show host

Education is the great equalizer. If you don't learn, no matter who you are, you'll fall behind. It's as true for the richest, most powerful people in the world, as it is for a kid.
Nathan Myhrvold chief technology officer, Microsoft

I've got a Ph.D. from Harvard, and 2 other degrees from Harvard, and it was a bit of a struggle. You've gotta push yourself.
Wade Davis explorer-in-residence, National Geographic Society

A really valuable skill is simply learning how to learn. It's lifelong learning. The whole idea behind a doctor's education is to get you started with the intention of learning for the rest of your life.
Greg Zeschuk game developer of the year

I'm not a particularly smart guy. Just an average guy raised on a farm in Indiana. **But I believe in working hard**, because that's what I was taught. I can't overemphasize hard work.

Randall Larsen founding director, Institute for Homeland Security

Of *The Top 8 Success Factors*, there are 3 often mentioned as being more important than being smart. The first is Work. Many people who are not intellectually smart or school smart still achieve great success thanks to a lot of hard work.

Jeong Kim is a good example. He started out working in a 7-Eleven store and ended up selling his technology company and pocketing $500 million, give or take a few million. He attributes his success to work, not smarts, saying there were lots of people smarter than him, but he compensated by working harder. David Zussman, president of the Public Policy Forum, told me he took the same approach: "I wasn't a particularly good student, or gifted, but I made up for it with hard work."

Nortel president Dave House got some good advice about work winning over smarts as he headed off to college. His father said, "Dave, there are going to be smarter guys at college, but just keep on working hard. Those smart kids will run out of ambition, or go see their friends, or decide to sleep in, and you'll move up a little bit. And the next thing you know, you'll be at the top of the class." Dave told me that advice turned out to be true: "I just worked real hard. I kept at it and I didn't let up. I worked weekends. I worked nights. And I won in the end."

Personally, I was never the smartest one in the room, but I compensated by working really hard. Other people may have had higher IQ numbers than me, but my numbers were higher when it came to hours worked. And, in the end, it paid off. The advantage for people like me is that smart folks may know a lot, but they may not know how to work hard, because everything comes to them so easily. Then when a tough situation arises they can't apply themselves, and the un-smart ones like me pull ahead.

The bottom line is, work wins over smarts. NCAA college football coach Lou Holtz summed it up well: "You might not be able to outthink, outmarket or outspend your competition, but you can outwork them." So, if you're not smart, remember that hard work can be your launchpad to success. And if you are smart, remember that even though you're a rocket scientist, you'll still have to work hard to reach the stars.

I was not necessarily the smartest kid, but I was the hardest working, because it's my ethic to work hard.

Nancye Green founding partner, Donovan and Green

I think that we're all born with a certain degree of intelligence, and mine is no greater than most, and a lot less than some. But I've always been willing to work hard. I attack things with great zeal.

Elliot Wahle, VP, manager Toys R Us, Times Square

Being intelligent is one thing, but being able to work really hard is another thing. I could coast through high school but I couldn't coast through university. I know lots of intelligent people who don't finish graduate school cause they just can't do the work associated with it.

Kim Rossmo criminologist

PERSISTENCE

WINS OVER **SMARTS**

It's not that I'm so smart, it's just that **I stay with problems longer**.

Albert Einstein world's most renowned physicist

The second of *The Top 8 Success Factors* that's more important than smarts is Persistence. Many successful people say they're not the smartest, but they still often go further than others simply because they keep persisting. Renowned economist Victor Fuchs says, "Most of the people around me were probably smarter than I am, but some of them were more erratic or irregular. They'd have streaks where they'd work hard for a while then they backed off. I just kept plugging away."

Persistence seems to win over smarts, not just for humans, but also for insects. Scientist Bob Full studies the biomechanics of creatures like cockroaches, so he can apply the same principles to multi-legged robots that he builds. When he was designing a robot for NASA that could maneuver over any terrain, even on the moon, Bob discovered it wasn't the smart robots with brains that did the best. The winner was a little robot with no brain and no sensors, so it didn't know where it was going and couldn't steer, but it had legs that just kept moving over and over and over. It wasn't the smartest, but it was the most persistent, and it ended up going places the smart robots couldn't.

The same goes for getting places in life. Sometimes it's better not to be too smart, because you do things that are logical and make sense, when hanging in there often makes no sense at all. Michael Wolff, journalist for *New York* magazine, says, "The logic is that you probably cannot do it, so you may as well give up. Intelligent, well-balanced people probably give up. And I seem not to have that kind of logic."

We think of Einstein as one of the smartest people the world has ever seen, yet the great man himself credited persistence not smarts for his success, when he said: "It's not that I'm so smart, it's just that I stay with problems longer." Neurobiologist Stanley Prusiner is another scientist who says he's not exceptionally smart, but he kept hanging in there looking for answers to what causes degenerative diseases of the central nervous system. His persistence paid off when he made the ground breaking discovery of a new class of disease-causing agents called prions, and was awarded a Nobel Prize.

The moral of the story? To light your way to success you don't need to be the brightest bulb on the tree, you just need to be the bulb that lasts the longest.

I don't consider myself especially brilliant. But I do have tenacity. Staying with it is important.
Gerald Durnell CEO, ProTech Publishing

In business, most of the people around me have accomplished more academically. But I'll tell you what I've done that they haven't. I never quit from a challenge. The tougher things get, the more I resolve to dig in and not let it beat me.
Nez Hallett III CEO, Smart Wireless

People of mediocre ability sometimes achieve outstanding success because they don't know when to quit. Most men succeed because they are determined to.
George Allen football coach, no losing season in 12 years

Nothing in this world can take the place of persistence... Genius will not; unrewarded genius is almost a proverb... Persistence and determination alone are omnipotent.
Calvin Coolidge 30th American president

IDEAS CAN TAKE YOU FURTHER THAN INTELLIGENCE, SO

SHOULD STAND FOR

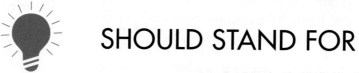

RATHER THAN INTELLIGENCE QUOTIENT

Imagination is **more important** than **knowledge.**

Albert Einstein world's most renowned physicist

The third Success Factor that is more important than smarts is the ability to come up with ideas. In fact, ideas are so important I think they should change the meaning of IQ from Intelligence Quotient to Idea Quotient. People who may not be intellectually or academically smart still achieve great success because they develop their ability to generate ideas.

Skills like observation, listening, and curiosity lead to ideas, and these are different than the skills emphasized in IQ tests and in school, such as reading, writing, and arithmetic. Both skill sets are important, but they're opposites. This explains why some people may not do well in school, yet do great in the real world. We've seen how Fred Smith only got a "C" in college when he came up with his great idea for overnight delivery, but in the real world that idea earned him an "A" when FedEx became a huge success.

I've worked with people in business who were considered very smart. They had photographic memories and could recite all kinds of facts, data, and statistics. Yet, not once, did I ever see them come up with an original idea. They were so concerned with getting the facts right that it held them back from creating anything new or innovative. Which brings us to a major difference between Intelligence Quotient and Idea Quotient – memory. A good memory is seen as an indicator of intelligence, and it certainly helps in school. However, memory can actually inhibit ideas, since it involves putting energy into repeating what already exists, rather than changing it into something new. Many creative people actually have terrible memories. Investor François Parenteau says, "I can't even remember my own zip code." Yet his ideas on investing made him the top independent analyst. Medical geneticist Josef Penninger told me he can't remember names or numbers: "I don't know my phone number. I have no idea what it is." Yet Josef's ideas uncovered the master gene for osteoporosis.

So, if you can't remember your phone number, it doesn't mean you can't succeed. Forget your Intelligence Quotient and work on your Idea Quotient. If you do have a good memory, set it aside once in awhile and give your mind the chance to come up with a new idea. Don't forget what the great scientist Einstein said: "Imagination is more important than knowledge." (Well, to be honest, I did forget. I had to look up his quote.)

I have a learning disability that makes it difficult for me to read a map or solve simple math problems. So I compensate by being creative, seeing things in a different way.

Jerry Della Femina one of the 100 most influential advertising people

If you aren't really familiar with a situation your ignorance can help you come up with an idea for a solution to a problem, because you try things based on common sense rather than a preconceived notion.

Wallace Eley president, Crossey Engineering

I don't think I'm a very smart guy. I can't read hard books and I can't do a lot of things that other people around me can do. So the only way I could remember things was to see their connections to other things in my mind's eye, and I developed the ability to see patterns.

Richard Saul Wurman creator of the TED conferences

MANY PEOPLE WITH **LEARNING DISORDERS STILL SUCCEED**

I performed poorly at school, when I attended, that is, **and was perceived as stupid because of my dyslexia.** I still have trouble reading.

Tommy Hilfiger fashion mogul

More proof that being intellectually or academically smart are not the top success factors, rests in the fact that people with learning disorders, such as dyslexia, still achieve great success. Even though their minds have a tough time making letters, words, and numbers compute, and they often do poorly in school and on standardized tests, they still reach the top in many fields.

- John Chambers, CEO of Cisco Systems, had dyslexia, and without a tutor probably would have flunked school.

- David Boies, a brilliant lawsuit lawyer, had dyslexia, couldn't read until the third grade, and preferred comics to books.

- Charles Schwab, the famous discount stock brokerage pioneer, had dyslexia, did poorly in English, and almost flunked out of college.

- Agatha Christie said, "I, myself, was always recognized…as the slow one in the family….Writing and spelling were always terribly difficult for me. My letters were without originality. I was…an extraordinarily bad speller and have remained so until this day." Gee, interesting how Agatha became the world's most popular mystery author.

So how did these people achieve incredible success in spite of dyslexia? Because, even though their brains are not wired for school smarts, they compensate by doing the 8 things that do lead to success. Peter Urs Bender credits WORK, "All my success is thanks to dyslexia, because in school I had to work my butt off, and then in real life when I worked my butt off, it worked." Virgin Records/Airways founder Richard Branson says having dyslexia forced him to put more WORK into being organized and writing things down. Craig McCaw says that dyslexia pushed him to use his imagination, so he became skilled at coming up with IDEAS, and that helped him become a pioneer in cellular communications. Actor Henry Winkler, who played "Fonzie" on *Happy Days*, had trouble with reading, spelling, and math, but he also says, "I'm very grateful for the struggle, because the struggle made me who I am." And, incidentally, he eventually got his Ph.D.

The success of all these people, in spite of dyslexia, is more proof that academic or intellectual smarts aren't critical to success. Sometimes it's the people who aren't seen as the smartest, that end up outsmarting everyone else.

I had to train myself to focus my attention. I became very visual and learned how to create mental images in order to comprehend what I read.

Tom Cruise popular actor

I couldn't read. I just scraped by. My solution back then was to read classic comic books because I could figure them out from the context of the pictures. Now I listen to books on tape.

Charles Schwab discount stock brokerage pioneer

I barely made it through school. I read real slow. But I like to find things that nobody else has found, like a dinosaur egg that has an embryo inside. Well, there are 36 of them in the world, and I found 35.

John R. Horner renowned paleontologist

IF YOU ARE SMART

PLAY DUMB

Never be the brightest person in the room because you won't learn anything.

James Watson Nobel Laureate, co-discoverer of DNA structure

We've seen that being smart is NOT a major factor in reaching success. So, what if you're one of those brainy people, a real rocket scientist or an "A" student? Well, that's great! Congratulations! Now forget about it. "What? Are you crazy? Why should I forget I'm smart?" Because, otherwise you might just sit back and rest on your intelligence and not achieve the success you could. That's why many smart people set their smarts aside.

Peter Drucker, a brilliant pioneer management consultant, says, "My greatest strength as a consultant is to be ignorant and ask a few questions." Richard Saul Wurman, creator of TED, the Technology, Entertainment, Design conference that brings together some of the world's smartest people, said to me, "I've worked hard at being stupid all my life. If I don't understand, I don't understand. I'm not afraid of being publicly dumb."

Being smart is all about knowing things, but as renowned architect Douglas Cardinal says: "Creativity has to come from not knowing, and when you come from knowing it just blocks all the opportunities and possibilities." Terry Gilliam, a very creative filmmaker and Monty Python member, told me, "If you're really dumb it helps. You always have to reach beyond what you think you're capable of and I'm dumb enough to think I can do it. That's the important thing."

Why is it that unsuccessful people are always trying to prove how smart they are, while successful people readily admit they're not smart? One reason is the successful ones know that being smart doesn't lead to success, so why brag about it? Another reason is, if you think you're smart, you may stop learning, because you think you already know it all. Nobel Laureate James Watson, famous co-discoverer of DNA structure, said to me, "Never be the brightest person in the room because you won't learn anything." And Satheesh Namasivayam, a smart guy who came from a small village in India and now has 3 Masters degrees, says, "I'm not smart, I'm just exploring and learning. I want to remain a fool all my life, so I'll keep learning. I admit my ignorance and that's my strength."

So, if you're smart and have a Master's degree, that's great. Now, to succeed in the real world, master the art of playing dumb.

I am more stupid about some things than others; not equally stupid in all directions; I am not a well-rounded person.
Saul Bellow
writer, Nobel Prize for literature

It is not what we know that is important, it is what we do not know....A man must have a certain amount of intelligent ignorance to get anywhere with progressive things.
Charles Kettering inventor, head of research for GM, over 300 patents

When I was a young reporter I tried asking profound questions and that didn't go anywhere, so you finally learn to just ask dumb questions.
Robert Hunter journalist, co-founder of Greenpeace

Some of the world's greatest feats were accomplished by people not smart enough to know they were impossible.
Doug Larson middle distance runner, Olympic gold medallist

All you need in this life is ignorance and confidence, and then success is sure.
Mark Twain humorist, novelist

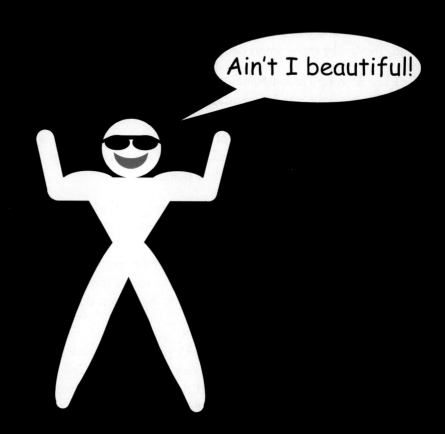

MYTH #2

LOOKS
LEAD TO
SUCCESS

294   **SUCCESSFUL PEOPLE ARE AVERAGE-LOOKING**

296   **EVEN MANY STARS LOOK ORDINARY**

298   **SPIKE'S LAW - THE UGLIER THEY ARE THE RICHER THEY ARE**

300   **GOOD LOOKS CAN BE A BARRIER TO SUCCESS**

302   **AVERAGE-LOOKING PEOPLE FIND OTHER WAYS TO STAND OUT**

304   **UNLIKE BEAUTY, SUCCESS IS MORE THAN SKIN DEEP**

| **MYTH** | **REALITY** |

SUCCESSFUL PEOPLE ARE
BLPs
BEAUTIFUL
LOOKING
PEOPLE

SUCCESSFUL PEOPLE ARE
ALPs
AVERAGE
LOOKING
PEOPLE

I don't see myself as pretty...It doesn't mean I don't love myself, but I do know what I am. **I'm a wonderful, bright, loving person, but I am not beautiful**.

Oprah Winfrey top talk show host

There's a myth that being a BLP, a Beautiful-Looking Person, is going to help you succeed. Well, if that's the case, how come most really successful people are ALPs, or Average-Looking People? I discovered this by accident when I started doing interviews at conferences attended by the rich and famous. I'd be standing there, looking around the room, wondering who to approach, and I'd spot a tall, good-looking man or woman, someone who had the image of an important person or company president. I'd stroll over and start chatting with them, only to discover they were the spouse of the person who was really successful, or they'd be a member of the video crew or media covering the event.

On the other hand, I was standing in line to go into a talk, and briefly chatted to an Average-Looking Person next to me. I asked him what he did and he said, "I'm in animation." Then we went into the talk, and he was the one giving it. It was Jeffrey Katzenberg, Hollywood powerhouse and producer of some of Hollywood's biggest animated hits, such as *Shrek*. Another time I shared a lunch table with an ALP named John Abele. Later I looked him up on the net and discovered he was worth over $5 billion. (If I'd known that I would have left him with the lunch bill.) Another Average-Looking Person I chatted with turned out to be Leonard Susskind, one of the world's top 3 physicists. And a woman who I didn't bother asking for an interview, thinking she was somebody's grandmother, turned out to be urban planning legend Jane Jacobs.

I'm a little slow to catch on, but eventually I learned to avoid the Beautiful-Looking People, the BLPs, and head straight for the ALPs, because the Average-Looking People are more likely to be the most successful ones in the room.

Looking back, I still remember the "Aha" moment when the whole looks myth dawned on me. I'd just come to a conference after auditioning actors to play the part of a company president in a film I was producing. So there I was, standing in a room full of extraordinarily successful people from many fields, and I thought, "Gee, none of these people would pass the audition to play the part of a successful person on TV or in an ad." It was at that moment I realized successful people in the media may be great looking, but successful people in real life are just everyday people. And that's not a bad thing. It's the media that has it all wrong.

I'm not saying looks won't help you get a date. I'm just saying looks aren't a key success factor. If you don't believe me, do the Limo Test. When I'm in New York or L.A. and a limousine the length of a football field pulls up to the curb, I always join the gawkers to see who will emerge. Maybe it'll be a gorgeous celebrity movie star. And who gets out but some everyday person — a real disappointment for the crowd, but always proof for me that looks DON'T lead to success. And if there is a Beautiful-Looking Person, it usually turns out to be the chauffeur for the Average-Looking millionaires.

The same applies to the Ferrari test. When a $300,000 Ferrari goes flying by, it's never a bombshell at the wheel. It's always an Average-Looking Person you wouldn't look at twice. But you look twice at them in the Ferrari, which I think is the point. Success and wealth are the great revenge for ordinary people.

EVEN MANY **STARS LOOK ORDINARY**

I was not a popular guy in high school. I did not have girls hounding me. But now I get up on stage and people are screaming, and I meet girls and they start crying and shaking. And it's still strange for me, 'cause **I'm not the kind of guy people were screaming about – ever**.

Ed Robertson musician, Barenaked Ladies

We tend to think celebrities are glamorous and different from we everyday people. However, many of the big stars are just Average-Looking People and we wouldn't notice them if we didn't know they were famous. Jay Leno became one of the top talk show hosts, but early in his career he was rejected for a movie part because he wasn't considered handsome enough. And, get this, the casting director said, while Jay was in the room, "We really like Jay, but we feel his face could be frightening to children." I wonder what that casting director's doing these days? Bob Dylan reached the top of the music world without being beautiful in either looks or voice. Once, when he was starting out, Bob couldn't get past his own security guards because they didn't recognize him. He simply said, "I can hardly blame them. Look at me."

I'm the world's worst celebrity spotter, because in real life they just look like ordinary people to me. Once, I asked a woman standing next to me for an interview. She agreed, so I started my recorder and said, "Please say your name." She said, "Naomi Judd." Boy, did I feel like a jerk! A famous country music star and I didn't even recognize her, because she looks just like you and me. Okay, much better than me. Another time, I bumped into famous actor Russell Crowe on the street and almost walked past him, until I realized who he was. Then, of course, I begged him for an interview. There are many other actors you could argue are better-looking, however, Russell's the Oscar winner, and it's a lot more than looks that got him there.

My celebrity non-spotting that really takes the cake was when I was at an event and Martha Stewart was standing right in front of me, but I didn't recognize her, because she didn't look like the woman we see on TV. Of course Martha is not bad looking, she even did some modeling to pay her way through school, but my point still stands. If she wasn't famous we wouldn't look twice at her. And when I interviewed her, she told me what put her on the map wasn't her looks but her books. She worked hard gathering information, writing books, and becoming a homemaking expert.

My experience tells me that most successful people don't have celebrity looks, and that also goes for many celebrities. So don't worry if you're an Average-Looking Person. Not winning the beauty pageant won't stop you from winning the success pageant.

> **So I'm ugly. So what? I never saw anyone hit with his face.**
>
> **Yogi Berra**
> legendary baseball player and manager

> **I can look pig ugly standing on my head – I'm plain, bony and brittle.**
>
> **Kristin Scott Thomas**
> actor

> **I was a fat kid and I struggled with body image the greater part of my life.**
>
> **Hawksley Workman**
> rock singer-songwriter

> **There's always a part of me that says someone's going to come along and find me out and discover that I'm really normal.**
>
> **Erin O'Connor**
> top fashion model

> **When I was a kid my ears stuck out. I just used to make fun of it. People would poke fun at me and I'd say, "Yeah, but I can hear better than you can." You just turn it to an advantage.**
>
> **Ian Craig** president, Nortel wireless division

SPIKE'S LAW OF LOOKS

THE **UGLIER** THEY ARE
THE **RICHER** THEY ARE

Here's 3 of the world's richest men: Warren Buffett, Bill Gates, and Rupert Murdoch – living proof that looks don't lead to success. Okay, I apologize for calling them ugly. They're not really ugly. They're just basic, average-looking guys, and that's a good thing. If they were great looking, it's unlikely they would ever have become as successful and as rich.

After doing much in-depth scientific research, consisting mostly of staring at thousands of successful people, I've come to the conclusion there is actually an inverse relationship between looks and success. The most successful people are rarely the best looking. This led me to develop "Spike's Law of Looks," which states: Less good looks leads to more success. Or to put it another way, the uglier they are the richer they are.

Just look at 3 of the world's richest guys: Bill Gates, Warren Buffett, and Rupert Murdoch – living proof that looks don't lead to success. Okay, to be honest they're not really ugly, but you get my point. They didn't make it on their looks. They're ALPs, Average-Looking People. I remember, long ago, when it first came out that Bill Gates was the richest person in the world, you could hear the gasps. Nobody could believe it. The media was saying, "How could this be? He's so, well, ordinary!" Yes and that's a good thing, because if Bill, or Warren, or Rupert were better looking they never would have achieved so much. Thomas J. Stanley backs this up in his book *The Millionaire Mind*. He studied hundreds of millionaires and many actually said they would not have become as rich if they were better looking.

Even in the entertainment field, where looks seem to really count, it's often the Average-Looking People who succeed. Barbra Streisand and Bette Midler weren't the most beautiful singers, but they made it to the top. Same goes for Mick Jagger. I first saw Mick on the Ed Sullivan show when I was a teenager and I remember thinking, "That's one ugly guy!" But he mesmerized me with his energy and charisma, and I still go to see him whenever I can. The Stones still always work incredibly hard to put on a great show because they can't sit back and coast on their looks. That's why they've outlasted all the pretty-boy bands, and risen to the top in terms of music and money. Other examples of Spike's Law in the world of entertainment are comedians such as Bob Hope, Phyllis Diller, Roseanne Barr, Rodney Dangerfield, and Jerry Seinfeld – all Average-Looking People who became millionaires because we average folks could relate to them. And they weren't afraid to poke fun at their looks. Henny Youngman joked: "I was so ugly when I was born, the doctor slapped my mother."

If you still believe that looks lead to success, just go to a website that lists the world's billionaires. There you won't find the names of the beautiful people we see on movie and TV screens. But you will find a lot of very Average-Looking People who make it happen behind the scenes, like director Steven Spielberg. One of the few stars with billionaire status is Oprah, and she became the top talk show host by being average-looking, not a glamour queen. Good for her. Oprah once said: "I don't see myself as pretty.... I'm a wonderful, bright, loving person, but I am not beautiful."

Spike's Law of Looks is great news for Average-Looking people. It means you can still become wildly successful. But what if you're a Beautiful-Looking Person and want to succeed? Well, you could always go for reverse cosmetic surgery: "Doc, can you make my nose a bit bigger and add more wrinkles." Or, instead, just focus on the 8 Steps that really lead to success instead of your looks. As Ann Turner, founder of Profile Recruitment Consulting says, "Successful people don't have time to look in the mirror."

BUT WHAT IF YOU ARE **GREAT LOOKING?**
MY SINCEREST CONDOLENCES!

If you're a Beautiful-Looking Person you automatically get noticed, so you may just sit back in your comfort zone.

Meanwhile, the Average-Looking People are working their butts off so they will be noticed. And that takes them much further than looks ever would.

Most successful people are ALPs, Average-Looking People. So, what if you were born a BLP, a Beautiful-Looking Person? Well, you have my condolences! What may appear to be an advantage can also be a huge disadvantage, because society often discounts people who are good looking. We envy them, but we discount them. It's the dumb blonde syndrome. If you're beautiful, you can't possibly be very smart or be able to do very much. This is nothing new. Long ago writer and art critic John Ruskin said, "Remember that the most beautiful things in the world are the most useless; peacocks and lilies for instance."

As a result of this prejudice, good looks becomes a barrier. Beautiful people often get shunted off into jobs based mainly on looks and get excluded from many fulfilling careers. They become the greeter at the PR event, not the one who produces the event. They become the one who models the designer clothes, but doesn't get the chance to design them. As someone once said, "Beautiful people don't go to medical school."

Good looks can even be a barrier in, of all places, Hollywood! It's interesting that Charlize Theron didn't win an Academy Award when she looked like a typical gorgeous Hollywood star. It was only when a lot of makeup was used to transform her into an Average-Looking Person in the movie *Monster*, that she took home the Oscar for Best Actress. Only when her beauty was hidden did she achieve the ultimate symbol of success in Hollywood.

Work, or lack of it, is one of the things that holds beautiful people back, because if you're good looking you may not learn to knuckle down and apply yourself. Actually, it's not your fault. You're pleasant to look at so you get preferential treatment in many little ways. Doors are opened for you. You get the best seats in restaurants. You're invited to all the parties. Recognition and appreciation come without having to do very much, so why should you bother to push yourself? There's a tendency to settle back in your comfort zone and, sadly, you may never live up to your full potential.

Meanwhile, the Average-Looking People, who don't get noticed, aren't distracted by a lot of attention, so they can be more focused and work harder at something that will give them the recognition and appreciation they're missing. They bust their buns doing what really leads to success and, in the end, that takes them further than looks ever would.

Of course there are examples of Beautiful-Looking People who achieve success in spite of their looks and these people deserve a special award, because they could have just married a millionaire. They could have hung around looking beautiful, like a nice painting on the wall. They could have sat back and coasted through life. But they didn't. They ignored their looks, worked their butts off, broke though the good looks barrier, and achieved something. Hats off to them.

The moral of the story is if you're beautiful and want to succeed it may not be easy. You'll need to work like a dog doing what really leads to success, and keep resisting that urge to coast on your looks. Take philosopher and writer Baltasar Gracian's advice: "A beautiful woman should break her mirror early." And that goes for men too.

AVERAGE-LOOKING PEOPLE FIND OTHER WAYS TO

STAND OUT

Why do so many Average-Looking People end up achieving great success? One reason is when you're not great looking you have to find other ways to stand out, or get a date.

When Farley Mowat, a best-selling author published in over 40 countries, was asked why he got into writing he said, "Well, I didn't have any other options, really. I was a short little character, ugly, mean. My eyes weren't crossed, exactly, but they didn't attract beautiful glances from women.... Since I couldn't do anything else that was useful, I discovered that I could sometimes hold a girl's attention for 2 or 3 seconds by telling stories, whispering in her ear. And that's what started me on my long career of being a storyteller."

Ben Saunders stood out by hauling a 400-pound sled 800 miles and becoming the youngest person to ever ski solo to the North Pole. When I went to meet Ben, I was expecting a huge guy with bulging muscles, and he turned out to be a nice, ordinary-looking guy who accomplished an extraordinary feat. He said to me, "Sometimes I'll go to speak at meetings and I'm accompanied by a fairly large guy who's a consultant. And when the two of us enter the room, people usually rush over and start shaking the big guy's hand and say, 'Oh, hi, you must be Ben Saunders.'"

Scott Shapiro stood out by becoming a top neurosurgeon. He performed surgery on Lance Armstrong when cancer had spread to his brain. But when Lance first met Scott he had to get past the fact that he just didn't look like the tall, handsome, well-groomed Hollywood version of a top brain surgeon. Lance writes: "I studied him: in addition to his resemblance to the sad-eyed Vigoda, there was the matter of what he was wearing: an Adidas sweatsuit with the signature stripes down the side and zippers at the bottom, over which he wore the more traditional lab coat. His hair curled over his collar. This guy is a brain surgeon? I wondered. He seemed entirely too casual to be a doctor at all."

Speaking of hair over the collar, Albert Einstein looked more like a homeless person than the world's most famous physicist. He was a plain-looking little patent clerk, but he stood out by discovering $E = mc^2$. Einstein refused to wear socks, dressed in shabby clothes and his hair was all over the place. Which prompted a little girl to write him the following letter:

DEAR MR. EINSTEIN, I AM A LITTLE GIRL OF SIX. I SAW YOUR PICTURE IN THE PAPER. I THINK YOU OUGHT TO HAVE YOUR HAIR CUT, SO YOU CAN LOOK BETTER. CORDIALLY YOURS,

ANN G. KOCIN.

I'm sure Albert appreciated Ann's concern, but didn't go for the haircut, because here's his philosophy when it comes to looks: "It would be a sad situation if the wrapper were better than the meat wrapped inside it." I think many successful people would agree.

UNLIKE BEAUTY

SUCCESS

REALLY IS MORE THAN SKIN DEEP

I really want to get the message across that good looks DON'T lead to success, because there are people out there who are literally killing themselves to become better looking. Even very successful people, like Micheline Charest. She was an ordinary looking person who, with her husband, created the Cinar children's TV show and became a multi-millionaire. *The Hollywood Reporter* once named Micheline the 19th most-powerful woman in Hollywood, ahead of Madonna and Barbra Streisand. She made it without being a beauty queen. But in spite of her great success, she still figured she needed to be better looking, so she went in for some nips and tucks, and died from complications following the plastic surgery. It's so sad, and all because of the looks myth.

I can relate, because for most of my life, I felt I was ugly. Recently somebody said to me, "Well, you're not really ugly," I said, "I don't know if I am or not. The important thing is, for much of my life, I thought I was." When I was young, scarlet fever left me with a weak eye, so at times I looked cross-eyed. Probably less than I imagined, but it seemed huge. Plus, my face was a minefield of zits ready to blow. And to top it off, I'm short. So, I definitely wasn't tall, dark, and handsome, the measure of a handsome guy in those days.

Another thing that I thought made me ugly was my nose. In hindsight it wasn't that bad, but I wished it was smaller. I felt that this thing sticking out on my face was somehow holding me back, which is ridiculous because I achieved success and became a millionaire with that nose. But it really bugged me, so when I had a lot of money I went for a nose job, and this was back when few men were doing it, so it was a big decision for me.

After the cosmetic surgery, I still wasn't tall, dark and handsome, but now my nose was smaller and I was expecting big changes in my life. You know, I'd get more respect, people would pay more attention to me, and I would become even more successful. And you know what happened? Nobody noticed. They didn't see any change. I'd go up to friends and say, "Notice anything different about me?" And they'd go, "You got a haircut?" Boy, after spending all that money, what a letdown! But it taught me 3 things: 1. We tend to exaggerate our flaws. 2. Other people don't care how you look, they only care how they look. 3. Being better looking won't change your life or make you more successful.

In fact, just the opposite happened. The minute I thought I was better-looking, I also became less successful. Why? Because it was one more factor in making me think I was a hotshot who'd made it. I figured I didn't have to work hard any more, so I sat back in my comfort zone and expected everything to come to me. And the only thing that came was a rapid downhill slide into failure. (See Myth #4.) I was actually more successful before the cosmetic surgery, because I focused on the things that really do lead to success, rather than my looks. For me that experience is personal proof that looks don't lead to success.

I can't be hypocritical and say don't have cosmetic surgery. If there's something about the way you look that really bothers you, do something about it. Get it out of the way so it ceases to be a distraction. Just don't think that being better looking is going to make you more successful. Because, unlike beauty, success really is more than skin-deep.

MYTH #3

LUCK
LEADS TO
SUCCESS

308 THERE'S NO LUCK IN SUCCESS

310 SURE SUCCESSFUL PEOPLE HAVE LUCK, BUT IT'S BAD LUCK

312 SUCCESSFUL PEOPLE TURN BAD LUCK INTO GOOD

314 LUCK DIDN'T MAKE ME A MILLIONAIRE

316 LUCK IS REALLY SPELLED W-O-R-K

318 LUCK = PREPARATION + OPPORTUNITY

320 SUCCESS IS NOT IN YOUR GENES

322 SPECIAL DOESN'T LEAD TO SUCCESS -
     SUCCESSFUL PEOPLE ARE ORDINARY PEOPLE

MYTH

SUCCESSFUL
PEOPLE HAVE
GOOD
LUCK

REALITY

THERE'S
NO
LUCK
IN SUCCESS

I don't believe in luck. I don't believe in fatalism. I believe in hard work and self-worth and doing it yourself.

Martha Stewart
Americas first female, self-made billionaire

One of the biggest myths about success is that it's all due to luck. I mean, that's the first thing we often say when we see others succeed, especially those who are obviously inferior to us: "Oh, they were just lucky!" However, in reality, luck has little bearing on success.

I'm not saying there's no such thing as luck. I'm just saying there's no luck in success. As award-winning science historian, author, and TV producer James Burke says, "Most people who are successful made their success. It may look like luck, because either they make it look easy, or because you misinterpret what is happening." Gerald Durnell, who made his fortune in the publishing business, says, "Luck doesn't really have anything to do with it. I don't believe in luck." Kimberly King, president of King & Associates Strategic Alliances, says, "I created a business, then lost that business, then made another one. The second one was the best, because when you rise again you know for sure that it wasn't a fluke. It wasn't timing. It wasn't luck. No one can say it was."

On the other hand, there are successful people who say they were lucky. Michael Stadtlander told me he considers himself "extremely lucky" to have reached the status of one of the world's top chefs. Acclaimed architect Will Alsop was telling me about his house in the Mediterranean, sitting there in the evening and thinking, "My God, I am lucky." But whenever people told me they were lucky, and we sat down and analyzed how they succeeded, it was always, I repeat always, because they followed the factors that really lead to success. So why do they believe they're lucky? First, because they don't think about their success, they just do it. And second, attributing their success to luck helps them stay humble. So rather than saying, "I worked my butt off and I deserve it, they simply say, "I was lucky." Humility is good, but I wish they'd stop using the L-word, because it sends the wrong message.

My mission is to eradicate the myth that luck leads to success, because if you believe in luck you may not do what really will lead you to success. I'm trying very hard not to use the L-word myself. I don't wish people "good luck" any more, and I'm asking you to do the same. Please help the cause and eliminate the word luck from your vocabulary right now. It won't be easy because it will just keep slipping out. But I know you can do it if you really try. And good luck with it.

> **As a rule, things don't just happen. There are some lucky moments, but you can't count on them to guide your life.**
>
> **Jerry Hayes** optometrist, founder, Hayes Marketing

> **Luck is a crook who ultimately destroys all those who are taken in by her.**
>
> **J.C. Penney** retail pioneer

> **Luck? I don't know anything about luck. I've never banked on it and I'm afraid of people who do. Luck to me is something else: Hard work – and realizing what is opportunity and what isn't.**
>
> **Lucille Ball** TV comedian

> **Someone receives a promotion, gets an important assignment, makes a major discovery, or moves into the president's office. "He's lucky," an envious person remarks…In reality, luck or the breaks of life had little or nothing to do with it.**
>
> **Kenneth Hildebrand** author

SURE SUCCESSFUL PEOPLE HAVE LUCK
BUT IT'S OFTEN
BAD LUCK

The only good luck many great men ever had was being born with **the ability and determination to overcome bad luck.**

Channing Pollock author

All the evidence shows that luck doesn't have much effect on success. Wait! I take that back. There is one kind of luck that does seem to affect success. Except it's not good luck, it's bad luck. Yes, successful people often experience more bad luck than good, for example a successful real estate developer, who prefers to remain anonymous, said to me: "When the oil business collapsed, I lost about $20 million. I had this friend who would call me and say, 'If it weren't for bad luck, you wouldn't have any luck at all.' I just started over and clawed my way back."

The great composer Beethoven had the bad luck of going deaf. Now, I'd say that being unable to hear is definitely not considered good luck when you're composing music or playing the piano. Yet Beethoven still made beautiful music and wrote some of the world's greatest symphonies. Another musician, Adrian Anantawan, had the bad luck of being born without a right hand, which could be a problem when you're trying to play an instrument like the violin. But it didn't stop Adrian and, with the help of an artificial hand, he became an acclaimed violinist. Oprah Winfrey had the bad luck of being born into poverty and was whipped and abused as a child. Whew! That's not good luck. More bad luck came along when, after a perm, some of her hair fell out and she ended up partially bald on the TV news. But all that bad luck didn't hold Oprah back and she went on to become one of the most successful people in broadcasting.

Many successful people have the bad luck of poor health, childhood disease, and accidents. Dennis Washington contracted polio when he was 8 years old. The other kids called him a cripple, but the little crippled kid went on to build an empire in construction, mining and railroads. Dale Chihuly had the bad luck of losing one eye in an automobile accident and, despite not being able to see in 3 dimensions, became one of the world's premier glass artists. Macy Gray had the bad luck of having a funny voice. Other kids poked fun at her, but Macy used her different voice to become a singing sensation.

Erik Weihenmayer had the bad luck of going blind at the age of 13. So, let's see... What would have been a good career choice for Erik? How about something where sight isn't really important, like music? So what does Erik pick? Mountain climbing! Now, correct me if I'm wrong, but is this not a sport where it might help to actually see where you're going? That's what I thought until I actually met Erik, well, sort of. My wife and I were climbing Mt. Aconcagua, the highest mountain on the American continent. At about 18,000 feet, we were struggling along when a climber passed us and, get this, he had bells on his wrist. I was hearing these bells ringing in my ears and thinking, "Am I delirious from the lack of oxygen at this height?" Then I realized the climber behind him was totally blind, and he was following the sound of the bells up the mountain. Turned out it was Erik Weihenmayer, and I can tell you, he's a much better climber without sight than I am with it. He passed my wife and me, beat us to the top, and has since become the first blind climber to summit Everest, the world's highest mountain.

I could fill many more pages with stories of other people who had incredibly bad luck and still reached great success in life. So if you're thinking you need good luck to succeed, forget it. You can succeed with good luck, bad luck, and no luck at all.

TURN BAD LUCK

INTO GOOD

People think good luck leads to success. Yet many people have amazingly good luck – health, wealth, everything going for them – and they fail miserably. Good luck can actually turn out to be bad because when it lands in people's laps they feel special. They think they don't have to go to any effort to make things happen, because good luck will take care of them. Las Vegas is full of down-and-out people who had good luck and made the big win when they were younger, then they sat back waiting for it to come again. And it never did. On the other hand, bad luck can be good for you because, like it or not, it pushes you to develop skills that good luck doesn't. When bad stuff happens you can't just sit back, you have to deal with it. So you learn how to put effort into things even when you don't want to. You learn how to problem solve and work your way out of difficult situations. You acquire skills that were missing when everything was going smoothly, and these skills help push you on to success. Bad luck never gets the credit it deserves, so on the next page let's look at some examples of rotten luck that ended up being good. (And I'm not being funded by the Bad-Luck Marketing Board – honest!)

Successful people often experience bad luck, but then they turn it around into something good. Ruth Handler was one of those people. After creating the Barbie doll, Ruth had the bad luck of being forced out of the company she founded. On top of that she got breast cancer. Talk about bad luck! But the experience taught her what women have to go through in coping with cancer, and she started a new company, Nearly Me, which sold prosthetic breasts. Her bad luck led her to success in an entirely new field.

We have no control over the situation we're born into, and landing in poverty is just plain bad luck. But Roberto Benigni turned that bad luck around and used it as a springboard to better himself, becoming one of the most popular comics of Italian cinema, and receiving 2 Oscars for his film *Life is Beautiful*. I'll never forget watching Roberto's acceptance speech at the Academy Awards: "First I must thank my parents for giving me the greatest gift of all, poverty."

Elizabeth Manley had the bad luck of catching the flu just before competing in figure skating at the Olympics. After years of preparation and training, that's about the worst luck she could have. Yet she says, "I honestly believe that one of the best things that ever happened to me was being sick...because I was feeling so miserable, I didn't get as nervous as I probably would have if I had been very healthy." And the reduced stress helped Elizabeth win an Olympic medal.

George Lucas' dream of being a race car driver ended when he had the bad luck of being involved in a nearly fatal car accident. But that bad luck turned his life around. Before the accident, George was going nowhere, and from the time he was in the hospital, his life started to accelerate, he took off into the world of filmmaking, and achieved great success with movies like *Star Wars*.

Steve Jobs had the bad luck of being thrown out of Apple computers, the company he founded. But, in hindsight, he says it was a great thing, as it pushed him to explore new creative areas. He started NeXT and Pixar, an animation studio that created *Toy Story*, the worlds first computer animated feature film. Then, in a cool twist of events, Steve took his new experience and NeXT technology back to Apple and steered it to a new generation of products and success.

Personally, I never think of myself as having bad luck, but I guess I've had my share. When I was a child I had the bad luck of having scarlet fever and I lost most of the sight in one eye. As a result, I see everything in 2D not 3D, which means I'm not great at any sport that involves balls flying at me. In grade school I loved baseball and would have given anything to be a ball player, but I was mediocre at best. However, the bad luck at ball sports turned out to be good luck in another area – photography. Since I see everything in 2 dimensions, the world always looks like a photograph to me. So, when I first picked up a camera, I was pretty good at photography right from the start, even without formal training, and later I became a successful advertising photographer.

So when bad luck falls in your lap, feel free to gripe about it for a while. But then turn it around and see if there's a way you can turn that bad luck into the springboard for your future success.

I'M SO UNLUCKY

BLACK CATS
ARE AFRAID
TO CROSS
MY PATH

A discussion of luck wouldn't be complete without a look at gambling and investing, since there's a myth that getting lucky in the stock market, casino, or lottery is the ticket to getting rich.

That's what I thought when I was a kid, so I tried my hand at gambling. What I didn't know is I have the world's worst luck. Well, maybe I'm not quite as unlucky as the forest ranger who's been struck by lightning 28 times, but I am unlucky. As a little kid, I used to go to the Bingo hall with my mother every week, but not once did I ever get to yell "Bingo!" Playing poker with my friends, I was always the first one out of the game. When I played the slot machines in Vegas I got nothing but a sore arm. I anxiously bought lottery tickets and waited for the big jackpot to land in my lap. It never did. Just as well. With my luck I would have been run over by the armored truck bringing me all the money.

Later in life, I started reading all those books about how people got rich by investing. Except nobody tells you the only people getting rich are the ones writing the books. They also don't tell you that investing is like going to Las Vegas, except you save the airfare. So I invested in the stock market, which turned out to be the signal for it to take the biggest, as stockbrokers say, "correction" since the Great Depression. I lost my shirt, which caused another great depression – mine. But, being a wise investor, I decided to seek help from the best financial advisors in the field. They helped me also lose my pants. Through all this, I learned why they call them stockbrokers. They helped me go broke. So I thought I'd invest in something safe like real estate, and I bought a commercial building. The real estate market immediately dropped like a rock.

Now, 15 years later, the building I bought is almost back to being worth what I paid for it.

I'm so unlucky, black cats are afraid to cross my path. But, being unlucky was the luckiest thing that ever happened to me. Because I stopped relying on luck to succeed, and started relying on me to succeed. I no longer wasted time gambling and investing, and I tossed away my lucky rabbit foot, since it wasn't any luckier for me than it was for the poor rabbit running around without one foot.

I had no control over luck, so I focused my energy on things I could control – doing what I loved, working very hard at it, serving others something of value, and following the other factors that lead to success. And that's what made me a millionaire – not luck. The same goes for other millionaires I've interviewed. They became rich the same way I did, not by investing, or gambling, or buying lottery tickets.

I'm not saying don't invest. (Because if I did I'd never be invited to speak at those big investment conferences.) The reality is most millionaires do invest, but usually only after they're rich and can afford to lose money. On the other hand, most millionaires don't gamble – period. I don't. I won't even buy a $5 lottery ticket, because I know the odds of winning are so low it's a total waste of money. There's a better chance I'll get hit by lightning – and, with my luck, that really could happen.

The bottom line is, if you want to get rich follow the 8 factors that really lead to success. And luck isn't one of them.

WORK LEADS TO LUCK

It really is true, **the harder you work the luckier you get.**

Donald Ziraldo co-founder, Inniskillin Wines

Luck doesn't lead to success but sometimes we think it does, because we never see all the work the so-called lucky person put into it. When I asked billionaire Gerry Schwartz if he believes in luck, he said, "I sure do. The harder I work, the luckier I get." Scores of other people reflect the same thought. Golfing legend Arnold Palmer said, "The more I practice the luckier I get." The oldest record I have of it being said is from U.S. president Thomas Jefferson in the 1700s: "I am a great believer in luck, and I find the harder I work the more I have of it." It's as true today as it was hundreds of years ago, if you want to get lucky, work hard.

Bob Ferchat, chairman of Bell Mobility, said to me, "I don't believe that luck is passive. Luck is something you work for. You say you're damned lucky because you achieved it, but you didn't sit there passively waiting for it. You went out and got it, dragged it in through the door, kicking and screaming, and then when it gets inside you say, 'Gee, I'm lucky.' But in the meantime, you've got scratches and bruises all over your body. That's luck."

There's a saying that luck is being in the right place at the right time. After doing this research, I'd say that luck is working hard to put yourself in many situations, some of which will end up being lucky ones – and if you're prepared you can take advantage of them. Those situations don't just happen. Effort and action come first, then luck might follow. Marine scientist David Gallo says, "I always have to take some action in order for the luck to happen. I go to a conference and I happen to sit next to somebody who can help me. Sitting next to them might be luck, but I had to take action and go to the conference first."

Success is something we work for, but luck is something we wait for, and if we sit around waiting for luck to land in our laps, we never do the work that really leads to success. Besides, sitting around waiting for luck to magically appear is just plain boring. The fun, the energy, the excitement comes from effort.

The moral of the story is, people talk about beginners luck, sheer luck, dumb luck, damn luck, blind luck, pot luck, lady luck – but when it comes to success, the only real luck is work-your-ass-off luck.

Luck is for Bingo Halls. Work is for life.

Rick Pitino prominent college basketball coach

I think luck comes to people who work hard. You've gotta work really hard.

Kevin Gilbert award-winning photojournalist

I worked hard and fortune smiled at me....Actually, it's what happens with a lot of hard work and just being tenacious.

David Oreck founder, Oreck Vacuum Cleaners

It's not luck. I think it's a lot of hard work, and it's a lot of focus, and being really determined.

Larry Burns head of Research and Development for GM

Luck is not going to come looking for you. They're not going to call you up and say, "Will you run for state senator?" It just doesn't happen. You've gotta put yourself in the way of success.

Bob Rogers founder, BRC Imagination Arts

LUCK
IS
BEING
PREPARED
WHEN
YOU
FALL
INTO
OPPORTUNITY

Luck is preparation meeting opportunity and the ability to recognize it...You can have preparation but not see opportunity. You can have opportunity but not be prepared. You need it all.

Pierre Lassonde president, Newmont Mining

It's not that successful people are luckier than other people. It's just that they're more prepared to handle the opportunities that come along. If you ask successful people the formula for luck, many will say, "Luck = Preparation + Opportunity." Back in the old days, that's what famous inventor Thomas Edison said. "We should remember that good fortune often happens when opportunity meets with preparation." More recently I was talking to Mickey Clagg, CFO of Bob Howard Investments, and he echoed the same thought, "Everybody used to say to me, 'Boy, you sure are lucky,' and I never felt like it was luck. Luck really is when preparation meets opportunity."

James Burke, award-winning science historian, author, and TV producer, told me about an opportunity that changed his life: "I was on a bus in Rome with a journalist friend, and he pointed out an ad in the paper that said a British television company required a director/reporter. And I said, 'If the bus stops, I'll phone them and make an appointment. If it doesn't stop, then I'll forget it.' The bus stopped, I got off and phoned them, got the job and here I am." That phone call led James to worldwide success with his famous TV series *Connections* and best-selling books. So I said to him, "It was pure luck that the bus stopped. What if the bus hadn't stopped?" James said, "I don't believe that life presents you with only one opportunity. A person lives 365 days a year for 60-plus years. That's a lot of days for opportunities to come along."

Yes, opportunities fly past every day, but they don't do us much good if we're not prepared to take advantage of them. It's like the baseball player who doesn't take the time to prepare and perfect his swing, then, when he has the good luck of being thrown an easy hit, he can't take advantage of it, and he strikes out. Joe Kraus, co-founder of Excite, says, "The traits of seeing an opportunity, building momentum, and having persistence, are critical elements to taking advantage of luck."

In the formula "Luck = Preparation + Opportunity," we have no control over the luck part. We only have control over what we do with the opportunities when they happen, and how we prepare for them. So don't sit back waiting for luck to happen. Prepare, prepare, prepare. Then, when the lucky star of opportunity zooms past, you'll be ready to reach out and seize it.

Successful people don't have more lucky breaks. They just work hard and recognize a positive opportunity in more situations than other people.

John Abele founder, Boston Scientific

You make your own luck. You see an opportunity and you take it, and you take it as far as you can.

Wayne Schuurman president, Audio Advisor

Every day prepare yourself for opportunities that are coming your way. I mean, it isn't about luck. It's about preparing yourself to be opportunistic – to seize the moment.

Pam Alexander CEO Alexander Ogilvy public relations

People talk about getting lucky, but a lot of it is just being receptive to what the world can offer and being prepared to take the gifts that come along. You need to be on the lookout for those gifts and be ready when they come.

Bruce Cockburn singer, songwriter

SUCCESS IS **NOT** IN YOUR **GENES**

SOME PEOPLE HAVE **GREAT PARENTS** → AND **DON'T ACHIEVE SUCCESS**

OTHER PEOPLE HAVE **TERRIBLE PARENTS** → AND **ACHIEVE GREAT SUCCESS**

You've got to do your own growing, no matter how tall your grandfather was.

Irish Proverb

The other day I heard a woman say, "Of course, he's successful. It's in his genes." I knew she wasn't talking about me, because I was wearing shorts. And I also knew she was wrong. Success is not in our genes. You can have the good luck of having great parents or the bad luck of having awful parents, but, either way, it doesn't have to affect your success.

Yes, the children of successful people are sometimes also successful, but it's not due to genes, it's due to copying. Kids learn by copying and imitating their parents. If your parents are successful, you spend many years watching them do the things that lead to success, and over time you automatically absorb the same things. I can't tell you how many times during my interviews successful people would say, "My parents told me a million times…" For example, surgeon Douglas Dorner told me, "One of my dad's sayings that I used to hate, just because I heard it so much, was 'A job worth doing, is worth doing well. If you're going to do something, do it well.'" With that kind of advice, no wonder Doug became a successful surgeon, just like his father.

My own dad had many sayings. One I heard over and over was: "If at first you don't succeed, try, try again." It ingrained in me that it's okay to fail and, knowing that, helped me succeed. He also told me work was important. Well, he never actually told me, he showed me. I could see he loved his work because he was always happily humming away while he worked. No wonder I turned out the same, except for the humming part. I love my work. On the other hand, my friend Billy's father hated work and did as little as possible. It's no surprise that Billy grew up avoiding work and, sadly, also avoiding success in life.

Of course, not all children of successful people become successful themselves. Many kids have everything going for them and end up total disasters. For whatever reason, they do none of the things that helped their parents succeed. Sometimes it's because their parents spoil them. Sometimes, kids being kids, they just go the other way. The sheer number of unsuccessful people who come from successful parents is proof that genes have nothing to do with success.

For further proof, look at all the people who reach incredible success even though their parents didn't. I mean, if success was in our genes, then Oprah could not have become one of the most successful people in broadcasting, because there was no history of big success in her family. Same with Quincy Jones. He told me his mother was carried away in a straitjacket when he was young, so there was little parental guidance to help him along, but he compensated by searching out successful people in the field of music and emulating them. Quincy said to me, "I watched people a lot. I got to watch Peggy Lee, Frank Sinatra, Picasso, Miles Davis. These people were good mentors." Quincy watched and learned from the greats and he too succeeded big time, winning an unprecedented 26 Grammy Awards.

You can't change your genes, but you can change the people you imitate. The choice is up to you, so why not imitate the best? In this book there are hundreds of great people to emulate and copy. They have terrific advice about what helped them succeed. Soak it up, jot down notes, and carry them around in your pants pocket. Then success will be in your jeans, even if it's not in your genes.

MYTH
SUCCESSFUL PEOPLE ARE
Special

REALITY
SUCCESSFUL PEOPLE ARE
ORDINARY

SUCCESS AND WEALTH ARE THE GREAT REVENGE FOR ORDINARY PEOPLE

I'm nobody special, I just followed a dream and achieved it...

Marc Gagnon speed skater, 3 Olympic gold medals

So, we've debunked the myth that smarts, looks, and luck lead to success. Now, there's one last myth we need to tackle – the myth of "special." Because, in the back of your mind you may think successful people are somehow special, and if you're just ordinary, well, you can kiss success goodbye. However, the reality is, most successful people are just ordinary, everyday people. Comedian Don Rickles says, "Famous people are deceptive. Deep down, they're just regular people. Like Larry King...One minute he's talking to the president on his cell phone, and then the next minute he's saying to me, 'Do you think we ought to give the waiter another dollar?'" Champion investor Warren Buffett, one of the world's richest men, admits he's nothing special: "I would not have been the most popular guy in the class, but I wouldn't have been the most unpopular either. I was just sort of nothing."

In the back of my mind I used to believe the *special* myth. When I started this book I was reluctant to approach famous people for interviews, because I thought they were special and I was just ordinary, so why would they want to talk to me? I believed they were born with special powers or some kind of hidden advantage. But the more I talked to them, the more I realized famous people go to the washroom, just like me. In fact, that's how I sometimes get interviews with them. At conferences, I just stand outside the washroom and wait for them to come out. Hey, I'd sit in the stall next to them, if it would get me an interview.

Now, after hearing hundreds of successful people tell me they're ordinary, I believe them. Like billionaire Gerry Schwartz: "I'm pretty much the same as everybody else. I put my pants on one leg at a time." Or this famous country music star: "There's really nothing special about Naomi Judd." Or media mogul and billionaire Rupert Murdoch: "I'm no different than other people." Or Emmy Award-winning news anchor Forrest Sawyer: "I'm just a guy. I screw up a lot. I try to make it through the day, like everybody else."

The message is this: Don't think you can't succeed just because you're not special. Being ordinary is the best starting point for success. Just do the same things successful people do, and you, too, can go from ordinary to extraordinary. Then someday I'll be standing outside the washroom waiting for you to come out.

You don't have to be a fantastic hero to do certain things...You can be just an ordinary chap, sufficiently motivated to reach challenging goals.
Edmund Hillary first climber to summit Mt. Everest

Some day they're going to find out that I am just your average Joe.
Gary Burton Grammy award-winning musician

I'm a human like everyone else, but I was being treated like I'm superhuman.
Michael Jordan superstar basketball player

You do not have to be superhuman to do what you believe in.
Debbi Fields founder, Mrs. Fields' Cookies

It's better to be an ordinary guy living an extraordinary life than the other way around.
Roy Siegfried & Roy, Masters of the Impossible

MYTH #4

REACH THE TOP AND STOP

SUCCESS

I REACHED THE TOP AND STOPPED DOING EVERYTHING THAT MADE ME SUCCESSFUL

The 4th Myth is what I call "Reach The Top and Stop." And, for this one I'll dig deep into my own personal experience. I'm just an ordinary guy, not smart, good-looking, or lucky, but by intuitively following *The Top 8 Success Factors*, I made it to the top of my field. Yes, I had a successful company, was winning the top awards in marketing and video, and I achieved millionaire status relatively early in my career. I was a true WorkaFrolic, who loved my work and had a lot of fun doing it. But then a funny thing happened, although it wasn't funny at the time.

Deep down in my gut I must have believed the myth that you reach the top and stop, because when I achieved success, I thought I should somehow change. I mean, isn't that what people do, make a few million, pack it in, and head for the beach? Or they reach success and now they're cool, so they go do some other cool thing. I didn't know what to think, but I guess I figured, since I'd made it to the top, I could just stop. I slipped into my comfort zone and, almost overnight, stopped doing all of the 8 things that had brought me success in the first place.

PASSION **TOOK ME TO THE TOP**

To reach success I always did what I loved and followed my passion for communicating information.

AND THEN I STOPPED

Then, after I reached success I started doing things I didn't love, like management. I'm the world's worst manager but figured I should do it since I was the president of the company.

WORK **TOOK ME TO THE TOP**

When I was reaching success I was a WorkaFrolic. I worked my butt off and had loads of fun doing it.

AND THEN I STOPPED

Once I was successful, I stopped working hard. I thought, "Hey, I've made it. Now I can relax."

FOCUS TOOK ME TO THE TOP

Reaching success, I ignored the money and focused on one thing – the client's project.

AND THEN I STOPPED

Buy me 20,000 shares!

But when I reached success I became distracted by the money. Suddenly I was more focused on the cash than on clients.

PUSH TOOK ME TO THE TOP

Reaching success I wasn't the driven type, but I kept pushing myself, even when I didn't feel like it.

AND THEN I STOPPED

But after I was successful I stopped pushing and sat back in my comfort zone waiting for everything to come to me.

IDEAS **TOOK ME TO THE TOP**

Reaching success I did all the things that lead to good ideas. But when I became successful I stopped doing them.

AND THEN I STOPPED

I thought I was a hot-shot creative guy and ideas should just appear like magic. But the only thing that appeared was creative block. I couldn't come up with any ideas.

IMPROVE **TOOK ME TO THE TOP**

Reaching success I always tried to improve whatever I did, and prided myself on quality. I wanted to produce the best.

AND THEN I STOPPED

It's good enough! On to the next project.

But with success came too much work. I found myself rushing projects just to get them finished and the quality fell rapidly downhill.

SERVE **TOOK ME TO THE TOP**

I reached success because I put all of my energy into serving clients. Making them successful is what made me successful.

AND THEN I STOPPED

Then, once I reached success, my ego expanded. I started thinking I was the important one, and I began to serve myself, rather than clients.

PERSIST **TOOK ME TO THE TOP**

Reaching success didn't happen overnight. It was a 10-year journey through failure, mistakes, criticism, rejection, prejudice and time. And I just kept persisting.

AND THEN I STOPPED

But once I reached success, I expected things to always work for me, and if they didn't, I wasn't willing to persist until they did. I just gave up.

I WAS **VERY SUCCESSFUL** AND ALSO **VERY DEPRESSED**

I thought the reason I'd become successful was due to the fact that I was, after all, just a very cool guy. It didn't occur to me that "I" had almost nothing to do with my success. It was all due to *The Top 8 Success Factors*, which I thought I no longer needed, since I'd "made it!"

I wasn't doing what I loved, working hard, or pushing myself. I had no focus, and couldn't come up with a good idea if my life depended on it. Improving myself was out of the question because I didn't know where to start. Gee, no wonder a black cloud appeared over my head and I grew steadily more depressed. But, being a guy, I knew how to fix it. I bought a fast car. It didn't help. I was faster, but just as depressed.

So I went to my doctor. I said, "Doc, I can buy anything I want, but I'm depressed. I never believed it until it happened to me, but it's true what they say: 'Money can't buy happiness.'" Doc said, "No, but it can buy Prozak." He put me on anti-depressants and the black cloud faded a bit, but so did all the work, because I was just floating along, and I couldn't care less if clients ever called.

And clients didn't call because they could see I was more interested in serving myself than in helping them. So they took their projects and money to others who would serve them better.

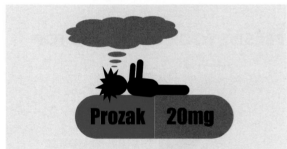

GOING FROM **SUCCESS** TO **FAILURE**

The bottom line is, after reaching success I sat back and stopped doing all the things that made me successful.

It didn't take long for business to drop like a rock. Our company was about to go under.

But, you know, facing failure was the best thing that could have happened. Because I went back to doing *The Top 8 Success Factors*.

THE JOURNEY BACK TO SUCCESS – – – – –

With no employees to manage, I went back to doing projects myself, which was what I really loved –being up to my elbows in a great project. Suddenly my **PASSION** returned, and that was step-one towards success.

Now **WORK** was fun again. So, instead of slacking off, I started to put in more effort and work harder. I re-discovered the satisfaction of work and turned into a WorkaFrolic once more.

We were rapidly going broke, and that was great! I mean, since there was no money coming in, I stopped being distracted by things like investments and started to **FOCUS** on clients and projects again.

The good thing about the adversity was it pushed me out of my comfort zone. But I had to **PUSH** myself through the setbacks and the huge self-doubt, that I could ever produce something great again.

PASSION

WORK

FOCUS

PUSH

TOOK 7 YEARS

SUCCESS

IDEAS

I felt like a washed-up creative guy whose idea-well was dry. But since we didn't have much work, I started exploring and experimenting in new areas. My eyes and ears opened up again. I began to listen and observe and suddenly the **IDEAS** started flowing once more.

IMPROVE

There weren't a lot of projects coming through the door, and that was also good, because it meant we could spend the time to **IMPROVE** each one. The quality of our work shot up and, we returned to the awards podium.

SERVE

Success had inflated my ego, but failure brought me crashing back to earth, and made me more humble. I realized it was actually more satisfying to **SERVE** others than to dwell on myself. I went back to bending over backwards for clients, and they sensed renewed passion and dedication, and returned with great projects.

PERSIST

The journey back to success didn't happen overnight. It required a lot of **PERSISTENCE** to hang-in through past failures, current mistakes, plus the criticism and rejection from others. I just kept my head down, took baby steps, worked my butt off, and moved relentlessly forward. And slowly, after 7 years of persistence, success returned.

THE TOP 8 FACTORS TOOK ME TO THE TOP

7 years to go from failure to success. Couldn't they build an express route?

And the thing is, I didn't succeed because I'm smart, good looking, or lucky. I'm none of those things, just an ordinary, everyday guy. And I was the same guy when I was failing as when I was succeeding. I didn't change. The only thing that changed were the things I did. When I was succeeding it was because I was doing the Top 8 things, and when I was failing I wasn't doing them. It's as simple as that.

I wish I could take credit for my success because, of course, I'm such a wonderful person, but the truth is I owe it all to *The Top 8 Success Factors*. And now, after many years of research, I realize they're the same factors that help most people succeed in life.

From what I read, they're nothing new. Throughout history, these same factors have been the key ones that have led people to success. And the great thing is, they're not complex. They're very simple things that anybody can do. I'm not saying success is easy, but I am saying the things that lead to success are easy to grasp.

Oh, and a little side benefit: Once I went back to doing what I loved and following the other success factors, the black cloud over my head disappeared altogether. I woke up one day and said, "I don't need Prozac anymore." And I threw it away and haven't needed it since. Except, of course, at income tax time.

EVEN THE BLACK CLOUD DISAPPEARED

SUCCESS IS A CONTINUOUS JOURNEY

When you achieve success, don't reach the top and stop. Success isn't a one way street, it's a continuous journey. Just keep doing the Top 8 things and that's how you'll continue to succeed. They'll take you on a journey to fun, satisfaction, wealth, ice cream, and maybe even happiness.

Enjoy the journey

As I sit here writing these last words I'm reminded of something Dave Lavery, the NASA whiz who sent Rover to Mars, said to me: "After working on a project for years to develop these machines, to actually see them sitting on top of a rocket in Florida, launching to Mars, is a very misty-eyed experience. Very steely, hard-edged, business and scientific guys have tears in their eyes as they watch the thing they have put so much time and effort into leave the ground."

And, you know, that's the way I feel, as I finish this book. Here I am, a grown man, actually crying. Tears are streaming down my face, mainly because after working on this book for so long, I'm on the verge of bankruptcy. I have no money, and I also have no friends since I neglected them for so long. Even my wife Baiba avoids me because she's afraid to hear the word success one more time. So, to the girl on the plane who started this, all I can say is thanks. It's been quite a journey.

ACKNOWLEDGEMENTS

THANKS

I'd like to thank all the people who were involved in the creation of this book. However, once they saw the title, most of them didn't want to be associated with it. But, let me just name a few people who made a big difference.

Thanks to my wife Baiba, for putting up with this thing that has taken over my life for so many years, and for her unquestioning support. Well, not exactly unquestioning. The usual question was: "When's it going to be finished?" But through it all, Baiba's constant good nature and laughs kept me going.

A big thanks to friend and business partner Thom Rockliff, who kept the lights on at the St. John Group and ran our company while I ran off to do this book. Thom is an amazing fountain of ideas and without his vast computer knowledge, I'd still be writing with a fountain pen.

Thanks also to all the great folks at the St. John Group, past and present, who pitched in and helped in so many ways, especially George Tunbridge and Seth Singer.

I'd be lost without Deborah Llewellyn. Well, actually it would be readers who'd be lost, since Deborah cleans up my language and punctuation and is our resident gramairian...grimmarean.... "Hey, Deborah, how do I spell grammarian?" Deborah also accurately typed most of the research that went into this book, no small feat when you consider the millions of words.

Thanks to producer Nicole Hillmer, who made it her personal goal to get this book out. A master of multi-tasking, Nicole is able to bounce from ideas, to writing, to editing, to graphic layout, to quote permissions, to her most difficult task – keeping me on track. How many times did I hear, "No, don't rewrite that for the hundredth time. It's fine. Leave it."

Thanks to business coach Joanne McLean. Writing is a lonely sport, and it's great to have somebody who will actually listen to me rant on and on about the stuff in this book. When I do it at Starbucks, people just walk away, but Joanne actually listens and helps me figure out what I'm really trying to say.

Thanks to great graphic designer and friend Frank Haveman for his frank criticism of my graphics and for help in improving them.

There isn't room enough here to thank all my friends who provided feedback and direction over the years. When nobody else in the world knows what you're doing, those few words of interest and support from friends help you keep going, and certainly make the trip less lonely.

Special thanks to all the test readers for slogging through various drafts of this book and giving fabulous feedback that made it what it is today. If you don't like it, blame them.

ACKNOWLEDGEMENTS

A sincere thanks to the hundreds of people who were kind enough to give me interviews, especially when I probably just walked up to you, shoved a recorder in your face, and asked, "What helped you succeed?" You knew nothing about me, or how I'd use your comments, but you seemed happy to help, and I can't thank you enough.

Sir Isaac Newton said, "If I have seen further it is by standing on the shoulders of giants." In my case, it's actually true. Because I'm so short, it's the only way I can see anything. I've stood on the shoulders of all the successful people in these pages. It's really your book. I'm just the scribe who records what you say, and tries to find the patterns that helped you all succeed.

If I interviewed you and your quotes are not here, it's my editor's fault for saying, "I don't care if they're great quotes, there's no room for them all!" So many quotes, so little space. Know that your interview made a valuable contribution to the research, and is standing by for future books. That sound in the background is my wife Baiba screaming, "No, no. Please, not another book!"

NOTE REGARDING TITLES: If you see a quote of yours in this book, the first thing you'll say is: "Hey that's not my current title." No, it isn't, because we could spend all our time just changing titles. So, the titles here are usually the ones people had when they were interviewed, either by myself or other sources. Thank you for understanding.

Richard St. John

Hank **Aaron** — **267** Original source of quote not found.

John **Abele** — **95, 319** Richard St. John

Dan **Ackroyd** — **31** Richard St. John

Sandra **Ainsley** — **155, 263, 277** Richard St. John

Karl **Albrecht** — **177** Karl Albrecht, Service Within: Solving the Middle Management Leadership Crisis, ISBN: 1556233531 Published by Irwin Professional Publishing,

Pam **Alexander** — **319** Richard St. John

Muhammad **Ali** — **254** Original source of quote not found.

Paul **Allen** — **57** Daniel Ichbiah and Susan L. Knepper, The Making of Microsoft (Rocklin, Calif.: Prima Publishing, 1991) (p.7)

Tony **Allen** — **112** http://www.nba.com/celtics/chat/allen_05010.html

George **Allen** — **285** Original source of quote not found.

Will **Alsop** — **309** Richard St. John

Robert **Altman** — **143** Roger Ebert, No one else would dare make this film, Special to National Post, December 21, 2001

Adrian **Anantawan** — **105, 251, 263** Richard St. John

Chris **Anderson** — **69, 83, 93** Richard St. John

Lance **Armstrong** — IT'S NOT ABOUT THE BIKE by Lance Armstrong, copyright © 2000 by Lance Armstrong **73** p. 196 **111** pp. 27,28 **115** p.244 **161** p.49 **165** pp. 221,222 **167** p. 21 **219** p.50 **239** p.184 **253** p.191 **265** p.220 **303** p.105 Used by permission of G.P. Putnam's Sons, a division of Penguin Group (USA) Inc.
163 CBC Radio News Report, Aug. 5, 2001, July 29

Neil **Armstrong** — **249** Original source of quote not found.

John **Bach** — **155** Jim O'Donnell, "The Stuff of an NBA Legend," Chicago Sun-Times, January 13, 1999

Francis **Bacon** — **147** Original source of quote not found.

Meredith **Bagby** — **79, 95, 159** Richard St. John

Janet **Baker** — **53** Richard St. John

James **Baker** — **211** Richard St. John

David **Baldacci** — **57, 212** David Baldacci, An overnight success, me? New Statesman, May 10, 1999

Lucille **Ball** — **309** Original source of quote not found.

Jim **Balsillie** — **75** Sean Silverthorne, editor, HBS Working Knowledge, "Research In Motion's Jim Balsillie's Wild Ride on a BlackBerry," special to MarketingProfs.com

Tyra **Banks** — **227** Original source of quote not found.

Roger **Bannister** — **115** Runner's World

Drew **Barrymore** — **199** A&E Biography: Steven Spielberg

Bill **Bartmann** — **115** Adrienne Sanders, Edited By Katarzyna Moreno, Forbes Magazine, "On My Mind: Success secrets of the successful", Nov 2 1998, Reprinted by Permission of Forbes Magazine © 2006 Forbes Inc.

Layne **Beachley** — **119** Courtesy of Nature, http://www.pbs.org/nature, a production of Thirteen/WNET New York

Diane **Bean** — **47, 99, 103, 233, 254** Richard St. John

Geoffrey **Beene** — **143** Fashion Television, Jan. 25, 2003

Jeanne **Beker** — **255** CBC Radio, Aug. 5, 2001, Dec. 20. 2000

Alexander Graham **Bell** — **77** Original source of quote not found.

Saul **Bellow** — **291** Original source of quote not found.

Ben & Jerry's **Ice Cream** — Thanks to Ben & Jerry's for permission to show their ice cream.

Peter Urs **Bender** — **289** Richard St. John

Roberto **Benigni** — **313** Roberto Benigni, Academy of Motion Picture, Academy Awards, 1998

Arthur **Benjamin** — **47, 59, 69, 93,181** Richard St. John

Janine **Benyus** — **93** Richard St. John

Yogi **Berra** — **131, 297** Original source not found.

Jeff **Bezos** — **51** Richard St. John

Keith **Black** — **27** On Stage, TED, 2000

Adam **Bly** — **23, 70** Richard St. John

Edward **Bok** — **185** Original source of quote not found.

Bono — **167** Bill Flanagan, U2: At the End of the World, Delta Publishing, August 1996

Nick **Bollettieri** — **267** http://visionarysports.com/tournaments.php

Jon **Bon Jovi** — **23** Passion is Key, Bon Jovi Tells Oxford Students, National Post, Associated Press, June 19, 2001

Sister Esther **Boor** — **255** Pam Belluck, "Nuns Offer Clues to Alzheimer's and Aging," The New York Times, May 7, 2001

Bjorn **Borg** — **254** Original source of quote not found.

Liona **Boyd** — **163** Jane Haughton : Conversations, as heard on CFRB Radio, Nov. 11, 2001

Ken **Bradshaw** — **103** Courtesy of Nature, http://www.pbs.org/nature, a production of Thirteen/WNET New York

Richard **Branson** — **103, 119, 161** Cal Fussman "What I've Learned: Richard Branson," Esquire, a Hearst Publication, Volume 137, Issue 1, January 1, 2002
147, 289 Pamela Wallin, Speaking of Success, (Toronto:Key Porter Books Limited, 2001), p.134

Craig **Breedlove** — **253** Original source of quote not found.

Sergey **Brin** — **225** Richard St. John

David **Brinkley** — **230** Original source of quote not found.

Martin **Brodeur** — **58** www.harryrosen.com

Joyce **Brothers** — **220** Original source of quote not found.

Haywood Hale **Broun** — **45** Original source of quote not found.

Bob **Brown** — **213** Original source of quote not found.

Deana **Brown** — **254** Richard St. John

Jamie **Brown** — **127** Richard St. John

John Seely **Brown** — **80, 81** Richard St. John

Theresa **Brown** — **178** Richard St. John

Robin **Budd** — **27, 59, 101, 106, 131, 157, 159, 207, 223, 225** Richard St. John

Michael **Budman** — **51** Richard St. John

Warren **Buffett** — **49** "Eye," Women's Wear Daily, October 10, 1985, p. 10
75 The Wall Street Journal, Sept. 30 1987, p.17
79 L. J. Davis, "Buffett Takes Stock" The New York Times Magazine, April 1 1990
193 Warren Buffett, CEO, Berkshire Hathaway, on stage, annual meeting, 1995
323 Beth Botts, et al., "The Corn-fed Capitalist," Regardie's, February 1986

Paul **Bunt** — **159, 198** Richard St. John

James **Burke** — **37, 107, 126, 127, 309, 319** Richard St. John

Philip **Burke** — **143, 215** Richard St. John

Edward **Burns** — **241** Bob Thompson, "This is not Woody's Manhattan," National Post, Nov 30 2001

Larry **Burns** — **85, 181, 317** Richard St. John

Charles H. **Burr** — **183** Original source of quote not found.

Gary **Burton** — **69, 99, 167, 195, 213, 323** Richard St. John

Edward **Burtynsky** — **117** Richard St. John

Lise **Buyer** — **37, 131, 234, 257** Richard St. John

John **Caldwell** — **83, 191, 251** Richard St. John

James **Cameron** — **103, 115** http://www.achievement.org/autodoc/page/cam0int-6 This page last revised on Feb 04, 2005 15:06 PDT ©2005 Academy of Achievement. All Rights Reserved.

Russell **Campbell** — **31, 95, 197, 225** Richard St. John

Douglas **Cardinal** — **291** On Stage - Idea City June 23, 2005

Dale **Carnegie** — **221** Original source of quote not found.

Ronda **Carnegie** — **179, 221** Richard St. John

Dr. Jean **Carruthers** — **133** CBC Radio, "Sounds Like Canada", with Shelagh Rogers, May 14, 2002

Carlos — **25** Richard St. John

David **Carson** — **29, 37, 53, 217** Richard St. John

Percy **Cerutty** — **118** Original source of quote not found.

John **Chambers** — **289** Original source of quote not found.

Ray **Charles** — **111** Quincy Jones, Q: The Autobiography of Quincy Jones, (USA: Doubleday, 2001) p.55 **231** Original source of quote not found.

Jay **Chiat** — **46, 55, 68, 129, 217, 241, 263, 257** Richard St. John

Julia **Child** — **145, 165** Mike Sager, "What I've Learned: Julia Child," Esquire, a Hearst Publication, June 1, 2000

Choclair — **57, 91** CBC Radio, Ontario Today, March 26, 2004

Agatha **Christie** — **289** Original source of quote not found.

Winston **Churchill** — **219, 235, 254, 281** Original source of quote not found.

Michele **Claeys** — **147** Richard St. John

Mickey **Clagg** — **189, 319** Richard St. John

Jimmy **Cliff** — **181** CBC Radio, August 8, 2004

Peter **Cochrane** — **249** Richard St. John

Bruce **Cockburn** — **159, 222, 319** Richard St. John

Paul **Coffey** — **59** Richard St. John

Ben **Cohen** — **9, 169, 195, 261** Richard St. John

David **Cohen** — **55, 161** Richard St. John

Naida **Cole** — **77, 263, 265** Richard St. John

Ornette **Coleman**   **143, 229** Original source of quote not found.

Carol **Coletta**   **36** Richard St. John

Joan **Collins**   **229** Original source of quote not found.

John Robert **Colombo**   **97** Richard St. John

Calvin **Coolidge**   **199, 285** Original source of quote not found.

Sherry **Cooper**   **45** Jacqueline Thorpe, Jazzing up the 'dismal science', Financial Post, May 6, 2002

Geoffrey **Cowan**   **159** Richard St. John

Ian **Craig**   **49, 161, 193, 197, 205, 297** Richard St. John

Russell **Crowe**   **22, 23, 51, 161, 261** Richard St. John

Tom **Cruise**   **103** Merle Ginsberg, "Risky Business," W Magazine, July 2002
289 Original source of quote not found.

Brian **Curtner**   **215** Richard St. John

Ken **Danby**   **59, 109, 181** Richard St. John

Bette **Davis**   **155** Original source of quote not found.

Elli **Davis**   **33, 53, 89, 91, 125, 137, 149, 183, 199, 205, 207, 225, 254, 263** Richard St. John

Lisa **Davis**   **98, 193, 197, 233,** Richard St. John

Steve **Davis**   **211, 265** Richard St. John

Wade **Davis**   **33, 51, 79, 179, 281** Richard St. John

Sky **Dayton**   **33, 75,125, 139, 217** Richard St. John

Bessie **Delaney**   **244** Amy Hill Hearth, Having Our Say: The Delany Sisters, First 100 Years, (Kodansha America, 1993)

Michael **Dell**   **201** Baiba St. John, meeting with Michael Dell

Robert H. **Dennard**   **137, 155** Jill Rosenfeld "Here's An Idea!",   Fast Company, issue 33, p.97

Daniel **Dennett**   **227, 229** Richard St. John

Simone **Denny**   **37, 51** Richard St. John

Jack **Diamond**   **49, 207** Richard St. John

Celine **Dion**   **109** Larry King Weekend, CNN, November 22, 1999 Interview, Aired April 7, 2001, 21:00

Thomas **Dolby**   **73** Richard St. John

Douglas **Dorner**   **71, 81, 103, 127, 145, 159, 161, 163, 187, 195, 215, 321** Richard St. John

Peter **Drucker**   **89, 227** Nortel Networks Management Conference, Oct. 2000
291 Original source of quote not found.

Faye **Dunaway**   **97** Mike Sager, "What I've Learned: Faye Dunaway," Esquire, a Hearst Publication, Volume 132, Issue 2, August 1, 1999

William **Durant**   **263** Original source of quote not found.

Gerald **Durnell**   **75, 97, 135, 195, 285, 309** Richard St. John

Bob **Dylan**   **297** Original source of quote not found.

Esther **Dyson**   **45** Richard St. John

George **Dyson**   **141** Richard St. John

Thomas **Edison**   **49, 53, 57, 111, 218, 221, 255, 317, 319** Original source of quote not found.
155 http://www.worldofquotes.com/topic/Science-and-Technology/1/
218, 355 Criswell Freeman, The Book of Florida Wisdom, Walnut Grove Press (March 1, 1996)

Brad **Edwards**   **119** Richard St. John

James **Ehnes**   **117** CBC Radio, "Richardson's Roundup", with Bill Richardson, May 1, 2002

Albert **Einstein**   **135, 181, 214, 225, 267, 259, 134, 135,284, 285, 286, 287** Original source of quote not found.
143 Original source of quote not found.

Michael **Eisner**   **123** Michael Eisner, Tri-State Camping Conference, American Camp Association, 2001
143 http://www.achievement.org/autodoc/page/eis0int-2 This page last revised on Feb 05, 2005 08:19 PDT ©2005 Academy of Achievement. All Rights Reserved.

Wallace **Eley**   **89, 127, 287** Richard St. John

Ralph Waldo **Emerson**   **183, 207** Original source of quote not found.

Eve **Ensler**   **47, 97, 109, 163, 165, 174, 175, 231** Richard St. John

Cathy **Enz**   **125** Jill Rosenfeld, "No Room for Mediocrity", Fast Company, Issue 50, p.160

Kevin **Eubank**   **227, 281** Richard St. John

Linda **Evangelista** **214** Original source not found.

Chris **Evert** **77** Criswell Freeman, The Book of Florida Wisdom, Walnut Grove Press (March 1, 1996)

David **Fairchild** **223** Criswell Freeman, The Book of Florida Wisdom, Walnut Grove Press (March 1, 1996)

Ralph **Famiglietta** **91** Richard St. John

Jerry Della **Femina** **123, 141, 221, 287** Hugh Delehanty - Editor-in-Chief, Modern Maturity, March-April 2000

Bob **Ferchat** **47, 95, 119, 135, 147, 195, 223, 229, 260, 317** Richard St. John

Emperor **Ferdinand** **231** Original source of quote not found.

Ruth **Fertel** **115** Adrienne Sanders, Edited By Katarzyna Moreno, Forbes Magazine, "On My Mind: Success secrets of the successful", Nov 2 1998, Reprinted by Permission of Forbes Magazine © 2006 Forbes Inc.

Richard **Feynman** "SURELY YOU'RE JOKING, MR. FEYNMAN!": ADVENTURES OF A CURIOUS CHARACTER by Richard Feynman as Told to Ralph Leighton. Copyright © 1985 by Richard P. Feyman and Ralph Leighton. **91** p.31 **131** pp.173,174 **275** p.247 Used by permission of W.W. Norton & Company Inc.

Debbi **Fields** **239, 323** Original source of quote not found.

Bernie **Finkelstein** **254** Richard St. John

Malcolm **Forbes** **213, 223** Original source of quote not found.

Henry **Ford** **60, 196** Original source of quote not found.
251 Criswell Freeman, The Book of Florida Wisdom, Walnut Grove Press (March 1, 1996)

Nick **Foster** **29, 281** Richard St. John

Michael **Frankfurt** **45** Richard St. John

Morgan **Freeman** **113** Jeanne Wolf, "With 3 Academy Award nominations, Freeman stands at the top of his Profession," The New York Times, reproduced in The National Post, April 6, 2001

Barry **Friedman** **107, 177** Richard St. John

Norbert **Frischkorn** **103, 104, 116, 119, 177, 264** Richard St. John

Victor **Fuchs** **285** Richard St. John

Robert **Fulford** **81, 193** Richard St. John

Robert **Full** **35** Richard St. John

Buckminster **Fuller** **227** Anthony Robbins, Unlimited Power, Simon & Schuster. Inc [New York: 1986]

Michael **Furdyk** **35** Richard St. John

Mary **Furlong** **125** Richard St. John

Marc **Gagnon** **322** Dave Stubbs "Toast of the nation", The Montreal Gazette, March 13, 2002

Cindy **Galbraigh** **137** Richard St. John

David **Gallo** **88, 129, 157, 317** Richard St. John

Jeff **Galloway** **251** Richard St. John

Alex **Garden** **158** Richard St. John

Gideon **Gartner** **56, 125** Richard St. John

Bill **Gates** **27** Michael W. Miller, "How Two Computer Nuts Transformed Industry Before Messy Breakup," The Wall Street Journal, August 27, 1986
39 Larry King: Millennium 2000, "Bill Gates Discusses Microsoft, Philanthropy and the Future of Computers," CNN, January 1, 2000
75 "Watching His Windows," Forbes ASAP, Dec. 1, 1997, p. 142
113 Lammers, Programmers at Work, Microsoft Pr (April 1, 1986)
123 James Kim, "Networking: On-line Will Be Key," USA Today, August 24, 1995
129 Janet Lowe, Bill Gates Speaks, John Wiley & Sons Inc., Copyright © 1998, p. 23, Reprinted with permission of John Wiley & Sons, Inc.
167 Bill Gates, "Column," The New York Times Syndicate, March 12, 1997

Frank **Gehry** **29, 101, 110** Richard St. John

Daniel **Gilbert** **213, 277** Richard St. John

Kevin **Gilbert** **37, 119, 129, 191, 317** Richard St. John

Terry **Gilliam** **57, 131, 143, 237, 291** Richard St. John

John **Girard** **81, 89, 105** Richard St. John

Rudolph W. **Giuliani**   **55** Rudolph W. Giuliani, Leadership (Hyperion: New York) pp. 210-211

William E. **Gladstone**   **229** Original source of quote not found.

Milton **Glazer**   **49** Richard St. John

Joseph Mark **Glazner**   **63** Richard St. John

Seth **Godin**   **185, 213, 241** Richard St. John

Baltasar **Gracian**   **301** Original source of quote not found.

Martha **Graham**   **163** http://womenshistory.about.com/cs/quotes/a/qu_graham_m.htm

Billy **Graham**   **277** Billy Graham, Just As I Am: The Autobiography of Billy Graham (Audio), Cassette (HarperAudio, 1997)

Richard E. **Grant**   **235** Richard E Grant, "The first cut is the deepest," Times On Line, August 11 2005

Macy **Gray**   **139** Muchmore music, Intimate and Interactive, Oct. 25, 2001

Don **Green**   **23, 183** Richard St. John

Nancye **Green**   **37, 159, 194, 283** Richard St. John

Wayne **Gretzky**   **49, 225** Original source of quote not found.

Susan **Grode**   **73, 79** Richard St. John

Matt **Groening**   **39, 128, 177** Richard St. John

Bill **Gross**   **74** On Stage, TED, 2000

Andy **Grove**   **227** Mike Sager, "What I've Learned: Andy Grove," Esquire, a Hearst Publication, May 1, 2000

Mark **Guibert**   **215** Richard St. John

Aman **Gupta**   **35, 179** Richard St. John

Paul **Haggis**   **221** Shelagh Rogers, "Sounds Like Canada," CBC Radio, August 31, 2005

David **Hajdu**   **147** Stephen Cole, "Folk heroes, flaws and all" National Post, June 12 2001

Monty **Hall**   **216** Original source of quote not found.

Nez **Hallet III**   **45, 161, 167, 181, 185, 227, 277, 280, 285** Richard St. John

Gary **Hamel**   **137** On Stage TED conference

Suzy Favor **Hamilton**   **157** USA Track & Field, Suzy Favor Hamilton teleconference quotes, May 22, 2001

Marvin **Hamlisch**   **159** Pamela Wallin, Speaking of Success, Key Porter Books Limited, Toronto P.243

Harvard   **281** Mary Vallis, 60-year study finds 7 keys to a long life, National Post, June 1, 2001

Derek **Hatfield**   **57, 111** On Stage idea City June 2005

Graham **Hawkes**   **25, 89, 251** Richard St. John

Michael **Hawley**   **33, 95** Richard St. John

Goldie **Hawn**   **96** Richard St. John

Jerry **Hayes**   **27, 35, 53, 63, 91, 97, 180, 181, 219, 309** Richard St. John

Ernest **Hemingway**   **133, 199** Original source of quote not found.

Heath **Herber**   **201** www.highgain.com, Highgain: The Business of Listening

Ken **Hertz**   **35** Richard St. John

Kenneth **Hildebrand**   **309** Original source of quote not found.

Tommy **Hilfiger**   **288** Original source of quote not found.

Austin **Hill**   **228, 264** Richard St. John

Edmund **Hillary**   **323** Original source of quote not found.

Sandy **Hillmer**   **277** Richard St. John

Conrad **Hilton**   **267** Original source of quote not found.

Oliver Wendell **Holmes, Jr.**   **123** Original source of quote not found.

Lou **Holtz**   **63, 283** Original source of quote not found.
255 Lou Holtz and John Heisler, A Championship Season at Notre Dame: The Fighting Spirit, Pocket; Rpt edition

Roy **Horn**   **323** Bill Zehme, What I've Learned: Siegfried & Roy, Esquire, a Hearst Publication, Volume 134, No. 2, Aug 1, 2000

John R. **Horner**   **289** Original source of quote not found.

Dave **House**   **109, 261, 267, 283** Richard St. John

Ron **Howard**   **51** CFRB Radio, Dec. 3, 2000

Michael **Howe**   **59** http://tinpan.fortunecity.com/harrison/ 624/practicetalent.htm, Original article by John Clare in The Daily Telegraph

Robert **Hunter**   **211, 291** Richard St. John

Robert **Hunter**   **291** Richard St. John

Lee **Iacocca**   **199** Original source of quote not found.

Irish Proverb   **320** Irish Proverb

Dave **Irvine-Halliday**   **253** Richard St. John

Pico **Iyer**   **147, 162** Richard St. John

Phil **Jackson**   **81** Phil Jackson and Hugh Delehanty, Sacred Hoops: Spiritual Lessons of a Hardwood Warrior, (Hyperion, New

York: 1995), p. 174.

263 Melissa Isaacson, "Head Master," Sporting News, April 27

Janell **Jacobs** — **61** Richard St. John

Douglas **Jacobs** — **191** Richard St. John

Willam **James** — **183** Original source of quote not found.

Anula **Jayasuriyk** — **75** Richard St. John

Mae **Jemison** — **130** On Stage, TED 2002

David **Jensen** — **23, 83, 91, 129, 169** Richard St. John

Norman **Jewison** — **69, 159** Richard St. John

Steve **Jobs** — **313** Steve Jobs, Stanford Commencement address, June 12, 2005

Colleen **Jones** — **37, 161** Robin Brown, Inside Track, CBC Radio, January 5, 2003

Franklin P. **Jones** — **231** Original source of quote not found.

Quincy **Jones** — Quincy Jones, Q: The Autobiography of Quincy Jones, (USA: Doubleday, 2001) **37** p.305 **107** p.194 **167** p.67 **191** p.303 **233** p.242

249 On Stage at TED 2002

81, 250, 321 Richard St. John

Michael **Jordan** — **39** Mark Vancil, "Playboy Interview: Michael Jordan", Playboy, May 1992, p. 51

49 Melissa Isaacson, "His Airness Shows He's Human" Chicago Tribune, March 20 1995

62 Original source of quote not found.

117 Michael Jordan, Rare Air, (Harper Collins: San Francisco, 1993), p.13

224 "Air Jordan on the Air," Chicago Tribune, July 17 1998

227 Bob Greene, Hang Time (New York: Double Day, 1992) p.154

231 Jan Hubbard interview with Michael Jordan, "One on One," Newsday, November 27, 1992.

323 Sam Smith, Second Coming: The Strange Odyssey of Michael Jordan: From Courtside to Home Plate and Back Again, (HarperCollins: New York), p. 90

Bill **Joy** — **109, 253** Richard St. John

Naomi **Judd** — **323, 257** Richard St. John

Steve **Jurvetson** — **32, 79, 89, 135, 143, 257** Richard St. John

Norma **Kamali** — **123** Fashion TV, June 1, 2001, Courtesy of FT-Fashion Television / CHUM Television, all rights reserved.

Dean **Kamen** — **69, 213** Richard St. John

Mitch **Kapor** — **35** Richard St. John

Francis **Kay** — **261** Richard St. John

John **Keats** — **221** Original source of quote not found.

Linda **Keeler** — **27, 199, 277** Richard St. John

Kevin **Kelly** — **264** Richard St. John

Charles **Ketterling** — **291** Original source of quote not found.

Chip **Kidd** — **25, 235, 239** Richard St. John

165 The Onion, June 2, 2004, Volume 40 Issue 22

Margot **Kidder** — **245** Margot Kidder, Toronto Star, August 18, 1979. p. G04

Nicole **Kidman** — **101** Lisa Gabriele, "Acting? What was I thinking?" National Post, interview from Britain's Radio Times magazine, Thursday, March 20 2003

113 John Hiscock, "Kidman carries on", National Post, May 7, 2001

Chris **Kilham** — **175, 185** Richard St. John

Jeong **Kim** — **101, 283** http://www.achievement.org/autodoc/page/kim1int-5 This page last revised on Feb 05, 2005 10:09 PDT©2005 Academy of Achievement. All Rights Reserved.

Gayle **King** — **137** Kenneth Best, "Q&A: Gayle King: on Television, for News and Talk, Too," The New York Times, March 29, 1998

Kimberly **King** — **54, 178, 309** Richard St. John

Stephen **King** — **38, 53, 79, 81, 99, 141, 149, 193, 241, 249** Reprinted with permission of Scribner, an imprint of Simon & Schuster Adult Publishing Group, from ON WRITING: A MEMOIR OF THE CRAFT by Stephen King. Copyright © 2000 by Stephen King

Martin Luther **King, Jr** — **121** Original source of quote not found.

Pannin **Kitiparaporn** — **139** On Stage at the AIC conference in Singapore

Ann G. **Kocin** — **303** Original source of quote not found.

Joe **Kraus** **210, 239, 319** Richard St. John

Kate **Laidley** **63** Richard St. John

Anne **Lamot** **259** Original source of quote not found.

Kathleen **Lane** **53** Richard St. John

Randall **Larsen** **53, 105, 282** Richard St. John

Jack Lenor **Larson** **35, 41,155** Richard St. John

Doug **Larson** **291** Original source of quote not found.

Pierre **Lassonde** **318** Diane Francis, "Miners in loafers' build golden empire," National Post, May 4 2002

Silken **Laumann** **61, 89, 225, 257** On Stage at the "Unique Lives & Experiences Series," Roy Thompson Hall, Toronto, Silken Laumann, World Champion Rower, Physical Activity Advocate and Author of Child's Play - Rediscovering the joy of play in our families and communities (Random House) www.silkensactivekids.ca

Dave **Lavery** **25, 47, 57, 107, 178, 221, 265, 275** Richard St. John

Mike **Lazaridis** **75** Deirdre McMurdy Fast Company, "Research in Motion Ltd.", issue 49, p.101

Norman **Lear** **157** Richard St. John

Jay **Leno** **297** Jay Leno, Leading With My Chin (New York: HarperCollins, 1996), p. 173

Dawn **Lepore** **34, 109, 217, 265** Richard St. John

Darlene **Lim** **37, 49, 101, 231** Richard St. John

Don **Lindsay** **193, 197** Richard St. John

Peggy **Lipton** **241** Quincy Jones, Q: The Autobiography of Quincy Jones, (USA: Doubleday, 2001) p.224

Brian **Little** **23, 155** Heather Sokoloff, "'Funny' Canadian Professor Voted Harvard's Favourite" National Post, May 13 2003

Jennifer **Lopez** **217** Entertainment Tonight, Feb. 14, 2003

Bill **Low** **123, 177** Richard St. John

Janet **Lowe** **27** Janet Lowe, Bill Gates Speaks, John Wiley & Sons Inc. Copyright © 1998, p. 2, Reprinted with permission of John Wiley & Sons, Inc.

Gord **Lownds** **75, 102, 125, 197, 248, 255** Richard St. John

George **Lucas** **265, 277** A&E Biography: George Lucas, Sunday January 27

Jerry **Lynch** **115** Runner's World Extr@,Friday, January 31, 2003

Douglas **MacArthur** **253** Original source of quote not found.

David **Macaulay** **95** Richard St. John

Joseph **MacInnis** **29, 69, 202, 219** Richard St. John

Elinor **MacKinnon** **11, 39, 61, 79, 125, 137, 149** Richard St. John

Margaret **MacMillan** **25, 135** On Stage, Idea City, June 2003

André **Malraux** **179** Original source of quote not found.

Elizabeth **Manley** **178** Lorna Jackson, World This Weekend, CBC Radio, January 26, 2002

313 CBC Radio, Lorna Jackson, World This Weekend, Saturday, January 26, 2002

George **Martin** **141** George Martin interviewed by Ed Bicknell , keynote for Canadian Music Week, Toronto, March 6, 1998

Linda **Martinez** **111** Richard St. John

Jennifer **Mather** **23, 75, 93, 259** Richard St. John

Jaymie **Matthews** **24, 52, 57, 73, 163, 274** Richard St. John

T.K. **Mattingly** **33,109** Richard St. John

Peter **Max** **69, 163, 164** Richard St. John

Albert **Maysles** **92, 93** Richard St. John

Eilish **McCaffrey** **95** Richard St. John

Paul **McCartney** Barry Miles, Paul McCartney, Many Years From Now, (1st American edition: Secker & Warburg Henry Holt & Company, 1997), **133** p.164 **163** p.171

157 CNN Larry King Live, Paul McCartney Discusses 'Blackbird Singing', aired June 12, 2001

Craig **McCaw** **287** http://www.achievement.org/autodoc/page/mcc0int-5 This page last revised on Feb 05, 2005 10:36 PDT ©2005 Academy of Achievement. All Rights Reserved.

William **McDonough** **55, 61, 89, 177, 211, 257** Richard St. John

Deborah **McGuinness** **71** Richard St. John

Don **McKeller** **27, 213** Richard St. John

Murray **McLaughlin** **159** Richard St. John

Brian **McLeod** **157** Shelagh Rogers, "Sounds Like Canada," CBC Radio, November 14, 2005

Alexander **McQueen** **23** Bridget Foley, "McQueen's Kingdom," W Magazine, July 2002
175 Courtesy of Fashion Television / CHUM Television, all rights reserved

Rick **Mercer** **39, 73, 105, 107, 165, 233** Richard St. John

Lorne **Michaels** **49** CBC Radio, As it Happens, June 18, 2002

Michelangelo **59** Original source of quote not found.

Ian **Miller** **197** CBC Radio, November 5, 1999

Wilson **Mizner** **51** Richard St. John
213 Original source of quote not found.

Isaac **Mizrahi** **207** Fashion Television, August 30, 2003, Courtesy of FT-Fashion Television (CHUM Television), all rights reserved

Catherine **Mohr** **129, 265** Richard St. John

Clement **Mok** **78** Richard St. John

Tom **Monaghan** **75** From SELLING THE INVISIBLE by HARRY BECKWITH. Copyright © 1997 by Harry Beckwith, By permission of Warner Books, Inc.

Louis **Monier** **69, 135** Richard St. John

Jean **Monty** **149,167,169,199** Richard St. John

Rick **Moran** **25, 201, 223** Richard St. John

Edwin **Moses** **77** Original source of quote not found.

Walt **Mossberg** **107, 197** Richard St. John

Farley **Mowat** **303** CBC Radio, "DNTO", with Sook-Yin Lee, July 9, 2005

Aimee **Mullins** **25** Richard St. John

Robert **Munsch** **33, 133, 165, 177** Richard St. John
113 CBC Radio, "Best of Richardson's Roundup", Bill Richardson, September 14, 2005

Rupert **Murdoch** **323** Richard St. John

Story **Musgrave** **31, 161, 165** Richard St. John

Nathan **Myhrvold** **83, 281** Richard St. John

Satheesh **Namasivayam** **179, 291** Richard St. John

Peter C. **Newman** **45, 245** Richard St. John

Jakob **Nielsen** **191** Richard St. John

Leslie **Nielsen** **267** CBC Radio, April 1, 2001

Drew **Nieporent** **51, 97** Richard St. John

Don **Norman** **71, 167, 255** Richard St. John

Greg **Norman** **160** Original source of quote not found.
235 Original source of quote not found.

Dr Izzy **Novak** **23** "Say What?", Elevate Magazine, New Year, 2003

Lisa **Nugent** **23, 55, 261** Richard St. John

Sherwin **Nuland** **50, 71, 154, 183** Richard St. John

Erin **O'Connor** **91, 297** Joan Lunden, Behind Closed Doors with Joan Lunden, A&E Television Networks, March 23, 2001

Greg **Olsen** **275** Elise Young, "Physicist Greg Olsen had an extra $20 million in his bank account," The Record, Hackensack, N.J. Knight Ridder/Tribune Business News, Mar. 30, 2004

Robert **Orben** **221** Original source of quote not found.

David **Oreck** **217, 317** Patty Kovacevich, "David Oreck Moves the Air," Airport Journals, August 2005

David **Ossman** **95** Richard St. John

Larry **Page** **45, 71, 179, 279** Richard St. John

Arnold **Palmer** **109 317** Original source of quote not found.

François **Parenteau** **45, 189, 219, 229, 275, 279, 287** Richard St. John

Louis **Pasteur** **211** Pauline Barrett, Success - Inspirational Quotations, Four Seasons Publishing

Jimmy **Pattison** **47** Tetsuro Shigematsu, "The Roundup," CBC Radio, August 1, 2005

George **Patton** **72, 256** Original source of quote not found.

Linus **Pauling** **127** Original source of quote not found.

Norman Vincent **Peale** **77** Original source of quote not found.

Gregory **Peck** **238, 259** Original source of quote not found.

Robert Young **Pelton** **85** Richard St. John

Kevin **Pennant** **199** Richard St. John

J.C. **Penney** **51, 309** Criswell Freeman, The Book of Florida Wisdom, Walnut Grove Press

Josef **Penninger** **71, 133, 166, 221, 261, 287, 259** Richard St. John

Irene **Pepperberg** **93** Richard St. John

Gail **Percy** **33, 135** Richard St. John

H. Ross **Perot** **255** Original source of quote not found.

Pablo **Picasso** **111, 139** Original source of quote not found.

139 Picasso and ceramics exhibit, Gardiner Museum of Ceramic Art, Toronto, ON

Steven **Pinker** **127** Steven Pinker, How the Mind Works, W. W. Norton & Co., New York & London, 1999

Rick **Pitino** **63, 105, 113, 147, 221, 211, 251, 263, 317,** Rick Pitino with Bill Reynolds, Success is a Choice, (Bantam Double Day Dell, Audio Publishing, 1997)

William **Plomer** **141** Richard Saul Wurman, Information Anxiety 2, Que

Channing **Pollack** **310** Richard St. John

Colin **Powell** **205** Original source of quote not found.

Lakshmi **Pratury** **113, 169, 183, 239, 249** Richard St. John

Steve **Prefontaine** **127** Runner's World Extr@, October 25 2002

Elvis **Presley** **231** Original source of quote not found.

Marcel **Proust** **131** Original source of quote not found.

Stanley **Prusiner** **285** Pamela Wallin, Speaking of Success, (Toronto:Key Porter Books Limited, 2001), p.91

Nido **Qubein** **105** Nido Qubein, international speaker, author, president High Point University

Karim **Rashid** **249** Nora Young, DNTO, CBC radio, Dec. 15 2001

John **Rawle** **177** Richard St. John

Cliff **Read** **83** Richard St. John, phone interview

Pam **Reed** **267** Scott Gold, "First Woman wins Badwater 135-Miler", Los Angeles Times, Jan. 6 2004

Joseph **Ricciuti** **193** Richard St. John

Ron **Rice** **55, 131, 216** Richard St. John

Don **Rickles** **323** Mike Sager, "What I've Learned: Don Rickles," Esquire, a Hearst Publication, Volume 135, Issue 1, January 1, 2001

Cathy **Rigby** **73** Cathy Rigby, Ten Words That I Never Forget, http://www.souloflife.com/tenwords.html, Sept. 12/04

Jason **Robards** **85** Original source of quote not found.

Ed **Robertson** **55, 103, 239, 296** Richard St. John

Chris **Rock** **51** A&E Biography: Chris Rock

John D. **Rockefeller Jnr.** **73** Original source of quote not found.

Thom **Rockliff** **113** Richard St. John

Anita **Roddick** **49** intro. **61** P.31 Anita Roddick, Body and Soul, (Crown Publishers, 1991), Permission granted by the author WWW.ANITARODDICK.COM

227 Anita Roddick, Business As Unusual, Thorsons, 2000, p.35, Permission granted by the author WWW.ANITARODDICK.COM

Bob **Rogers** **71, 149, 190, 263, 317** Richard St. John

Alexander **Rose** **110** Richard St. John

Harry **Rosen** **181, 201** Richard St. John

Kim **Rossmo** **71, 283, 259** Richard St. John

Paul **Rowan** **169, 193, 229** Richard St. John

J.K. **Rowling** **107** Margaret Weir, "Of Magic and Single Motherhood," Salon.com, March 31, 1999 Lindsey Fraser, Conversations With J.K. Rowling, Scholastic Inc, USA, October 2001 **167** p. 21 **275** p.17

Susan **Ruptash** **35, 45, 55, 69, 107, 159, 169, 177, 179, 264** Richard St. John

John **Ruskin** **301** Original source of quote not found.

Stefan **Sagmeister** **97, 101** Richard St. John

Joan **Samuelson** **105** Joan Samuelson, Running for Women, Rodale Press

Carl **Sandburg** **31** Original source of quote not found.

Tim **Sarnoff** **179** Richard St. John

Ben **Saunders** **29, 39, 55, 89, 91, 103, 178, 223, 253, 303** Richard St. John

Forrest **Sawyer** **129, 211, 249, 323** Richard St. John

Robert J. **Sawyer** **240** Richard St. John

Steve **Schklair** **55, 89, 254** Richard St. John

Michael **Schrage** **101, 261** Richard St. John

Wayne **Schuurman** **63, 93, 138, 168, 201, 319** Richard St. John

Charles **Schwab**   **289** Original source of quote not found.

Daniel **Schwartz**   **183** Richard St. John

Gerry **Schwartz**   **157, 219, 317, 323** Richard St. John

Steven **Schwartz**   **91, 93, 142, 163, 235, 241** Richard St. John

Albert **Schweitzer**   **183** Original source of quote not found.

Patricia **Seemann**   **267, 258** Richard St. John

Seth   **99, 101, 213** Seth, "A good artist must be torn between arrogance and self-loathing," National Post http://peteashton.com/mirror/seth/seth4.html

Eve **Shalley**   **113, 197, 251** Richard St. John

Issy **Sharp**   **27, 29, 61, 109, 146, 161, 175, 191, 195, 207, 239, 249** Richard St. John

Lindsay **Sharp**   **77, 82, 140, 178, 183, 229** Richard St. John

Martin **Short**   **49** "The Ground Breakers", Elm Street Magazine, October 2001

Paula **Silver**   **25, 39, 123, 175** Richard St. John

Peter **Silverberg**   **147, 199** Richard St. John

Gene **Simmons**   **61** Two Hundred Greatest Pop Culture Icons, VH1, 2003

Russell **Simmons**   **245** Russell Simmons with Nelson George, Life and Def, (Three Rivers Press, New York, 2001) p. 146

Neil **Simon**   **261** Richard St. John

Sinbad   **147, 213, 223** Richard St. John

Spike   **214** Original source of quote not found.

Laurie **Skreslet**   **81, 105, 115, 139, 163, 251** Richard St. John

Samuel **Smiles**   **143, 213** Original source of quote not found.

Fred **Smith**   **155, 235, 277** http://www.achievement.org/autodoc/page/smi0int-3 This page last revised on Feb 05, 2005 12:24 PDT ©2005 Academy of Achievement. All Rights Reserved.

John F. **Smith**   **201** Original source of quote not found.

Rick **Smolan**   **129, 239** Richard St. John

Lee **Smolin**   **27, 277** Richard St. John

Art **Spiegelman**   **139** CBC Radio, Eleanor Wachtel, Writers and Company, Jan. 6, 2002

Steve **Spurrier**   **227, 252** Criswell Freeman, The Book of Florida Wisdom, Walnut Grove Press

(March 1, 1996)

Baiba **St. John**   **65** Richard St. John

Richard **St. John**   **200, 314** Richard St. John

Michael **Stadtlander**   **89, 204, 267, 309** Richard St. John

Thomas J. **Stanley**   Thomas J. Stanley, The Millionaire Mind (Kansas City: Andrews McMeel Publishing, 2000) **279** p. 118   **299** p. 388

Robert J. **Sternberg**   **275** From SUCCESSFUL INTELLIGENCE by Robert J. Sternberg. Copyright 1996 by Robert J. Sternberg. Reprinted by permission of Simon and Schuster Adult Publishing Group.

Martha **Stewart**   **44, 135, 308** Richard St. John

181 Speaking at the TED 11 conference, Feb. 2001

Oliver **Stone**   **219, 255** Richard St. John

Ted **Stout**   **33, 133** Richard St. John

Bill **Stumph**   **135** On Stage, Idea City, June 2003

Joseph **Sugarman**   **219** www.usdreams.com, The Web's Resource On The American Dream

Sam **Sullivan**   **155, 191** Richard St. John

Leonard **Susskind**   **45, 123, 277** Richard St. John

Donald **Sutherland**   **101** Barrett Hooper, "I'm Not a Redford Type," National Post, Wednesday, May 28 2003

Jessica **Switzer**   **53, 101, 195, 201, 206, 229, 257** Richard St. John

Amy **Tan**   **155, 277** Richard St. John

117 http://www.achievement.org/autodoc/page/tan0int-4 Feb 05, 2005 12:31 PDT ©2005 Academy of Achievement. All Rights Reserved.

Don **Tapscott**   **135** Richard St. John

Ron **Tarro**   **187** Richard St. John

Bill **Tatham**   **75** Peter MacDonald, PROFITeer: The e-newsletter, Volume 4, Number 8 Dell Publishing

Julie **Taymore**   **55** Krista Smith, "An IrresistibleForce," Vanity Fair, a Conde Nast Publication, p. 123, February 2003

Sashi **Tharoor**   **179** Richard St. John

Freeman **Thomas**   **23, 35, 119** Richard St. John

Kristin Scott **Thomas**   **297** Original source of quote not found.

Anthony **Tjan**   **186, 187** Richard St. John

Rip **Torn** | **91, 233** Scott Raab, "What I've Learned: Rip Torn," Esquire, a Hearst Publication, May 1, 2001

Brian **Tracy** | **189** Original source of quote not found.
Ulrich **Trechsel** | **213** Richard St. John
Amber **Trotter** | **114** Runner's World Extr@, Friday January 17 2003

Cynthia **Trudell** | **111, 136** Richard St. John
223 Speech at the Sheraton Centre, Toronto,1999

James **Truman** | **100** Richard St. John
Donald **Trump** | **124** Original source of quote not found.
23, 254 Donny Deutsch,The Big Idea, CNBC, June 1, 2005

Alexander **Tsiaras** | **233, 249** Richard St. John
Kenneth **Tuchman** | **61, 73** Adrienne Sanders, Edited By Katarzyna Moreno, Forbes Magazine, "On My Mind: Success secrets of the successful", Nov 2 1998, Reprinted by Permission of Forbes Magazine © 2006 Forbes Inc.

Ted **Turner** | **45** "Southern Ocean Racing Circuit," New York Times, p. 46, Mar. 30 1966
45 Gary Smith,"What Makes Ted Run?", Sports Illustrated,p.78, June 23, 1986
49, 253 Peter Ross Range, "Playboy interview: Ted Turner", Playboy, August 1978, P.74
85 Maynard Good Stoddard, "Cable TV's Ted Turner: Spirited Skipper of CNN", The Saturday Evening Post, March, 1984
122 Turner Vows Worldwide CNN as Cable's Coming Tops Edinburgh Agenda," Variety, Sept. 8 1982, p.96

Ann **Turner** | **191, 207, 211, 233, 266, 299** Richard St. John
Shania **Twain** | **192, 193** Adam Sternbergh , "Pop's well-built cabinet" National Post, April 5 2003
Mark **Twain** | **251** Pauline Barrett, Success - Inspirational Quotations, Four Seasons Publishing
291 Original source of quote not found.
John **Tyson** | **48** Richard St. John
John **Updike** | **125** Original source of quote not found.
Jane **Urqhuart** | **97** CBC Radio, with Avril Benoit, November 5, 2001
Stephan **Van Dam** | **103** Richard St. John

Mies **van der Rohe** | **81** Original source of quote not found.
Maurizio **Vecchione** | **107, 157** Richard St. John
Craig **Venter** | **25, 38, 185** Richard St. John
Eva **Vertes** | **73, 105, 275** Richard St. John
Bruce **Vilanch** | **133** Richard St. John
Roger **von Oech** | **223** Original source of quote not found.
Marilyn **Vos Savant** | **131** Original source of quote not found.
Elliot **Wahle** | **199, 283** Richard St. John
Pamela **Wallin** | **229** Pamela Wallin, Speaking of Success, (Toronto:Key Porter Books Limited, 2001), p.234

Sam **Walton** | **132** Original source of quote not found.
Robert **Ward** | **31, 94, 211** Richard St. John
Andy **Warhol** | **125, 233** Original source of quote not found.
John **Warnock** | **249** Richard St. John
George **Washington** | **111** Original source of quote not found.
Omar **Wasow** | **111, 135, 175, 264** Richard St. John
James **Watson** | **91, 115, 235, 261, 275, 290, 291** Richard St. John
Wendy **Watson** | **259** Richard St. John
Alan **Way** | **159** Richard St. John
Howard **Weaver** | **253** Richard St. John
Erik **Weihenmayer** | **33, 167** Touch the Top of the World by Erik Wehenmayer, copyright © 2002 by Erik Weihenmayer. Used by permission of Dutton, a division of Penguin Group (USA) Inc.

Jack **Welch** | **47** Janet Lowe, Jack Welch Speaks, John Wiley & Sons Inc. Copyright © 1998, Reprinted with permission of John Wiley & Sons, Inc.
123 Charles R. Day Jr. and Polly LaBarre, "GE: Just Your Average Everyday $60 Billion Family Grocery Store," Industry Week, May 2, 1994.
157 Jack Welch, speech to shareholders, General Electric annual meeting, Erie, PA, April 25, 1990.
177 On Stage at the Seventh Annual Awards Dinner of the Work in America Institute
227 Janet Lowe, Jack Welch Speaks, John Wiley & Sons Inc.Copyright © 1998, p. 78,

Reprinted with permission of John Wiley & Sons, Inc.

237 Janet Guyon, "GE Chairman Welch, Though Much Praised, Starts to Draw Critics," The Wall Street Journal, August 4, 1988.

Leslie **Westbrook** **89, 119, 137** Richard St. John

Nan **Wilkens** **178** Richard St. John

Warren **Williams** **131** Dave Feschuk, National Post, Mar 23 2001

Ted **Williams** **156** Original source of quote not found.

Bruce **Willis** **51** New Idea

Oprah **Winfrey** **55** Joanna Powell, "I Was Trying to Fill Something Deeper," Good Housekeeping, October 1996, p.80

115 Dana Kennedy, "Oprah: Act Two", Entertainment Weekly, September 9, 1994, p.20

159 George Mair, Oprah Winfrey: The Real Story (Secaucus, N.J.: Birch Lane Press, 1994) P. 344

226 Myrna Blyth, "Advice from Oprah" Ladies' Home Journal, February 1995, p. 10.

233 Larry King Live, "Oprah Winfrey Discusses Her Success," CNN, September 4, 2001

281 "Oprah Winfrey Gives Another Million to Morehouse College: Graduates Call Her 'An Angel,'" Jet, December 8, 1997, p.22

294, 299 Mary-Ann Bendel, TV's Super Woman, Ladies' Home Journal, March 1988, p. 124

253 Bob Greene and Oprah Winfrey, "How She Did It: Winfrey's Fitness Success Is Detailed in a Five Part Series," St. Louis Post Dispatch, Jan 6, 1997, p. 1E

Henry **Winkler** **289** Original source of quote not found.

Sheldon **Wiseman** **47, 99** Richard St. John

Tom **Wolfe** **214** Original source of quote not found.

Michael **Wolff** **285, 259** Richard St. John

John **Wooden** **161** On Stage, Ted, Feb 2001

Coach John Wooden with Steve Jamison, Wooden (Chicago: McGraw-Hill

Contemporary, 1997), **165** p.144 **225** p.73 **262** p.80

Ken **Woodrow** **69, 97, 239, 263, 275, 279** Richard St. John

Tiger **Woods** **24, 77** Larry King Weekend, "Tiger Woods: A Golf Legend," CNN, April 15, 2001

99 Cam Cole "Golf's favoured son," National Post, June 13 2001

Hawksley **Workman** **157, 167** Aaron Wherry, He Just Wants You to Listen, National Post, Monday, December 22, 2003

297 DNTO, CBC radio, November 5, 2005

Frank Lloyd **Wright** **263** Vincent Scully, Sterling Professor Emiritus of the History of Art, Yale University

Richard Saul **Wurman 29, 97, 137, 141, 157, 241, 287, 291** Richard St. John

Sandra **Yingling** **25** Richard St. John

Henry **Youngman** **299** Original source of quote not found.

Babe Didrikson **Zaharias** **77** Criswell Freeman, The Book of Florida Wisdom, Walnut Grove Press (March 1, 1996)

Greg **Zeschuk** **45, 109, 161, 281** Richard St. John

Zig **Zigler** **182** Original source of quote not found.

Donald **Ziraldo** **169, 316** Richard St. John

Moses **Znaimer** **57, 249** Richard St. John

David **Zussman** **139, 149, 195, 223, 283** Richard St. John

WHY BLANK PAGES?

You may be wondering why the blank pages? Joe X, the nice man who printed this book, told us that due to technical reasons, adding blank pages would make a stronger book. Well, his exact words were: "Your writing could be stronger, but since we can't expect miracles, we'll just add some blank pages." Use them as you will.